THE COAL BLACK SEA

THE COAL BLACK SEA

WINSTON CHURCHILL AND THE WORST NAVAL CATASTROPHE OF THE FIRST WORLD WAR

STUART HEAVER

The History Press

This book is dedicated to the memory of my grandmother:
Lily Louisa May Heaver (née Potter).

I would that with sleepy, soft embraces
The sea would fold me—would find me rest,
In luminous shades of her secret places,
In depths where her marvels are manifest;
So the earth beneath her should not discover
my hidden couch—nor the heaven above her—
As a strong love shielding a weary lover,
I would have her shield me with her shining breast.

Adam Lindsay Gordon (1870)

Cover illustrations: Front: A watercolour of HMS *Cressy* and the Broad Fourteens disaster, produced in 1920. (Courtesy of Chatham Historic Dockyard) *Back:* Winston Churchill in 1911, the year he was appointed First Lord of the Admiralty. (GRANGER/Alamy Stock Photo)

First published 2022

The History Press
97 St George's Place, Cheltenham,
Gloucestershire, GL50 3QB
www.thehistorypress.co.uk

British Library Cataloguing in Publication Data.
A catalogue record for this book is available from the British Library.

ISBN 978 0 7509 9960 1

Typesetting and origination by The History Press
Printed and bound in Great Britain by TJ Books Limited, Padstow, Cornwall.

MIX
Paper from responsible sources
FSC www.fsc.org FSC® C013056

Trees for Life

CONTENTS

FOREWORD

BY ADMIRAL SIR GEORGE ZAMBELLAS, GCB DSC DL

Stuart Heaver, himself a former Royal Navy officer, has triumphed with *The Coal Black Sea.*

If ever there was a catastrophe waiting to happen, amid the inherent and structural inefficiencies of the pre-First World War Royal Navy, with its undisciplined mix of politics, personalities, ageing technology and technical naivety, this was it. And HMS *Cressy*, and her sister cruisers, fell foul of that horrid mess.

Stuart Heaver brings this complex story alive, and painfully so in the case of the officers and men of HMS *Cressy* as they battle with the boredom and ordinariness of pre-war life at sea, until the reality and practical horror of the German submarine threat is unleashed upon them, and their sister cruisers. With almost nothing with which to fight back, the vulnerability of these great warships and their crews is brutally exposed to the horror of the freezing North Sea.

All around this graphic and personalised account, masterfully captured by the author, are the ebb and flow of naval and national politics, and particularly the character and ambition of Winston Churchill. And the politics continue into the aftermath, as spin and reputation are themselves positioned for survival.

The Coal Black Sea is, ultimately, a factually accurate account about a family – the naval family – from the most senior to the most junior, and the collective failure to understand the nature of contemporary threats. Perhaps nothing changes. It is sobering, and a great read.

ACKNOWLEDGEMENTS

If I had known how arduous and protracted the journey would be to complete this book, I would probably have never taken the first few steps. An idea first conceived in a pretty English village in Suffolk during the summer of 2014 took several unexpected turns before the final manuscript was submitted from a quarantine hotel in Hong Kong in autumn 2021.

Before a long-postponed trip to my grandmother's childhood home of Westleton, Suffolk, I contacted my cousin, David Heaver, and he suggested I might like to have a look at the village war memorial while I was there.

Emerging into the summer sunshine after lunch at the Crown Inn, I crossed the road to the memorial 'sacred to the memory of 18 brave men of Westleton who gave their lives for their country in the great War, 1914-1918'. I quickly recognised a familiar name on the short list etched into the stone tablet:

Potter William J. Seaman Gunner HMS *Cressy*

Will Potter was my paternal grandmother's elder brother but, despite my service in the Royal Navy, no one in the family had ever mentioned that my great-uncle lost his life at sea in the First World War.

Further down the same list was another name:

Spindler David. Stoker HMS *Cressy*

It occurred to me that two men from this small village had lost their lives on the same ship, on the same day, in an incident I had never heard of. I didn't know it at the time, but this was the start of an eight-year journalistic journey to uncover the truth about what happened to Potter, Spindler and their shipmates in the southern North Sea on 22 September 1914.

Writing this book was often a solitary business but it could never have been completed without the support and industry of others.

Firstly, David Heaver, whose casual suggestion had initiated my interest in the events leading to the loss of HMS *Cressy*, became an invaluable proofreader of several versions of the copy and remained steadfast in his support throughout.

I would like to acknowledge the role of Henk van der Linden, who was instrumental in telling the story of HMS *Aboukir*, *Cressy* and *Hogue* and founding the Live Bait Squadron Society, a network for the families of descendants of those who served that day. It was Henk who organised the centenary commemoration of the event at Chatham Historic Dockyard on 22 September 2014, which I attended. This book is intended to be a continuation of the journey that he initiated.

Gerry Bartlett was an enthusiastic advocate from day one and has been a trusted friend and mentor since he recruited me into SSAFA, the Armed Forces charity, as a case worker and press officer. Without Gerry's support I would not have become a professional writer and his experience as a veteran Fleet Street reporter and his background as a Major in the TA were priceless.

Gavin Greenwood is also due a special debt of gratitude. Gavin is an experienced writer/editor with a military background and a passion for naval history. His contributions, tactful suggestions and edits improved my copy no end. I am embarrassed to admit that some of my favourite turns of phrase in the book were his suggestions.

Paul Harrison and Mick Atha PhD read through early versions and former Royal Navy submariner (and my old shipmate) Commander Tony Dolton kindly scrutinised the sections about submarine warfare.

I would like to thank Anna West, the cousin I didn't know I had (Will Potter was her uncle). She contacted me via the Ancestry website in 2019 and provided invaluable background detail and some timely encouragement on more than one occasion.

David Whittle and his dedicated colleagues at the Harwich Society opened up their museums and archives for me during the Covid-19 restrictions in the summer of 2020. Roger Jones and the dedicated team of volunteers at the HMS *Ganges* Museum in Shotley gave me unrestricted access to their library and supplied tea and biscuits for my wife while she waited patiently for me.

Thank you to Admiral Sir George Zambellas for writing the Foreword. Sir George was First Sea Lord in 2014 and presided at the commemorative event at Chatham Historic Dockyard. We both joined Cunningham Division, BRNC Dartmouth, on the same day in September 1980.

The staff at The National Archives, the Imperial War Museum Library, the Caird Library at the National Maritime Museum in Greenwich and the Royal Navy Submarine Museum in Gosport were all helpful. Thanks are also due to Chatham Historic Dockyard for allowing me to use a watercolour image for the book cover.

Thanks also to my mother-in-law, Dr Katharine Draper, for her encouragement, to my family and friends for their tolerance and support – and, finally, to my wife, Sarah, for her love and for her faith in me.

1

NORTH SEA PATROL

There are no roses on a sailor's grave,
No lilies on an ocean wave
The only tribute is the seagulls' sweeps
And the teardrops that a sweetheart weeps.[1]

Complete darkness engulfed the tiny cabin of 30-year-old Lieutenant Commander Edmond P. Gabbett as he enjoyed his last blissful moments of slumber.

No one will ever know what Gabbett, navigating officer of HMS *Cressy*, was dreaming of before being abruptly woken by a bridge messenger to stand watch on the bridge of the British armoured cruiser as it ploughed through the southern North Sea on 22 September 1914.

Perhaps he dreamt of his wife, Alicia, or their 9-month-old baby daughter. The Gabbetts' marriage in rural Gloucestershire, held on a bitterly cold day in January 1913, was described in the local newspaper as the 'fashionable wedding at Wotton-under-Edge'.[2] While Gabbett's dreams must remain the subject of conjecture, his fate is not.

Gabbett was one of 1,459 men who lost their lives on three British armoured cruisers on a single gloomy morning in the frigid North Sea – a longer casualty list than that sustained by the entire British Fleet at the Battle of Trafalgar – making it the worst naval catastrophe of the First World War.

As he regained consciousness, lulled by the steady motion of the 12,000-ton armoured cruiser, the grim reality of his wartime naval existence came slowly back into focus. He would doubtless have noticed that the heavy rolling and pitching of the ship had eased overnight, as the fierce equinoctial storms that had battered the ship relentlessly for the previous three days were easing at last. Frequent gales creating sharp mountainous seas, driving rain and poor visibility made the North Sea a hostile and forbidding environment for even the most experienced professional mariner.

'The North Sea is at its best a dull place, as winter begins to come on, it is a most Godforsaken hole, with continual rain, mist, fogs, alternating with gales and rough weather,' wrote Midshipman Alexander Scrimgeour, serving in HMS *Crescent*, flagship of the 10th Cruiser Squadron and operating in a more northerly sector of the North Sea, in a letter to his mother dated four days earlier.[3]

At 2300 on 4 August 1914, the British Admiralty had flashed the signal, 'Commence hostilities against Germany' and, ever since, the British public had been eagerly anticipating a decisive naval engagement and a glorious victory. A modern-day version of the Battle of Trafalgar in 1805 was generally envisaged, where the supposedly invincible Royal Navy would crush their German enemy and safeguard the empire in time for Christmas. Few foresaw a protracted naval stalemate or the development of the endless slog of bloody trench warfare on land along the Western Front.

The reality of the war at sea in the late summer of 1914 was proving to be considerably more complicated and less decisive than anyone had forecast. The big ships, big guns and big personalities mostly remained at a safe distance except for rare offensive sorties and sweeps. They remained within reach of Scapa Flow in the Orkneys, while the dirty work of routine, and often arduous, patrols to enforce the distant blockade of Germany was left to their less-celebrated colleagues – like Gabbett.

Gabbett had a wiry frame and sharp angular features topped by receding dark hair. He was not from a traditional naval background. This officer could not trace his ancestors back to Nelson's band of brothers, nor did he possess much in the way of aristocratic credentials or royal connections, generally thought to be a prerequisite for scaling the higher echelons of the service.

His father was a successful civil and mechanical engineer, a member of Britain's affluent new technocrat middle classes. The family home was in

Wellington Gardens, in the old village of Charlton, in Kent. It was a fine villa not far from the site of what is now The Valley, home of Charlton Athletic Football Club. Gabbett spent much of his childhood at his grandmother's home in the market town of Dursley in rural Gloucestershire. Born in 1884, he joined the Royal Navy as an Officer Cadet on 15 January 1900.

The Royal Navy's contribution to war by the autumn of 1914 had been largely conducted by smaller or older ships of the Third Fleet like HMS *Cressy*. They boarded unarmed merchant vessels to ensure they were not carrying contraband or acting as covert minelayers or commerce raiders. They also presented a shield to the eastern approaches to the English Channel. This had been the task of *Cressy* and her sister ships of the Third Fleet's 7th Cruiser Squadron since hostilities commenced. Under the original War Orders of 28 July 1914, cruisers were deployed 'in order to ensure the presence of armoured ships in the Southern approaches to the North Sea and the Eastern entrance to the Channel, and to support the 1st and 3rd Flotillas (comprising destroyers and light cruisers) operating in that area from Harwich'.[4]

The force reached full complement by Admiralty orders of 27 July 1914 and, after a rapid mobilisation at Chatham Dockyard, *Cressy* and her sister ships, HMS *Aboukir* and HMS *Bacchante*, sailed in company on 5 August 1914. But instead of a much-anticipated glorious battle, *Cressy* endured a monotonous and exhausting routine of patrols and boarding, interrupted only by the filthy and exhausting process of coaling ship to refuel.

'Coaling, coaling, coaling, always fucking well coaling' was often sung by the sailors as they lugged sacks of coal to the tune of the well-known hymn 'Holy, Holy, Holy',[5] though we can safely assume the godlier members of the ship's company like George Collier, the naval chaplain, would have declined to join in the irreverent chorus.

It was still early days but the prospect of the formidable Royal Navy playing a tedious bit part in a major war was unthinkable to all ranks from the most junior seaman to the First Lord of the Admiralty and his senior commanders at sea. 'This roaming about the North Sea, day after day with no prospect of meeting an enemy vessel, I think is the heaviest trial that could be laid on any man,' wrote the pugnacious young Admiral, David Beatty, in a letter to his wife, the glamorous American heiress Ethel Tree, in September 1914.[6]

The charismatic Beatty, whose histrionic good looks graced many newspapers and magazines during the war years, had made an unorthodox marriage to the wealthy divorcee, whom one biographer politely described as 'free ranging in her affections'.[7]

Gabbett was the ship's navigating officer, pilot, or 'Vasco', as his fellow officers would have referred to him, after the Portuguese navigator and explorer, Vasco da Gama. As such, he was responsible to the ship's commanding officer, Captain Robert Warren Johnson, for all aspects of the safe navigation of the ship. His first task on sailing from Chatham on 5 August had been to navigate *Cressy* to the patrol area known as the Broad Fourteens in the southern North Sea. Six weeks later the ship was back again in this familiar and forbidding seaway, some 25 nautical miles off the coast of the Netherlands.

The Broad Fourteens patrol zone (so named because the area was 14 fathoms deep), had no precisely defined limits, but the Haaks Light Vessel, 30 nautical miles west of the Texel, and the Maas Light Vessel, 10 nautical miles west of The Hague, were considered its rough northern and southern limits. The sea area is about 60 nautical miles long by 20–30 nautical miles wide and runs parallel to, and about 25 nautical miles from, the Dutch coast. It is about 90 nautical miles due east of the English coast of Suffolk.

In between the first patrol of 5 August and the later one, which had commenced on 30 August, the ships had been busy operating as part of what was known as Cruiser Force C. It had been a demanding but ultimately unfulfilling few weeks helping to protect the British Expeditionary Force during its first crossings of the Channel to France and supporting the Harwich flotillas during the Grand Fleet's sweep of the North Sea on 16 August.

At the outbreak of hostilities, the 7th Cruiser Squadron was originally composed of four *Cressy*-class (also referred to as *Bacchante*-class) armoured cruisers: *Cressy*, *Bacchante*, *Hogue* (joined on 11 August) and *Aboukir*. The squadron was under the direct command of Rear Admiral Henry Hervey Campbell, flying his flag in *Bacchante*. It became Cruiser Force C after Rear Admiral Arthur Henry Christian was appointed in command of all Royal Navy forces in the southern North Sea (the so-called Southern Force) on 15 August. He joined the cruiser force in his flagship, another *Cressy*-class cruiser, HMS *Euryalus*, and the light cruiser HMS *Amethyst* was also attached. This created the highly unusual situation of two seagoing Admirals in two flagships within one small force of patrolling cruisers.

And there were more flag officers with indirect responsibility for Cruiser Force C. It was supposed to act as a supporting force for two destroyer flotillas (1st and 3rd) consisting of thirty-five L-Class and *Ariel*-class destroyers and two flotilla cruisers, based at Harwich, under the command of Commodore Reginald R. Tyrwhitt. Commodore (T), as he was designated, was supposed to report to Commander-in-Chief Admiral John Jellicoe, although in effect he reported directly to the Admiralty War Staff in London but also 'nominally' to Christian.[8] Tyrwhitt was also obliged to confer with the more senior Commodore, Roger J.B. Keyes, who was also based at Harwich as commanding officer of the ten submarines of the 8th Submarine Flotilla. Though officially in charge of submarines, the energetic and highly regarded Keyes often flew his flag in surface ships and took a direct interest in North Sea patrols. It was Keyes who wrote to the Admiralty War Staff on 21 August requesting that the cruiser patrols be terminated as they put the ships at great risk for no apparent tangible benefit.

The elaborate and top-heavy chain of command was a classic case of 'too many cooks', or perhaps even 'too many chiefs', or more likely both. It was further confused when Admiralty orders were sent directly to ships without informing or consulting the flag officers supposedly in charge. At noon on 26 August, for example, when the ships of Cruiser Force C, including *Cressy*, were dispatched by the Admiralty to Chatham to embark a detachment of Royal Marines and land them in Ostend in Belgium, Admiral Christian, the flag officer in charge, was not even informed.[9] An unfortunate case of an Admiral not knowing where his ships were.

On completion of the successful landings in Belgium in late August, Cruiser Force C was dispatched to support the Heligoland Bight operation. This offensive was a rare attempt by the Royal Navy in the early weeks of the conflict to mount a daring initiative to engage German naval forces. It was targeted in and around the German naval base at the small Friesen Island of Heligoland. The operation was ultimately successful but only avoided being a complete disaster by a large slice of good fortune.

Cressy and Cruiser Force C did not actually come into action at Heligoland Bight but were of assistance in towing and escorting the damaged ships back to Sheerness and rescuing and landing German naval prisoners of war. 'We never saw a German until the Heligoland fight. We came up when this was going on and we saw the sinking of the *Mainz*. We cruised about picking up Germans who were swimming about or hanging on to pieces of wood, or anything else that would support them. We picked up about 223 of them and most of them seemed scared to death at us,' Stoker William Wake of *Cressy* told his local newspaper.[10]

Cressy had returned to its familiar patrol at the Broad Fourteens on 30 August. Gabbett had celebrated his 30th birthday in the ship's wardroom the same day, just twenty-six days after war had been formally declared. On patrol in rough seas and with a young wife and baby daughter at home, his birthday celebration would have been a subdued affair. A bottle of 'fizz' shared with fellow officers, perhaps, and a half-hearted rendering of 'Happy Birthday' before he turned in.

Apart from the periodic dash to Sheerness to coal ship, the ships of Cruiser Force C had been patrolling either the Broad Fourteens or the Dogger Bank patrol area to the north since that muted birthday celebration on 30 August. Buffeted by the fierce equinoctial gales and sandwiched between a German minefield to the north and the low-lying Dutch coast to the south-east, and with no sight of the enemy, it was not glamorous work. By 16 September, weather forecasts indicated that the often-inclement weather of the North Sea would turn particularly foul and a series of events started to unfold that were to decide the fate of three ships of Cruiser Force C.

HMS *Euryalus*, *Cressy* and *Bacchante* were jointly operating on the Dogger Bank patrol as the weather started to deteriorate. Admiral Christian was granted permission by the Admiralty to keep two cruisers at Dogger Bank and to send one south to the Broad Fourteens. Instead, Christian stated his preference to keep his force concentrated, ready to support either patrol area as required. His decision became a moot point because the weather turned so foul late the following day, 17 September, that all destroyers were ordered to return to port. Christian reported he was patrolling Dogger Bank in *Euryalus* in company with *Hogue* and *Aboukir*, *Cressy* having gone in to coal at Sheerness and *Bacchante* to Chatham for docking and repairs.

Bacchante was the flagship of Admiral Campbell of the 7th Cruiser Squadron[11] and it was to become significant that he was permitted to leave the patrol for coaling and repairs to the wireless telegraph (WT) aerials that had been damaged in the relentless gales. It meant that, when disaster struck later, the Admiral in command of the 7th Cruiser Squadron was sipping tea in Chatham Dockyard, oblivious to the fate of his own ships.

By the morning of 19 September, the weather had moderated and HMS *Fearless* led out eight destroyers from Harwich to the Broad Fourteens to join the larger cruisers. However, the weather steadily grew worse again. By noon that day, it was again blowing a gale from the north, with a violent heavy sea, and at 1915 *Fearless* and the destroyers returned to port.

The frightening violence of equinoctial storms in the North Sea are almost impossible to imagine if they have not been experienced. It should be noted that HMS *Fearless*, an *Active*-class scout cruiser and flotilla leader for the 1st Destroyer Flotilla, based at Harwich, was not a small ship. Commissioned in October 1913, it was 405ft (123.4m) long with a beam of 41ft (12.5m) and displaced 3,340 tons (3,394 tonnes). That it was not considered safe for this powerful modern cruiser to be at sea in wartime gives an indication of how unforgiving the weather conditions were. There was a 'big gale, cabins and mess decks flooded', noted Surgeon Captain H.W.B. Shewell of HMS *Euryalus* on 18 September 1914.[12]

On 19 September, an Admiralty telegram terminated the Dogger Bank patrol and ordered the cruisers to continue south for the Broad Fourteen patrol without screening protection from destroyers, which remained confined to port due to the weather conditions. 'Dogger Bank patrol need not be continued. Weather too bad for destroyers. Arrange with cruisers to watch Broad Fourteens,' read the order from London. This signal proved to be fatal.

The cruisers were supposed to be supporting the patrols of the Harwich flotillas by adding firepower to the lightly armed destroyers in the event heavier German warships ventured out to challenge them. They were never supposed to be the patrol itself, which was now the reality on 19 September.

By the time Gabbett guided *Cressy* from Sheerness to rejoin the three sister ships on 20 September, those four large armoured cruisers represented the entire Southern Force of the Royal Navy in the very rough and turbulent North Sea. These were not the Royal Navy's most prestigious, fastest or most modern warships by any means, but they could pack a punch and were proven to be good sea boats capable of weathering the worst conditions the North Sea could conjure up.

Designed originally for service on the China Station in Hong Kong, *Cressy* was launched in December 1899 and was the first of class. At 12,000 tons and with an overall length of 472ft (143.9m),[13] she, like the sister ships in her class, was a big ship. Constructed at Govan on the Clyde in Scotland by the Fairfield Shipbuilding Company, *Cressy* was fitted with a protective 6in belt of armoured Krupp steel installed along each side, above and below the waterline. More importantly, perhaps, this class of ship was armed with two 9.2in guns, one forward and one aft, capable of projecting a 375lb (170kg) shell more than 7 nautical miles (14km). It was quite a punch but the sophisticated fire-control systems that were slowly becoming the norm in modern warships were not yet fitted, meaning accuracy was poor, particularly in rough weather and at night.

The main armament was supplemented by twelve 6in guns installed in rotating turrets port and starboard and twelve standard 12-pounders. The 6in gun casements were often flooded in poor weather, which in the North Sea in autumn and winter meant most of the time. Coaxed by Engineer Commander Robert H. Grazebrook, the ship's two, four-cylinder, triple-expansion steam engines, officially capable of 21 knots, could muster a maximum speed of about 18 knots. But in order to conserve precious coal, 10–12 knots were deemed more feasible for prolonged periods.

Cressy carried a maximum load of 1,527 tons of coal, and its thirty Belleville-type boilers located in four boiler rooms, each overseen by a chief stoker or engine room artificer, consumed a great deal of it; stokers stripped to the waist shovelled relentlessly into the ship's furnaces twenty-four hours a day. Apart from providing power for the ship's two propellers, the steam produced by the coal-fired furnaces also powered the two Normandy distillers, capable of producing up to 82 tons of fresh water per day. Generators provided electricity for everything from lighting to boat davits. Conservation of coal was of paramount concern to Grazebrook, who encouraged the men to grow beards (or 'full sets' as they were known in the Royal Navy) to save precious fresh water and the coal used to produce it.

Coaling ship was a physically exhausting and filthy task that was hated by everyone on board. It covered every part of a ship in a film of black dust and employed almost all of the entire ship's company while in harbour, transferring hundreds of sacks of coal from a collier, berthed alongside. It required all officers (except the captain and commander and some watchkeepers) to take part, in a rare demonstration of naval egalitarianism. With no official uniform or rig required, sailors wore any sort of fancy dress, often donning silly hats, and after a few hours they resembled the cast of a music-hall show.

Consumption of coal and the need to frequently coal ship was a key limitation of naval operations in 1914 and the Admiralty had been seriously considering the alternative of oil. If a ship's speed was limited to 9.5 knots, those of the *Cressy* class would burn 66 tons of coal per hour, could travel to a range of 5,244 nautical miles and remain at sea for twenty-three days. (In practice it was much less time because no commanding officer would allow his ship to remain at sea with less than an adequate reserve (30–40 per cent) of coal in case of unforeseen events or emergencies.)

At its theoretical maximum speed of 21 knots, ships like HMS *Cressy* could achieve a range of 1,500 nautical miles and remain at sea for only three days before their coal ran out.[14] Quite simply, the faster a ship steamed, the quicker it ran out of coal and had to cease its patrol duties to return to port for the universally dreaded task of coaling ship.

Assisting Grazebrook in the hot, noisy and claustrophobic machinery spaces was a contingent of sweating stokers and engine room artificers, whom Midshipman Scrimgeour referred to in his diary as the 'saints down below'. They were supervised by two specialised engineer officers, Lieutenant Commander Fred Richard Monks and Lieutenant Stacey Wise.

Wise was a young, blond-haired, angelic-faced, 22-year-old engineering officer serving in *Cressy*, while his elder brother, Lieutenant Edward Selby Wise, aged 27, was on board HMS *Severn*, a *Humber*-class monitor designed for shore bombardments in shallow waters. The monitor's shallow draft made her a death trap in heavy seas and Wise must have been hoping that his elder brother was securely berthed alongside somewhere during the recent gales.

Having coaled ship at the Nore (Sheerness), *Cressy* was required to rendezvous with Admiral Christian's flagship *Euryalus* near the Maas Light at 0500 on 20 September. It was Gabbett's job to ensure they arrived on time. Given the poor weather conditions, with ships darkened and long before the advent of radar, GPS or radio navigation aids, even this relatively simple task would have presented a challenge.

Shortly after *Cressy*'s arrival, Admiral Christian informed the patrolling ships that he was leaving station to coal and his signal subsequently became the subject of immense official scrutiny:

> *Aboukir* will be in charge of patrol in absence of *Euryalus* who is going to coal. When patrolling and squadron is spread it is left to Captains to carry our alterations of course to guard against submarine attack. Suspicious vessels should be boarded if weather permits, especially those coming

> from the north and north east. No destroyers will be out on patrol at the present.[15]

In the absence of Admiral Christian and Admiral Campbell, the senior officer present, Captain John Edmund Drummond of *Aboukir* took command of the isolated three-ship force. Despite the apparent oversupply of flag officers and their overlapping responsibilities for operations in the southern North Sea, not one was present. Neither was any senior authority in direct contact with any of the three isolated cruisers operating in the foul weather of the North Sea by the late morning of 20 September 1914.

After the departure of *Euryalus* on that Sunday morning, Gabbett continued to navigate *Cressy* up and down the same patrol line running north-east and south-west along the neutral Dutch coast, in company with *Aboukir* and *Hogue*. It was boring, tiring and predictable. It was also highly hazardous. Not only was there a minefield to the north of the patrol zone, at its eastern limit the ships were about 130 nautical miles from the main German submarine base at Wilhelmshaven.

Having risen from his bunk in the early hours of 22 September and donned sea boots and wrapped himself in layers of warm clothing, Gabbett took a tentative sip from his steaming mug and exited his cabin. The navigating officer cast a ghostly shadow as he made his way through quiet, lantern-lit passageways towards the bridge as the rivets and steel deck plates groaned under the relentless assault of the North Sea. It was common practice to burn oil lamps at night so that, in the event of a power failure, the ship's internal compartments would not be plunged into complete darkness.

Gabbett would have proceeded along the ship's boat deck and negotiated his way up the final steel ladder to the open bridge. The accepted naval wisdom of 1914 was that if Nelson had stood on an open deck at the Battle of Trafalgar, so could modern seaman officers. Only freezing half to death and blinded by driving rain and spray, cutting into them like a whetted knife for hours on end, could a seaman officer possibly appreciate the full meteorological and tactical situation that confronted him.

Once on the bridge and shielded from the bitter wind and spray of the North Sea at night by only a brass guardrail and a canvas screen, Gabbett confirmed the ship's position. The ship was 25 nautical miles west of Hook of Holland, now out of sight on their port beam, and they were steaming on a south-westerly course at a speed of about 10 knots in company with the two remaining sister ships, *Hogue* and *Aboukir*. The Maas Light vessel would have been visible 8 nautical miles on the port quarter, as a sequence of four flashing white lights, as they steamed steadily south-west.

Gabbett chose the morning watch (0400–0800) because the three ships would reach the south-western limit of their patrol zone shortly after 0400. As navigating officer, he would have considered it his duty to be on hand to supervise the sixteen-point turn in company with her two sister ships. If the skies cleared it might also offer him the opportunity to confirm the ship's position using his sextant to conduct star sights against the emerging horizon at twilight. Accompanied only by the silent shadowy silhouettes of the bridge lookouts, on-watch signalmen, bridge messenger and midshipman of the watch – all hunched against the prevailing weather and the sound of the buffeting wind and the rolling billows of the sea – it was a desolate place to be.

The midshipman of the watch was an acting Midshipman and one of ten teenage cadets from Britannia Royal Naval College, Dartmouth, who were attached to the ship at the outbreak of war to make up the numbers and give the officers under training valuable operational experience. All those aboard *Cressy* were 16 years old but, with one exception, those serving on *Hogue* and *Aboukir* were only 15.

One of those serving in *Cressy* was John Aubrey Froude, from Kingsbridge in Devon, only a stone's throw from the naval college in Dartmouth on the other side of the River Dart, where he had been studying. He was 16 years old but, judging by his photograph, looked much younger.[16] Parents of cadets and acting midshipmen like Froude were still being charged £50 per year for their sons' training while they were serving at sea in wartime. Some parents were even sent bills after their sons' deaths.

While the Midshipman or 'Snotty' kept the morning watch on the bridge, his colleagues from the ship's gunroom stood watch in the machinery spaces or, if off-watch, slept soundly below in hammocks. Also sleeping below decks, in hammocks located in large sprawling unventilated mess decks, were hundreds of sailors, stokers and marines who made up the ship's company of 797 officers and men.

Gabbett and his fellow officers could at least enjoy the privacy of their own small and sparsely furnished cabins. While there was no heating and only poor ventilation, subject to the availability of fresh water, which was always scarce, they could in theory at least take a bath in a tin tub, with water brought in by their servant. They could also relax in the officers' mess or 'wardroom', furnished along the lines of an intimate gentleman's club with chintz sofas and sumptuous armchairs and a well-stocked bar. It was said that it was a court-martial offence if any officer in the Royal Navy allowed his warship to run out of ammunition, but it was a capital offence to run out of gin.

By contrast, the mess decks were so crowded that the sailors sleeping in hammocks would often complain that, if a neighbouring messmate sneezed or coughed, they were often rained on by his exhaled mucus. It meant tuberculosis was still a common ailment in warships. As little as 18in was allowed between clew hooks (used to hang hammocks to deck heads). Although hammocks were comfortable enough once in them, the art of entry and exit had to be mastered and there was no natural light or private storage space. Not surprisingly, some sailors preferred to sleep in passageways or even gun turrets and returned to their mess decks only to eat their meals with their mates. There was very little in the way of comfort on the lower deck for sailors on board a warship in 1914.

'The life of the bluejackets and stokers in our finest ships of war around the British coasts and in the North Sea is one of pitiable discomfort,' reported Winston Churchill shortly after being appointed First Lord of the Admiralty in 1911.[17]

The seamen's mess of *Cressy* was dominated by reservists from the Royal Fleet Reserve (RFR) and Royal Naval Reserve (RNR), which made up more than 60 per cent of the ship's company. It would be misleading to imply the reservists were somehow less competent or committed than their regular Royal Navy shipmates, but they had only seven weeks in which to familiarise themselves with their ship. 'The reserve men throughout seem a splendid lot of men and far beyond anything I expected,' wrote Admiral Sir Rosslyn Wemyss of HMS *Euryalus*, later in the year.[18]

The RFR was founded in March 1901 and required former Royal Navy personnel who had completed their twelve-year standard engagements to continue with some form of naval training and be available in time of war, in order to qualify for a modest pension. Just before the outbreak of hostilities, Admiral Jellicoe informed the Second Sea Lord that the Royal Navy had 36,636 RFR reservists, who had all served a term as regulars in the Royal Navy.

Typical of the RFR men in the seamen's mess were men like Leading Seaman William John Potter. Potter was from the pretty village of Westleton in Suffolk and had originally joined the Royal Navy in December 1898 on his 18th birthday on a standard twelve-year engagement. His motivation for pursuing a naval career was little to do with romantic notions of travel and adventure, or the supposed glamour of life in uniform as a bluejacket. As the second eldest of fourteen siblings, his career choice was driven by the need to escape the acute poverty of rural England. The only realistic alternatives to 'the Andrew' (as sailors referred to the Royal Navy) for men like Potter, growing up in rural Suffolk, were trying to scratch a living as a farm labourer, as a longshore fisherman working the small clinker-built boats that lined the pebble beach at Dunwich, near his childhood home, or joining the fleet of herring fishing boats at nearby Lowestoft.

According to his service records, despite joining on his 18th birthday, Potter grew 1½in in height during his naval service, presumably due to the drastic improvement in his diet. As one of only a few ardent Christians on board, he would have been well known to the ship's chaplain, Rev. George Collier, informally referred to by sailors as the 'sky pilot' or the 'sin bosun'.

The RNR men were different. Established by the Naval Reserve Act of 1859, this pool of seamen were typically professional mariners working in the merchant marine or fishing fleets who could be called upon during wartime to serve in the regular Royal Navy. Originally, the RNR was exclusively a reserve of seamen, but it was expanded in 1862 to include reserve officers. These men completed four weeks of naval training every year in return for a modest financial retainer of £6 per year and a pension of double that. By 1865, about 17,000 men had enrolled and the numbers increased steadily. They were considered an essential part of British naval manpower and supremacy.

Typical of the RNR contingent on board were the Penn brothers, from Deal in Kent. Louis Sidney Penn was single, 25 years old and a boatman from Custom House Lane in Deal, then an important maritime town and the traditional epicentre for smuggling operations during the previous century. Deal serviced the Downs anchorage. Here naval and merchant ships anchored in the sheltered waters of the English Channel before proceeding to the nearby Royal Navy dockyards at Sheerness and Chatham or the gateway to the commercial port of London, at Gravesend. Louis joined *Cressy* as an Able Seaman, as did his elder brother Hubert and his younger brother Alfred. The three Penn brothers, like their father and his father before him, worked as boatmen transferring pilots, customs officers, liberty men and cargo to and from ships anchored in the Downs. Only one of them survived the day.

There were eight RNR sailors aboard *Cressy* from the small oyster fishing town of Whitstable on the north Kent coast, who were more used to handling the sails of the oyster smacks that dredged the Swale estuary than the guns of an armoured cruiser. A photograph in *The Whitstable Times*, dated August 1914, shows a large group of the town's naval reserves being called up at Gladstone Road. The newspaper listed 37 RNR oystermen from Whitstable who were serving in the fleet by late September 1914.

The reservists serving aboard *Cressy*, *Hogue* and *Aboukir* were all professional seamen through and through, recruited from the ports and naval towns of Britain. These 'old salts' were often mature family men, in their 30s or 40s, and often teased their regular (and usually younger) counterparts with the (not totally unfair) taunt that the Reserves fought the Navy's wars while the regulars just manned the ships and kept them clean during peacetime.

Shortly before 0515 GMT (there was no such thing as British Summer Time in 1914), high above the sprawling mess decks on the exposed bridge of *Cressy* and as a raw and chilly dawn produced only a miserable gloom, Gabbett scanned the scene. Braced rigid against the cold wind now stinging his face, he observed only the four familiar funnel stacks of *Aboukir* and *Hogue* on his starboard side, both belching black smoke, and a monochrome vista of a hostile sea merging with a distant grey horizon.

Sometime around 0600, Captain Robert Warren Johnson, Royal Navy, commanding officer of *Cressy*, appeared unannounced on the upper bridge to inspect the scene. Johnson was a career naval officer from an esteemed naval family. His father was Admiral John Ormsby Johnson, who died in 1881, the same year that Johnson joined the Royal Navy. It must have been a source of bitter regret to him that his father, the Admiral, never saw him pass out of Britannia Royal Naval College, Dartmouth.

Though 46 years old, Johnson had retained the athletic build and angular good looks of his youth. He was from a subtly different social class to Gabbett and from a different social universe to the likes of Potter and the Penn brothers. The Captain had been expensively educated at public school and scored 1,362 marks in the competitive examinations for cadetships in the Royal Navy, coming first out of his batch of twenty applicants. He was also trained as a torpedo officer and was one of few commanding officers trained in war strategy, having attended the War Course at HMS *President* from March to June 1914, shortly before assuming command of *Cressy*. Unlike most of his fellow officers, he also possessed first-hand experience of submarines, having until 1913 commanded the 7th Submarine Flotilla from the submarine depot ship HMS *Vulcan*, based in Dundee.

What Johnson did share in common with Gabbett, Potter, and many of his ship's company, was that he was also a family man. He and his wife, Grace, lived in a large cottage in Havant, near Portsmouth, and were parents to three young children. He had been forced to miss the first birthday of his youngest daughter, Elisabeth, eleven days earlier.

Throughout the ship, Captain Johnson was referred to as 'the old man' or 'father'. He would need all the benefits of his privileged education, training and experience at sea to deal with the events that were about to engulf him that frigid grey morning in the southern North Sea. As he assiduously scanned the grey horizon with his binoculars from the upper bridge of *Cressy*, he was totally unaware that a German submarine was submerged ahead of his ship, like a covert predator waiting patiently for its prey.

2

A SINGLE U-BOAT

When *U-9* had left the port of Heligoland at 0415 on 20 September 1914 under the command of 32-year-old Lieutenant Commander Otto Weddigen, the weather was appalling.

Weddigen was a handsome man with a heavy jaw, large nose, cleft chin and high cheek bones. He had recently married his childhood sweetheart, Miss Prete, on 18 August 1914 at his brother's house in Wilhelmshaven.[1] 'Within twenty-four hours thereafter I had to go away on a venture that gave a good chance of making my new wife a widow,' he wrote.[2]

Weddigen's naval career began in 1901, during the course of which he found himself stationed at Tsingtao, the German international concession and naval base in China, in 1906–07. In September 1910, he was appointed U-boat commander and was given charge of *U-9* in October 1911. If conditions at sea in HMS *Cressy* were challenging in heavy North Sea gales, the degree of discomfort and squalor for sailors serving in a First World War submarine offered a different level of hardship.

Commissioned in April 1910, *U-9* was a relatively old submarine in terms of this rapidly advancing technology. For surface use, the 57.4m-long U-boat could produce a top speed of 14.2 knots, powered by two Körting eight-cylinder and two Körting six-cylinder two-stroke kerosene engines that were located in the engine room. The air required by these engines was drawn in through the conning tower hatch, while the exhaust was led overboard through a long demountable funnel. When the U-boat was submerged, two Siemens-Schuckert double-acting electric motors and two other electric motors could produce a maximum speed of 8.1 knots.[3] Its cruising range was 1,800 nautical miles at 14 knots on the surface, and 80 nautical miles at 5 knots underwater. The submarine's complement was four officers and thirty-one ratings.

In his vivid written account of life on board a First World War U-boat, contained in the memoir *Six Years of Submarine Service* published in 1929, Johannes Spiess, first watch officer of *U-9*, revealed some of the unique challenges and discomfort of being a submariner at war in 1914, namely that it 'was particularly wet and cold'.[4]

He describes the layout of the submarine, starting with the forward torpedo room, complete with two torpedo tubes and two reserve torpedoes, in the cylindrical pressure hull. Furnished with two bunks for the quartermaster and machinist, the warrant officers' compartment was further astern, followed by the commanding officer's cabin. Weddigen's tiny cabin was fitted with only a small bunk and clothes closet:

> Whenever a torpedo had to be loaded forward or the tube prepared for a shot, both the Warrant Officers' and Commanding Officers' cabins had to be completely cleared out. Bunks and clothes cabinets then had to be moved into the adjacent officers' compartment, which was no light task owing to the lack of space in the latter compartment.[5]

Spiess wrote of the 'certain degree of finesse [that] was required' on board, including the inconvenience of the watch officer's small bunk:

> He was forced to lie on one side and then, being wedged between the bulkhead to the right and the clothes-press on the left, to hold fast against the movements of the boat in a seaway. The occupant of the berth could not sleep with his feet aft as there was an electric fuse-box in the way. At times the cover of this box sprang open and it was all too easy to cause a short circuit by touching this with the feet.[6]

The officers' compartment was divided by the main passageway, where a folding table and camp chairs could be erected for the officers to eat their meals. 'While the Commanding Officer, Watch Officer and Chief Engineer took their meals, men had to pass back and forth through the boat, and each time anyone passed, the table had to be folded.'[7] As for the provisions for the rest of the crew, a small electric range short-circuited each time it was used, meaning meals had to be prepared on deck while the submarine was surfaced, while:

> The crew space had bunks for only a few of the crew – the rest slept in hammocks, when not on watch or on board the submarine mother-ship while in port.
>
> The living spaces were not cased with wood. Since the temperature inside the boat was considerably greater than the sea outside, moisture in the air condensed on the steel hull-plates; the condensation had a very disconcerting way of dropping on a sleeping face, with every movement of the vessel. Efforts were made to prevent this by covering the face with rain clothes or rubber sheets. It was in reality like a damp cellar.[8]

The atmosphere was always humid and fetid. Fresh produce embarked in Heligoland would start to go rotten within forty-eight hours and any bread was quickly covered with green mould.

Detailing the other everyday inconveniences of life on board, Spiess describes how:

> The storage battery cells, which were located under the living spaces and filled with acid and distilled water, generated gas on charge and discharge: this was drawn off through the ventilation system.Ventilation failure risked explosion, a catastrophe which occurred in several German boats. If sea water got into the battery cells, poisonous chlorine gas was generated.
>
> From a hygienic standpoint the sleeping arrangements left much to be desired; one 'awoke in the morning with considerable mucus in the nostrils and a so-called "oil-head"'.[9]

Being a submariner in 1914 was a life-threatening occupation, even before an enemy was encountered. Every man would also reek of fuel and human body odour within a few days in the absence of any washing facilities or spare clothes.

The central station was abaft the crew space, 'dosed off by a bulkhead both forward and aft'.[10] The gyrocompass, depth rudder hand-operating gear (used to keep the submarine at the required level) bilge pumps, the blowers for clearing and filling the diving tanks, and the air compressors were located here.

'In one small corner of this space stood a toilet screened by a curtain and, after seeing this arrangement, I understood why the officer I had relieved recommended the use of opium before all cruises which were to last over twelve hours,' wrote Spiess.[11] The operation of submarine toilets was a complex procedure of valves and levers and one small error could trigger a highly unpleasant blowback event. This would cause the unfortunate submariner to be subject to an unwelcome and high-powered spray of human excrement. The trademark submariner's jersey would often be seen with a faint but distinguishable pebble-dashed pattern caused by this unwelcome accident.[12]

The after-torpedo room was in the stern of the boat, right aft. It held two torpedo tubes but no reserve torpedoes. In total, the U-boat was equipped with four 45cm (17.7in) torpedo tubes (two in the bow and two in the stern) and carried six torpedoes. Originally, the boat was equipped with a machine gun, which was upgraded to a 3.7cm (1.5in) Hotchkiss gun when war was declared.

Submarines were lethal but imperfect weapons. While capable of firing a torpedo when submerged, the maximum speed while running on battery power was limited and the endurance short before the vessel had to surface and run on the petrol or diesel engines to recharge the batteries. Submarines were fitted with periscopes, but the technology was still in its infancy and offered very limited visibility; neither were they feasible for night attacks. It was essential for a submarine commander to locate his boat ahead of his target to avoid the risk of being overhauled by faster surface ships as he sought to achieve his firing position.

According to Spiess, the conning tower was the 'battle station' for both the commanding and watch officers. This area held the two periscopes (search and attack), a platform for the helmsman, the 'diving piano' (a bewildering array of twenty-four levers on each side that controlled the valves for releasing air from the tanks), indicator glasses and test cocks. Also described are the 'electrical controlling gear for depth steering, a depth indicator; voice pipes; and the electrical firing device for the torpedo tubes'.[13]

Spiess continues:

> Above the conning tower was a small bridge which was protected when cruising under conditions which did not require the boat to be

> in constant readiness for diving: a rubber strip was stretched along a series of stanchions screwed into the deck, reaching about as high as the chest. When in readiness for diving this was demounted, and there was a considerable danger of being washed overboard.
>
> The Officer on Watch sat on the hatch coaming, the Petty Officer of the Watch near him, with his feet hanging through the hatch through which the air for the gas engines was being drawn … The third man on watch, a seaman, stood on a small three-cornered platform above the conning tower; he was lashed to his station in heavy seas.[14]

With some exceptions, this was the general arrangement for all seagoing boats at this time. There is a wonderful oil painting by the former submarine commander George Bradshaw, 'On Patrol', painted around 1918. It once adorned the wardroom of the Royal Navy submarine base and training school at HMS *Dolphin* in Gosport and now hangs in the RN submarine museum. It captures the vulnerability of a First World War submarine pictured against the powerful energy of an azure but wild North Sea.

It was evidently a dirty, challenging, dangerous and claustrophobic environment. However, had Weddigen left his wife standing on the quayside with the full knowledge of just how hopelessly inadequate the Royal Navy's anti-submarine warfare measures were, she would have felt less anxious about his departure. Crushed inside with his crew and despite the inherent risks of being a submariner in 1914, Weddigen was a great deal safer than he could possibly have hoped.

In the view of British Admiral Sir Arthur Wilson, submarines were 'underhand, unfair and damned un-English'. His reactionary attitude was typical for the time and demonstrated a negligent disregard by the British naval establishment for adapting naval weapons and strategy to meet the obvious threat that submarines posed.

It was also Admiral Wilson who opined in the early 1900s, when Controller of the Navy, that 'we intend to treat all submarines as pirate vessels in wartime and we'll hang the crews'.[15] It was this oft-quoted antiquarian view that inspired the naval tradition of any submarine achieving a kill flying the Jolly Roger when returning to port. The practice was initiated by the British submarine commander Max Horton, who became the Royal Navy's most celebrated submariner of the First World War.

At the beginning of the twentieth century, the submarine had been damned by many and underestimated by many more – but now it was giving the Royal Navy the jitters.

A false submarine alarm at Scapa Flow on 1 September 1914 was taken very seriously because, almost incredibly, the main base of the Grand Fleet had no submarine defences of any kind. It was a fact that caused Admiral Jellicoe as many sleepless nights as the chronic pain of his haemorrhoids. We can only assume, as did Admiral Sir Percy Scott,[16] that the German Navy could just not contemplate the possibility that their enemy would be so inept as to base their finest ships in such a vulnerable anchorage with several deep-water entrances and no submarine nets.

With the complete absence of anti-submarine measures, the fear of submarine attack had developed into what was known in the Royal Navy as 'periscopitis' by early September 1914. The symptoms of this febrile condition were characterised by false sightings of submarines and random attacks on seals, driftwood and even small fishing boats, in the mistaken belief that they were potentially deadly U-boats.

On 30 August 1914, reliable information was received by the German Navy command of the presence of heavy British warships in the Firth of Forth, on the east coast of Scotland, which were expected to depart soon. This intelligence referred to Admiral Moore's two battlecruisers. It was further gathered in Germany that the *Town*-class light cruiser HMS *Liverpool* had landed some of the prisoners taken from the *Mainz* at Leith after the Heligoland Bight action of 28 August 1914. The conclusion was reached that the British intended to make greater use of the Firth of Forth and it was decided to dispatch the two available submarines, *U-20* and *U-21*, to the area to penetrate the estuary and attack British warships.

According to the classified official account,[17] after attempting to enter the Firth of Forth at 0320 on 5 September 1914, *U-21* sighted a cruiser to the south-east of the port entrance. This was HMS *Pathfinder*, flotilla leader of the Forth Destroyer Patrol (8th Flotilla). The cruiser soon disappeared, but at about 1500, *U-21*'s commanding officer, Lieutenant Commander Hersing, sighted her again. Royal Navy North Sea patrols tended to repeat the same course for days and weeks on end, so if a U-boat missed the first opportunity to strike they could simply wait for the target to make the reciprocal return patrol leg a few hours later.

Three-quarters of an hour later, *U-21* torpedoed HMS *Pathfinder* at a distance of 1,500m, 10 nautical miles south-east of May Island. The cruiser was travelling slowly (about 5 knots) because of a shortage of coal, so it made an easy target. The torpedo exploded a magazine and the *Pathfinder* sank in four minutes, suggesting that watertight doors were not closed at the time of the attack. It cost the lives of 259 members of the ship's company. At first it was thought that the ship had been mined, but Captain Martin Leake, who was wounded and saved, reported that his ship had been torpedoed by a submarine. *Pathfinder* was the first British warship to be sunk by a submarine during the war and the first warship to be sunk by a submarine-launched torpedo in the history of naval warfare.

In spite of the efforts of the patrolling destroyers, *U-21* escaped unscathed. *U-20* and *U-21* returned to their base at Heligoland on 7 September, and curiously there followed a brief hiatus of German submarine activity. The German Navy at this date possessed twenty-four submarines, namely, *U-5* to *U-12*, *U-14* and *U-16* to *U-30*.[18]

The incident was a game-changer in terms of naval warfare but at the time few saw it as such, at least on the British side. After the sinking of *Pathfinder*, there should have been a heightened consciousness of the submarine threat and anti-submarine measures should have been put in place throughout the fleet. Instead, this historic moment in naval warfare was largely ignored by the Admiralty. It was bitter taste of things to come.

The sense of denial about the threat of submarines was not, however, confined to the upper echelons of the service. In his diary entry for 12 September 1914, written from the 10th Cruiser Squadron, operating in the northern North Sea, Midshipman Scrimgeour refutes the modified reports that *Pathfinder* was sunk by a submarine (not a mine, as previously reported by the Admiralty): 'The report that the *Pathfinder* was sunk by a submarine, and not a mine, is completely untrue and a fabrication.'[19]

Despite a heightened awareness of the submarine threat after the sinking of *Pathfinder*, there were still no formal instructions issued by the Admiralty on what patrolling ships should do to counter it. Neither was there any such thing as an anti-submarine weapon in 1914. Indeed, it would be some considerable time before air reconnaissance and depth charges were introduced as complacency and inertia at the higher echelons of the Admiralty took a firm grip.

There were dissenting voices, of course. The energetic reformist First Sea Lord, Admiral 'Jacky' Fisher, recognised that the submarine 'must revolutionise naval tactics'[20] and wrote as early as 1904 in a letter to Admiral May, then Controller of the Navy: 'It's astounding to me … how the very best among us absolutely fail to realize the vast impending revolution in naval warfare and naval strategy that the submarine will accomplish.'

The 1912 set-piece naval manoeuvres showed the capability of the submarine and impressed the First Lord of the Admiralty, Winston Churchill. But despite the enthusiasm of the First Lord, never reluctant to advocate new technology and methods, and the enthusiasm of Fisher, who was rarely far away from the Admiralty, even in retirement, the view that the submarine threat had been exaggerated prevailed among their principal naval colleagues.

While employed by the Admiralty to improve director firing systems for ship's gunnery, something that he had been pioneering for decades despite Admiralty opposition to any innovation or change, Admiral Sir Percy Scott became increasingly occupied with the problem of detecting and attacking submarines. Scott was an iconoclast and a technical visionary but he discovered to his great frustration that the Admiralty had little interest in the issue. It is worth quoting from Scott's memoir at some length because these views and experiences recalled by a widely admired senior naval officer at the advent of the First World War are revealing:

> I took the liberty of pointing out to the Admiralty that the Germans were building many submarines and large ones.
>
> I found that their Lordships did not realize the potentialities of the submarine or the deadliness of the torpedo, their theory being that the submarine was an untried weapon and that the torpedo was inaccurate. That this view should have been held at the Admiralty, I considered a danger to the country, for it was obvious that if their Lordships did not recognize the power of the submarines they would not consider any anti-submarine measures necessary.
>
> The official view was the more surprising since in all frequent manoeuvres the submarine had over and over again demonstrated its deadliness of attack and it should have been apparent to everyone that the introduction of these vessels had revolutionized naval warfare and put into the hands of the Germans a weapon of far more use to them than their fleet of battleships.[21]

In desperation, Scott had written a provocative and highly prescient letter to *The Times* on 4 June 1914 in an attempt to get the Admiralty to take the threat of submarines seriously. He was widely vilified for doing so and accused of being both ignorant and a scaremonger. The general consensus within Admiralty circles at the outbreak of war was that the submarine might have limited potential as a coastal or port defence weapon but in its current form it was little more than an experimental toy.

Scott's suggestion that, unless a means of attacking submarines was found, the entire British fleet would remain largely confined to harbour and remain fearful of setting foot outside because the threat of submarines and mines was considered ridiculous. Yet he was proven to be correct on all counts. 'What surprised me was that five admirals rushed into print to tell the world how little they knew,' he wrote.[22]

A committee had been at work on the subject of anti-submarine weapons since 1910 but produced nothing tangible. Suggestions had verged on the bizarre, including the training of seagulls to defecate on submarine periscopes in order to obscure their view. When Admiral Scott was belatedly appointed as head of a unit set up to progress anti-submarine measures, the war had already been under way for 120 days and several ships had been lost to torpedo attack. 'With regard to attacking submarines, as the Admiralty before the war regarded them as little more than toys, it was only natural that no progress had been made in the direction of taking measures for destroying them,' wrote Scott.

Despite official ambivalence to the submarine and its potential, it would be wrong to imply that the Royal Navy did not construct submarines or train people to operate them, in what was known as 'the trade'. This was a snobbish, pejorative term, implying that it was a trade rather than a profession as far as the Royal Navy's snooty 'gin and bitters' club was concerned.

At the commencement of hostilities, Britain possessed seventy-four submarines[23] and France seventy. Germany only had twenty-three, though production was quickly ramped up as the war progressed. Weddigen would only have had very limited information regarding the lack of preparedness of the Royal Navy for submarine attack. It is unlikely he was aware of the complete non-existence of any effective anti-submarine measures, despite the submarine being a well-established naval weapon.

The first recorded experiment in submarine operation was made by the Dutch inventor Cornelis Drebbel, who in 1624 constructed a one-man submarine operated by feathering oars, which made a successful underwater trip from Westminster to Greenwich on the Thames. One of the first military missions for a submarine occurred during the Revolutionary War in North America, when David Bushnell used the American Turtle, a one-man submarine, to almost sink a ship in New York Harbor in 1776.

The technology had been introduced to popular culture by Jules Verne's ground-breaking book *Twenty Thousand Leagues Under the Sea*, published in 1870, featuring the fictional hero Captain Nemo. Gottlieb Daimler designed the first successful petrol-driven submarine in 1885 and the Royal Navy launched its first such craft in October 1901, designed by the Irish American designer John Phillip Holland. After twelve years of service, *Holland 1* sank near the Eddystone Lighthouse on the south-west coast of England while being towed by tug to the scrapyard. Luckily, no one was aboard, and the tow rope was quickly released to prevent any damage to the tug boat.

In April 1981, the wreck of *Holland 1* was discovered on the seabed by the minesweeper HMS *Bossington* and was eventually raised into dry dock in Devonport in November of the same year. The fully restored and conserved submarine can be visited at the Royal Navy Submarine Museum in Gosport, England.

Despite the increasing technological options, the modern submarine remained a rather underdeveloped naval technology that was untested in combat and considered by many as primarily the stuff of science fiction. But there was nothing fictional about *U-9*. Johnson and his bridge team scanned the horizon, oblivious to his presence.

Surprisingly, nothing was known by the German High Command about the predictable and largely pointless patrols by Cruiser Force C in the Broad Fourteens and on Dogger Bank. On 16 September, *U-24* and *U-8* were ordered to reconnoitre as far as the Haaks Light Vessel but, although they came safely through yet another North Sea gale, they discovered none of the patrols.

Admiral Christian later accused the Queenborough (near Sheerness) to Flushing mailboat of passing information about the patrols to the German Navy but there is no evidence that any merchant ship passed intelligence about the cruiser patrols to Berlin. Instead, Weddigen was chosen for an entirely different mission and only stumbled upon Cruiser Force C by chance. He was tasked with interrupting the transport of British troops to the Belgian coast and he was ordered to proceed to the position likely to afford the best results, between the West Hinder Light Vessel and Ostend.

The weather was so poor after the departure of *U-9* in the early morning of 20 September that navigation was almost impossible. The situation was made worse by a malfunctioning gyrocompass. During the afternoon, in order to fix his position, Weddigen turned due south from his westerly course to make land, which he sighted at 0730 on 21 September, near Ameland, one of the low-lying west Friesen islands, on the north Dutch coast.

Throughout the day and the greater part of the night of 21 September, *U-9* steered along the coast of the Netherlands on the surface. Weddigen attempted to rest his weary and sodden crew by lying the boat on the bottom of the Broad Fourteens at a depth of 30m, which was no easy task. Spiess wrote:

> To place the submarine on the bottom without undue shock requires a certain amount of expert handling on the part of the commanding officer. The boat is brought down by horizontal rudders until contact with the ground is slowly made and then after stopping the engines the regulating tanks are flooded until the boat is heavy by several tons and remains anchored by its own weight.[24]

On this occasion, there was a considerable seaway even at this depth and the attempt had to be abandoned because the boat bumped so heavily against the seabed.

About midnight on 21 September, as Lieutenant Richard Harrison RNR was making his way back from the bridge of *Cressy* to his cabin having stood the first watch, and as the strong wind had started to ease, Weddigen sighted a vessel without lights 1,000 yards off and thought it advisable to submerge to 15m, alter course to the south-west and continue submerged cruising. It is highly probable that the ship sighted by *U-9* was one of the patrolling cruisers still on the south-westerly leg of their patrol.

The three cruisers had been patrolling on a NE by N course during the day, running parallel with the Dutch coast, examining steamers and trawlers. At sunset, the three armoured cruisers were near the northern limit of the patrol area, off the Haaks Light Vessel. The squadron then turned 16 points and steered down towards Maas Light Vessel until midnight, when unknowingly they came into close contact with *U-9* for the first time.

Shortly after, their course was altered slightly to the westward until 0400, when the squadron again turned to the north-eastward to start the next leg of the patrol. Now at the southern end of the beat, Captain Drummond of HMS *Hogue*, in temporary command of the Force, had little apprehension of submarine attacks.

The ships were steaming on a steady course at 9 or 10 knots, when *U-9*, also steering for the Maas Light Vessel, sighted them, approaching from the south-west on the return leg of their patrol. The submarine had blown its tanks and engaged its kerosene engines at 0445 to charge the batteries, sending plumes of white smoke into the twilight. 'On coming to the surface on the morning of the memorable 22 September we were agreeably surprised,' recalled Spiess.[25]

Like Gabbett on the bridge of *Cressy*, Spiess also noticed that the weather was clearing and the wind had already dropped considerably. He had the watch while Weddigen and the chief engineer paced the deck of the casing to get some much-needed fresh air and exercise, as he and the bridge lookouts scanned the horizon with prismatic binoculars. The boat was proceeding in a zigzag course to avoid his view being obscured by the smoke from the engines. It was Spiess who detected the mast of a warship on the distant horizon. He immediately stopped the engines and called for Weddigen, who had just proceeded below for his breakfast.

Arriving on the bridge, the U-boat commander did not need a second look. Without hesitation, he calmly ordered the boat to dive. 'Could this be the first sight of the enemy that we would have during the war?' asked Spiess.[26] Weddigen also described the moment in his account:

> I had sighted several ships during my passage, but they were not what I was seeking. English torpedo boats came within my reach, but I felt there was bigger game further on, so on I went. I travelled on the surface except when we sighted vessels, and then I submerged, not even showing my periscope, except when it was necessary to take bearings. It was ten minutes after six [0510 GMT] on the morning of last Tuesday [22 September] when I caught sight of one of the big cruisers of the enemy.[27]

British accounts suggest that Weddigen's first belief was that the three cruisers composed part of the screening vessels of a fleet. It was not until the last moment, when there was still no sign of a main body to be seen, that he decided to attack the ships before him rather than wait for a more valuable victim. Weddigen's own account makes clear he was delighted to detect three large British cruisers and regarded them as a big potential prize, though he initially misidentified them as the smaller *Town*-class cruisers.

By 0512, as the skies brightened, he was positioned perfectly: about 2 miles north-east of the approaching cruisers illuminated by the rising sun as they obligingly closed towards him in formation, on a steady course and speed:

> I had been going ahead partly submerged, with about five feet of my periscope showing. Almost immediately I caught sight of the first cruiser and two others. I submerged completely and laid my course so as to bring up in the centre of the trio, which held a sort of triangular formation. I could see their grey-black sides riding high over the water …

Though *U-9* was still low on battery power due to the submerged cruising overnight, he dared not rush:

> When I first sighted them, they were near enough for torpedo work, but I wanted to make my aim sure, so I went down and in on them. I had taken the position of the three ships before submerging, and I succeeded in getting another flash through my periscope before I began action. I soon reached what I regarded as a good shooting point.[28]

Steering first for the *Aboukir*, which was in the centre of the three-ship formation, Weddigen skilfully manoeuvred *U-9* within the three cruisers without being detected and was now positioned only 500 yards on the port beam of HMS *Aboukir.* At this time, attacks had to be launched very close to their target (approximately 300–500 yards) as the running distance of early German torpedoes was limited. Adopting a firing position close to the central cruiser required considerable skill and patience.

During the approach to the firing position, it was vitally important that the submarine remained at exactly the correct depth. Too deep and Weddigen could not check his position with the periscope; too shallow and he would be seen, and the game would be over – and maybe his life, too.

'There is no room for mistakes in submarines – you are either alive or dead,' wrote Vice Admiral Max Horton, who as a young commander was the Royal Navy's most distinguished submariner of the First World War. As a Lieutenant Commander, he was in command of HMS *E9*, the submarine well known for torpedoing SMS *Hela*, a German warship, from a range of 600 yards in September 1914.

The torpedo used by Weddigen on board *U-9* was most likely the C/06, introduced in 1907. It was big. At 5.65m long and weighing 773kg, it was not easy to manhandle within the confines of a U-boat. Its four-cylinder engine emitted compressed air, which propelled the torpedo and its explosive payload of 122.6kg of TNT over a maximum range of 1,500m at 34.5 knots. It was the first German torpedo fitted with a gyro-angle setter so that the submarine did not have to be head on or stern on to its target when releasing the weapon from its torpedo tubes. This feature was to greatly open up the field of torpedo tactics.

The small amount of explosives in the warhead made an explosion at 500 yards safe for the attacking U-boat, unless of course the target was carrying explosive cargo such as ammunition or gasoline. However, *U-21* had reported that the concussion from the attack on HMS *Pathfinder* at 1,200 yards range had been very severe, so there was considerable anxiety on *U-9* about the potential damage to the U-boat from any hit at close range.

At about 0625, Weddigen gave the order to fire one torpedo from the forward tube.

'First tube FIRE. Periscope in,' was the order given and, having unscrewed the protective firing cap in readiness, Spiess stabbed the firing button with his right thumb and heard the distinctive hiss of the weapon leaving the tube en route to HMS *Aboukir.*

'Then I loosed one of my torpedoes at the middle ship. I was then about twelve feet underwater, and got the shot off in good shape, my men handling the boat as if she had been a skiff,' boasted Weddigen.

The first indication of the presence of *U-9* on board the bridge of *Cressy* was the sound of a muffled explosion that fractured the usual professional hush.

3

WHITEHALL AT WAR

Far from the windswept bridge of HMS *Cressy* and remote from the brutal realities of submarine attacks and North Sea patrols, the man responsible to His Majesty's Government for the war at sea was growing restive. After a near-perfect start, maritime matters in the opening six weeks of the conflict were proving to be somewhat frustrating.

The war at sea was planned and executed by the Admiralty – the vast government ministry responsible for all aspects of the Royal Navy from weapons and shipbuilding contracts to ship design, pay and uniform. The man who was its political chief, the First Lord of the Admiralty, ultimately responsible for all aspects of the Royal Navy including the successful prosecution of the war at sea, was Winston Churchill. Appointed in October 1911 at the age of 39 and already a seasoned political veteran, he was the man tasked with preparing the Navy for war and obtaining victory for the nation. He warmed to the challenge with his characteristic energy and vigour. 'I can now lay eggs instead of scratching around in the dust and clucking,' he explained at the time.[1]

In stark contrast to the sailors, stokers and marines crammed into the stuffy and often swamped mess decks of HMS *Cressy*, the First Lord lived in a splendid eighteenth-century official residence in Whitehall. Admiralty House came with the job and boasted two 35ft drawing rooms, a library and seven bedrooms. His wife, Clementine, the mother of his two young children and pregnant with their third, did not share his enthusiasm for the huge rooms and ugly furniture, but Churchill loved what he described as 'his mansion'.[2]

In common with many of the ships' companies at sea in the three *Cressy*-class cruisers, Churchill also had the safety and well-being of a young family to worry about. When Churchill rushed back to London from his family holiday on the eve of war, his heavily pregnant wife had been left with the children at Pear Cottage in the remote Norfolk coastal village of Overstrand, where the family had been staying. Their daughter, Diana, was 5 years old and Randolph was 3 in August 1914. There was official concern that they presented a security risk in such an isolated location on England's east coast, where they might be vulnerable to abduction by German special forces.

'It makes me a little anxious that you should be on the coast. It is 100 to one against a raid – but there is still a chance and Cromer has a good landing place near,' he wrote to his wife on 9 August.[3]

From the moment Churchill returned to Admiralty House he ploughed ferociously into his prodigious workload. In the same letter, he wrote to his wife: 'I am over head & ears in work & am much behind-hand.' Churchill kept unorthodox working hours, preferring to work late into the night and rise late. Having his private quarters on site made this more feasible. In the mornings, his staff would routinely bring papers and signals for inspection and signature at his bedside, which he would sign in a flourish of red ink while puffing on an enormous Corona cigar and sipping warm water.

'A most extraordinary spectacle, perched up in a huge bed with the whole of the counterpane littered with dispatch boxes, red and all colours and a stenographer sitting at the foot,' was how Chief Naval Censor, Captain Douglas Brownrigg, described his boss.[4]

The opening weeks of the First World War at sea were widely regarded as a disappointment for Britain. The initial febrile public excitement and patriotic sense of expectation that greeted the outbreak of the conflict had gradually diminished. Instead of a glorious gunnery engagement waged by an immaculate formation of capital ships, the Royal Navy's powerful Grand Fleet, commanded by Admiral Sir John Jellicoe, had largely withdrawn to Scapa Flow in the Orkney Islands, out of harm's way. 'So, we waited and nothing happened. No great event immediately occurred. No battle was fought,' wrote Churchill.[5]

Jellicoe, known as 'Silent Jack', was the man Churchill described as someone 'who could lose the war in an afternoon'.[6] Widely admired and respected by his peers and tortured by chronic haemorrhoids, Jellicoe was the principal exponent of a defensive mentality based on the fear of losing numerical superiority in warships over Germany that permeated the higher echelons of the service. The strategy of enforcing a blockade from a safe distance, while maintaining superiority, was undoubtedly shrewd but it did not make for great news copy. Like a top football team, one-nil up in the second half of a major cup semi-final, the Royal Navy, under the command of 'Silent Jack' Jellicoe, was playing it safe.

Caution did not come naturally to Churchill. The prime minister, Herbert Asquith – who appointed him to the job in 1911 – described him as having 'a pictorial mind brimming with ideas'.[7] Except for the office of prime minister, his was arguably the most prestigious and influential government appointment in wartime. Given the perceived importance and size of the Navy compared with the Army, it was arguably a more vital Cabinet post than Secretary of State for War, the position occupied in 1914 by another celebrity public figure, Field Marshal Kitchener.

Britain traditionally retained a huge navy and small army, and all issues naval or maritime were widely considered to be of vital national interest. There was good reason for this. Maritime trade was essential to the economic well-being of an island nation with an extensive overseas empire, economically dependent on trade. Its immense mercantile power and prosperity could only be protected by warships, capable of exerting mobile influence on a global canvas.

Churchill was considered to be more than qualified for this crucial Cabinet post. This fearless, provocative and opinionated trouble-shooter had the Midas touch. He seemed to be the perfect candidate to be at the head of the Navy in wartime – First Lord of the Admiralty.

By the time of his appointment, he had participated in, or at least observed at close hand, four wars, in three continents, as an Army Second Lieutenant or as a war correspondent. He had been an MP since the age of 25 and was dubbed 'Pushful, the Younger' by one witty newspaper journalist.[8] He had already served as President of the Board of Trade and, after the 1910 election, was appointed, at the age of 35, as the youngest Home Secretary since Robert Peel.

While the Admiralty appeared to offer him the perfect vehicle for his lofty ambition, he inherited a highly conservative and complacent institution obsessed with tradition and hierarchy and fractured by bitter internecine warfare. The task of reform and modernisation had been initiated in 1904 by Admiral John 'Jacky' Fisher, First Sea Lord between 1904 and 1910. 'The danger that is eternally present to the Navy is over confidence in our preparedness for war,' Fisher wrote in 1904.[9]

Churchill described Fisher as 'ruthless, relentless, and remorseless' and a 'veritable volcano of knowledge'.[10] He was a ferocious and unforgiving zealot who saw with clarity that the principal function of the Royal Navy was to win battles at sea with the latest in technology. Most remembered for his introduction of the 18,000-ton *Dreadnought* class of battleship, he also sought to modernise the service, revolutionise training, scrap obsolete ships and focus on a future war in the North Sea and Atlantic Ocean – not cocktail receptions in the far-flung corners of empire. 'He shook them and beat them and cajoled them out of slumber into intense activity,' wrote Churchill.[11]

But by offering no quarter in his restless quest to prepare his beloved Royal Navy for a new era of high-technology warfare, Fisher alienated the traditionalist wing of the Navy during his tenure as First Sea Lord. 'In carrying through these far-reaching changes, he had created violent oppositions to himself in the Navy and his own methods, in which he gloried, were of a kind to excite bitter animosities which he returned and was eager to repay,' wrote Churchill.[12] This animosity became so acrimonious that it erupted into a divisive national scandal, the aroma of which still lingered in the corridors of Admiralty House four years after Fisher's retirement.

The bitter disputes were waged broadly between two camps: the advocates of the ruthless modernist Admiral Fisher, nicknamed the 'Fishpond', and the traditionalists, represented by Admiral Lord Charles Beresford, named the 'Beresfordites'. Beresford was Commander-in-Chief of the Channel Fleet and a Member of Parliament and was generally an extremely well-connected and popular public figure. He was also a classic reactionary who resented modification and believed professional training and new technology remained a poor substitute for tradition, courage, strict discipline and personal 'pluck'.

The schism at the Admiralty and within the Navy reached a climax at the gunnery exercises in Portland in 1907. At this time, Rear Admiral Scott, a supporter of Fisher, was commanding the 1st Cruiser Squadron, with Beresford as his superior officer as Commander-in-Chief of the Channel Fleet. In November, it was planned for Kaiser Wilhelm II to view the fleet at Spithead and Beresford, a great advocate of ceremonial customs, signalled the whole fleet to be moved to Portland for a tidying up. One of Scott's ships, HMS *Roxburgh*, was undertaking gunnery practice. Her captain asked Scott whether he should abandon the practice and enter Portland under Beresford's instruction, to which Scott replied insubordinately with, 'Paintwork appears to be more in demand than gunnery, so you had better come in to make yourself look pretty by the 8th'.[13] Beresford was furious and decided to severely reprimand Scott publicly, refusing to listen to any explanation and sending a message to the fleet:

> The signal made by the Rear-Admiral commanding 1st Cruiser Squadron is contemptuous in tone and insubordinate in character. The Rear-Admiral is to issue orders to the *Good Hope* and *Roxburgh* to expunge the signal from their signal logs and report when my orders have been obeyed.

Beresford reported the incident to the Admiralty and requested that Scott be removed from his post. Fisher denied his request, but the whole affair soon became public knowledge and was splashed across the press, developing into a national scandal. Beresford made increasingly hostile comments towards the Admiralty Board, and the feud between Fisher and Beresford eventually resulted in a parliamentary sub-committee that undermined Fisher's authority and forced him to retire early in 1910.

This background is significant because when Churchill assumed responsibility for the Admiralty in 1911, it was not only a complacent organisation despite Fisher's zealous efforts, it was also a bitterly divided, dysfunctional and toxic place, with senior officers still split between Beresford and Fisher. The Chief of Staff, Sturdee, was a protégé of Beresford and therefore hated by Fisher, who still advised Churchill unofficially from the wings. It was far from an ideal environment at the advent of war and Churchill was acutely aware of it.

'A deplorable schism was introduced into the Royal Navy which spread to every squadron and to every ship,' wrote Churchill,[14] who resisted the temptation of inviting Fisher, whom he greatly admired, to return as First Sea Lord in 1911 because it would have reopened old wounds.

'The jealousy and quarrelling in Service circles in England during the war was a valuable asset to our enemies,' wrote Scott.

Churchill relished the challenges presented by his high-profile role and immersed himself in every detail of naval affairs as he prepared the nation for war. He achieved a great deal but the autocratic hands-on management style that he adopted was a radical change that was not to everyone's taste. 'His curiosity about the service for which he was responsible seemed to many of the older officers almost indecent,' wrote Admiral Sir William James, who first met Churchill while serving as Gunnery Lieutenant of HMS *Queen Mary* in 1912.

The account of the ship visit is illuminating because it reveals the attitude of naval officers to this new brand of First Lord of the Admiralty. According to James, naval officers expected a First Lord who merely presented the naval estimates to Parliament and 'abided by the advice of his professional colleagues on all technical matters, on strategy and on training'. By 1912 this mould had already been broken and it was never likely to have been a viable operational model for someone as dynamic as Churchill.

'The First Lord is responsible to crown and parliament for all the business of the Admiralty. In virtue of this he delegates to an eminent sailor the responsibility for its technical and professional conduct. But he cannot thus relieve himself either in theory or in fact. He [the First Lord] is held strictly accountable for all that takes place; for every disaster he must bear blame,' wrote Churchill.[15]

It meant that when Churchill visited HMS *Queen Mary* in 1912 to witness night gunnery exercises at Portland, he was given something of the cold shoulder by the officers on board. James related that when the exercise was complete, Churchill met with officers around the fireplace in the ship's wardroom, firing technical questions about improvements to gunnery performance late into the night. Before long, the assembled audience was won over by the sheer force of his enthusiasm and energetic personality.[16]

Churchill could win people over and persuade them of almost anything, but his highly unorthodox hands-on management style flew in the face of the tradition and precedent that was the foundation stone of the Admiralty.

Churchill may have been the most flamboyant character in the government, as the eminent naval historian Arthur Marder described him, but he was generally unpopular with senior officers in the Royal Navy. Those working in the Admiralty mostly regarded him as bumptious, erratic, impetuous and, as Jellicoe later wrote, 'entirely ignorant of naval affairs'. As early as December 1913, the German naval attaché reported: 'The sea officers of the British Navy are often enraged against Mr Churchill.'[17]

The First Lord of the Admiralty thought nothing of rebuking senior naval officers like junior cadets for their poor use of grammar in official reports, sending detailed operational instructions to seasoned commanding officers who, to paraphrase Churchill, were captains afloat when he was in his cradle. He longed to be in charge of front-line operations at sea; introduced madcap ideas and pet theories at a bewildering velocity; indulged in political intrigue to get his own way; and sacked popular senior officers with decades of experience in favour of his preferred appointees.

The sacking of Admiral Callaghan as Commander-in-Chief of the Home Fleet, a few days into the war, caused widespread resentment within the Navy and was universally opposed by all quarters, including Admiral Jellicoe, the man who replaced him. It was unprecedented for a politician to sack a Commander-in-Chief during wartime, particularly one who was widely admired and guilty of no apparent failing. It deeply offended the Royal Navy's sense of order, hierarchy and tradition.

Churchill was also a former Army officer – a 'bloody pongo', in modern naval parlance – from a distinguished military family that included John Churchill, 1st Duke of Marlborough and the victor of a string of battles, including Blenheim, during the War of the Spanish Succession. This did not endear him to senior naval officers, who had their own family traditions going back to Nelson's band of brothers and beyond.

Churchill was thought to be much more enthusiastic and knowledgeable about military strategy and tactics than the naval equivalents. This did not temper his direct interference in all naval matters, as he wrote:

> I interpreted my duty in the following way: I accepted full responsibility for bringing about successful results, and in that spirit, I exercised a close general supervision over everything that was done or proposed. Further, I claimed and exercised an unlimited power of suggestion and initiative over the whole field, subject only to the approval and agreement of the First Sea Lord on all operative orders, right or wrong this is what I did and it is on this basis that I wish to be judged.[18]

In 1832, a reforming First Lord of the Admiralty abolished the Navy Board, bringing all its functions under the superintendence of 'Their Lordships' –

the Board of Admiralty whose head was the First Lord, the minister who was the political master of the Navy. 'Robed in the august authority of centuries of naval tradition and armed with the fullest knowledge available, the Board of Admiralty wielded unchallenged power,' wrote Churchill.[19]

In the eighteenth century, the department moved to the building in Whitehall, which is still called the Old Admiralty. In organisational terms, in 1914 the Admiralty was still archaic, bureaucratic, conservative and paralytically slow at implementing change, and Churchill was determined to prepare it for war. 'I intended to prepare for an attack by Germany as if it might come next day,' wrote Churchill and he set about dragging the Admiralty edifice into the twentieth century, if not kicking and screaming, then at least sulking and obfuscating.

Churchill reappointed the Navy Board and set up a professional War Staff to plan and administer a future war at sea but, perhaps most significantly, he did his utmost to focus this giant government ministry on preparing for war. 'Upon the wall behind my chair, I had an open case fitted [and] within those folded doors spread a large chart of the North Sea,' he wrote, and he made it a rule to look at that chart once every day when he first entered his office.

'I did this less to keep myself informed, for there were many other channels of information, than in order to inculcate in myself and those working with me a sense of ever-present danger,' he wrote, and there was to be no tolerance of complacency in Churchill's Admiralty.[20]

Churchill might have been frustrated at times by the slow pace of reform at the Admiralty but he took delight in the perks of the job, not least the use of the official First Lord's yacht. HMS *Enchantress* was a lavishly fitted 4,000-ton steam-powered yacht with a 196-man crew, which was capable of undertaking ocean passages.

More importantly, perhaps, it was the perfect floating platform for entertaining in sumptuous style. The Churchills were not ultra-wealthy like many of their aristocratic contemporaries, but Churchill had the unfortunate combined traits of expensive taste and financial incontinence. He was accustomed to an opulent lifestyle but did not always have the means to finance it. *Enchantress* allowed him to indulge his passions for intense industry and lavish socialising, simultaneously and legitimately, at the taxpayer's expense. In the three years prior to the outbreak of hostilities, Churchill spent about eight months on *Enchantress*, often with his wife supporting his efforts to entertain, badger and influence military leaders, diplomats and senior government figures. He revelled in it. Churchill was 'easily satisfied with the best', as his close friend and political ally F.E. Smith put it.

While some found Churchill's apparent enthusiasm for war a little distasteful at the start of the conflict, the naval war plan was implemented successfully and his decision along with that of the First Sea Lord, Prince Louis of Battenberg, the professional head of the Royal Navy, to dispatch the Grand Fleet to Scapa Flow in the Orkney islands before the official outbreak of hostilities proved to be a prescient move.

Prince Louis (the brother of the King of Bulgaria) was described by Marder as 'brilliant'.[21] According to Churchill, 'Prince Louis was a child of the Royal Navy'. He certainly had impeccable aristocratic credentials and was widely respected. Battenberg was regarded as a capable and sound senior officer but not always an effective brake on the relentlessly impetuous Churchill. Ultimately, the First Sea Lord could not prevent his political boss running the show.

It was also very fortunate planning on the part of Battenberg and Churchill that by electing to mobilise the naval reserve in July instead of merely engaging in the usual annual routine manoeuvres, the manning of the ships of the Second and Third fleets (which relied on the recall of naval reservists) was already tested and the men at the ready.

On 18 July, leave was cancelled and the reserve ships of the Third Fleet, like HMS *Cressy*, retained in commission. It must have been a big disappointment to reservists expecting to spend the August bank holiday with their families but, in retrospect, it was a master stroke. It meant that when hostilities were formally declared on 4 August, the British fleet was, to a large extent, fully manned and ready.

According to Marder, the Second Sea Lord, Vice Admiral Sir Frederick 'Freddy' Hamilton, was rather a lazy officer of no great distinction who enjoyed great popularity in the fleet. He owed some of his success to his court entrée through his sister, who was married to Vice Admiral Sir Colin Keppel in command of HM Yachts. The Third Sea Lord, Rear Admiral Sir Frederick Tudor, was described as a 'competent officer'. The Fourth Sea Lord was Commodore Cecil F. Lambert, an old-school seagoing officer and traditionalist described as having a 'face like a seaboot or a scrubbed hammock' who was saturnine to subordinates and inflexible with almost everyone else.

Churchill's Permanent Secretary at the Admiralty was the highly respected civil servant William Graham Green. According to his obituary in *The Times*, Greene 'was a conscientious, zealous, and greatly experienced officer, but his modest nature deprived him of the strong personality which might have given him greater influence in the conduct of affairs'. He served at the Admiralty until 1917, when he left to rejoin Churchill at the Department of Munitions.

In addition to the all-powerful Admiralty Board and the Commanders-in-Chief of the various stations, there was a War Staff tasked with prosecuting the war at sea. Vice Admiral Sir Doveton Sturdee became Chief of War Staff in August 1914, largely because of his reputation as an expert in the history of naval warfare. According to Marder, Sturdee's main weakness was that he thought he was the only naval officer in Britain who knew anything about war. As a consequence, he largely ignored the advice and recommendations of his juniors, including experienced commanders at sea like Commodore Roger Keyes and Commodore Reginald Tyrwhitt, who had pleaded with him on several occasions to remove the *Cressy*-class cruisers from the Broad Fourteens patrol.

Between its creation in January 1912 under Churchill's tenure and the end of the First World War, some 930 individuals served on the Admiralty War Staff.[22] Research by Nicholas Duncan Black, of Imperial College London, indicates these was a various assortment of men and women, military and civilians, of whom 621 served in the Royal Navy in one form or another.[23] Many retired senior officers were recruited to the Admiralty at the start of war and not all to good effect. It was old fashioned, unwieldy and mostly ineffective.

The other key operational figure at the Admiralty was the Director of Operations (DOD), Rear Admiral Arthur Cavenagh Leveson, a stocky broad-shouldered domineering bully and authoritarian, equally immune to input from more junior officers or those on the front line. It was Leveson to whom Keyes wrote on 21 August, urging him to remove the *Cressy*-class vessels from the Broad Fourteens patrol.

By the time hostilities commenced in 1914, the day-to-day running of the war was delegated to Churchill's War Group. This ad hoc committee largely bypassed the unwieldy War Staff and met in the War Room once, sometimes twice, a day and issued a plethora of signals, instructions, memos and wireless telegraph signals. While individuals were invited as required, the running of the war at sea was essentially down to Churchill, Prince Louis, Sturdee, sometimes Leveson and the Permanent Secretary, Green.

'It happened in a large number of cases that seeing what ought to be done and confident of the agreement of the First Sea Lord, I myself drafted the telegrams and decisions in accordance with our policy and the COS [Chief of Staff, Sturdee] took them personally to the First Sea Lord [Prince Louis] for his concurrence before dispatch,' wrote Churchill.[24]

Prince Louis, often observed in his office leafing languidly through the daily newspaper, was known in the service as 'I concur'. Who could blame him given the relentless torrent of signals, innovations, observations, obsessions, thoughts and misgivings emanating from the First Lord?

In effect, the Admiralty Board became redundant for wartime decision-making and the Second, Third and Fourth Sea Lords took little active or operational part in the war. This was Churchill's war and Prince Louis was tasked with the futile mission of restraining his over-imaginative intellect and force of personality. It was US President Roosevelt who much later described Churchill as having 'a hundred ideas a day, of which at least four are good', and often the challenge was working out which four they were.

The War Group became extremely centralised, insular and largely cut off from the new realities of war at sea, and unresponsive to the requirements of those who were fighting it. It was dominated by Churchill.

It was not unusual in the eighteenth century for senior naval officers to hold the position of First Lord. Anson, Hawke, St Vincent and Barham are all examples but, at times, Churchill, the journalist, soldier and politician, seemed to be confusing himself with a battle-hardened Admiral with decades of experience at sea. 'It was undeniably the case that during this period from August to October 1914, Churchill was the dominant voice in Admiralty decision-making and politics. This inevitably created problems with which others, including members of the War Staff, had to grapple,' writes Black.[25]

As war progressed the Admiralty became rapidly overburdened with paperwork, so it recruited the services of a series of retired Admirals. Some of these were labelled the 'charity admirals' by Fisher. The most famous of these officers was Sir Arthur Wilson. According to an anonymous letter, dated 22 February 1917:

> The Staff was … merely a nondescript collection of officers. Many of them were retired officers who had been recalled in the war and who were as ignorant of the principles of staff work as they were of strategy and operations.[26]

According to Black, the failure to develop a coherent submarine policy in the years immediately prior to the First World War lay less with any weaknesses in the War Staff itself than with the manner in which Churchill ran his department.

'Now we have our war. The next thing is to decide how we are going to carry it on,' wrote Churchill, and while some saw this as an indictment that the Royal Navy was not prepared for war, the statement did him something of a disservice. 'The Duke of Newcastle himself could not have made a more damning confession of inadequate preparation for war,' recorded the Assistant Director of Operations (ADOD), Herbert Richmond, in his diary at the time.

However, while there might have been many serious shortcomings in the Navy's readiness for a full-scale, high-technology modern conflict and with the combat experience among its ranks, the pre-war planning in terms of deployment of assets and personnel was just about spot on.

As Lord Kitchener, who was hardly a devotee of Churchill, later wrote to him: 'There is one thing at any rate they cannot take from you: The fleet was ready,' and Jellicoe wrote after the war: 'Fortunately, the Admiralty in the last days of July 1914, placed us at once in a strong strategic position. For this action the nation should be grateful to the First Lord and First Sea Lord.'[27]

Thanks to Churchill's relentless vigour, the plan was sound enough, but implementing it, which included the co-ordinated operations of some 1,000 vessels around the world, proved more challenging.

The Royal Navy remained ill prepared for modern naval warfare and its officers had no direct experience of it. Its senior officers, such as Beatty and Jellicoe, had only seen action ashore during anti-foreigner uprisings such as China's Boxer Rebellion and on the River Nile in the Sudan. The international legation at Peking (Beijing) was under siege in 1900 and had to be relieved by a multi-national task force. They had very little, if any, direct first-hand experience of modern warfare at sea.

The joint Anglo-French naval bombardment of Russian fortifications at the Battle of Kilburn, during the latter stages of the Crimean War in 1855, was the most recent occurrence of British guns fired in anger and there were no enemy ships involved in that. The few sea battles involving armoured ships and modern gunnery like the Battle of Yalu River in 1896 during the Sino-Japanese War and the Battle of Tsushima in 1905 between Russo-Japanese War combatants did not involve the British, who could only spectate from afar.

The Navy still thought in straight lines and remained obsessed with the notion of classic gunnery actions undertaken between immaculately spaced formations of warships, as Admiral Nelson commanded at the Battle of Trafalgar in 1805. The Admiralty was too dismissive of new technology like mines and submarines and their future impact on naval warfare.

Naval technology had advanced rapidly and was incomparable in terms of anything Nelson would have recognised 109 years earlier. Ships were now constructed of steel, not oak. They were powered by steam engines rather than wind-driven sails, capable of speeds of up to 30 knots with guns able to hurl a 3,000lb (1,360kg) high-explosive shell from the pitching deck of one ship onto a moving target more than 15 nautical miles (27.78km) away, guided by semi-automated fire control systems that the Royal Navy was slowly adopting.

Scott stated:

> In addition, we had no up-to-date minelayers, nor an efficient mine, no properly fitted mine sweepers, no arrangements for guarding our ships against mines, no efficient method of using our guns at night, no anti Zeppelin guns; no anti-submarine precautions; no safe harbour for our fleet and only a few ships (eight) were fitted with a proper method for firing their guns. Our torpedoes were so badly fitted that in the early days of the war they went under the German ships instead of hitting them.[28]

New capabilities to communicate with and control the Royal Navy's huge fleet of warships were presented by the introduction of wireless telegraphy, first used operationally by the Royal Navy in set-piece manoeuvres during 1900. It gave the Admiralty the opportunity to communicate directly with individual warships and bypass the long-established chains of command. Many of the service's senior officers had learned their trade under sail and not everyone in the higher echelons embraced the new era of technology with enthusiasm.

There was no shortage of bravery, but wide swathes of the Navy had degenerated into a snobby peacetime cruising club. Ships' companies were often better trained in the arts of complex seamanship evolutions and elaborate ceremonial rituals in far-flung outposts of the British Empire than fighting wars at sea. Officers excelled at desultory small talk at lavish cocktail parties as part of what Marder called 'showing the flag and policing the seas with no thought of fighting a maritime war'.[29] The Navy's glowing reputation had been earned in another era against another foe, and Churchill rued the lack of commanding officers schooled in the art of combat at sea.

'At the outset of war, we had more captains of ships than captains of war. In this will be found the explanation of many untoward events,' he wrote.[30]

Polishing immaculate ships and sand stoning decks was the order of the day. 'The fact is that in 1914 the Royal Navy was almost totally unprepared for war and remained in that condition for most of the period 1914–18,' wrote Commander Stephen King-Hall.[31]

The China station had been *Cressy*'s first commission in 1901. It was about as far removed from war in the North Sea as can be imagined. These ships based in Hong Kong in the pre-war era were unlikely to be threatened by anything more powerful than the muzzle-loaded antique carronade of a local pirate's sailing junk. Commanders of ships like *Cressy* traditionally earned their promotion on the prettiness of their ships and often invested their own salaries in special cleaning materials. Ceremonial rituals and spit and polish ruled the Navy in a world dominated by cocktail parties, diplomatic receptions, sporting competitions and regattas. 'The cleanliness of the ship and the state of the men's bedding were still regarded as the most important factors of efficiency,' wrote Scott in disgust.[32]

'Fundamentally, the backward state of the Navy stemmed from the fact that it had for nearly a century enjoyed a peace routine and that Britain's title of Mistress of the Seas had not been seriously challenged,' wrote Marder.

At the apex of the mammoth antique of a government department, cloaked in history and hierarchy and plagued by inertia and bitter division, and overseeing a large Navy with no experience of modern warfare was the high-energy, ambitious, impetuous, impatient, determined, vain and irrepressible autocrat that was Churchill. It was difficult to envisage a less compatible or more dangerously dysfunctional combination.

4

THE MORNING WATCH

The sudden and unexpected noise of an explosion was the first indication on the bridge of *Cressy* of the torpedo attack by *U-9* on *Aboukir.*

It was quickly followed by a much larger blast, which rattled the wheel-house windows and caused everyone on the upper deck to stop short and gaze intently to starboard. *U-9* had scored a hit and still had five torpedoes left, three more already loaded in the tubes and two in reserve.

As Weddigen manoeuvred his boat for the kill, snatching only the occasional glimpse through the Zeiss attack periscope, his entire crew had waited in anxious silence as the torpedo made its way to the target. 'Under the greatest suspense, everyone in the boat was counting the seconds,' recalled Spiess.

This was the first time Weddigen had deployed a live torpedo in wartime but he had already developed a reputation as something of a torpedo expert within the German submarine service. As the flotilla torpedo officer, all questions regarding the use of torpedoes in wartime were referred to him. In addition to his technical expertise, he was greatly admired and respected by his small crew, with whom he lived at very close quarters. In *U-9*, there was insufficient room, or time, for unnecessary formalities.

In many ways, Weddigen represented the opposite of the traditional British naval officer shunning technical expertise in favour of character and social connections and enjoying a gilded existence which his men could only dream about. 'I was able to learn a great deal from him during the cruises under his command as he allowed his junior officers a great freedom of action and I was never made to feel as a subordinate but rather a younger comrade,' recalled Johannes Spiess, who was his executive officer in *U-9*.[1]

Thirty-one seconds after Spiess's thumb stabbed the button and the torpedo hissed away from the submarine, guided by its internal gyroscope, the entire crew heard and felt the unmistakable impact.

Weddigen told Spiess to take the submarine down to 15m as soon as the torpedo was fired. Early U-boats had an unfortunate habit of surfacing like a frolicking porpoise once the weight of a torpedo had been launched from the forward tubes. 'At once we heard a dull blow followed by a clear crash. Could that be the torpedo hit?' wrote Spiess. Nothing could be confirmed because they were at a depth of 15m and the periscope was run in, but a spontaneous cheer rippled through the boat.

The U-boat commander ordered one of the two 773kg reserve torpedoes to be loaded to replace the one that had been fired. In the confines of the submarine this was no mean feat. On 16 July 1914, this boat had performed the same procedure for the first time in history.

As *U-9* ascended carefully to periscope depth, Weddigen stole a quick view of the damage – Spiess and the rest of his crew had performed their duty well:

> There was a fountain of water, a burst of smoke, a flash of fire, and part of the cruiser rose in the air. Then I heard a roar and felt reverberations sent through the water by the detonation. She had been broken apart, and sank in a few minutes. The *Aboukir* had been stricken in a vital spot and by an unseen force; that made the blow all the greater.[2]

The torpedo took effect just abaft the foremost funnel and flooded two adjoining compartments. The ship listed at once to about 20 degrees. Steam power was lost immediately and the boom boats could not be hoisted out. The only boat available was one small cutter for a ship's company of some 800 men. The other sea boat was shattered by the explosion and the remainder of the boats had been landed on the outbreak of war.

From the upper deck of *Cressy*, a huge plume of black smoke could be seen rising from *Aboukir*'s side. The ship appeared to be losing way in the water and was already listing at an alarming angle. Captain Johnson assumed, as did Captain John Drummond of *Aboukir*, that the ship must have struck a mine. They remained ignorant of the presence of a German U-boat.

Yeoman Webb, in charge of the signalling on the bridge of *Cressy*, announced that *Aboukir* had hoisted the flag signal 'two pennants number eight', which meant 'close on me', and Johnson immediately issued the required helm orders in his calm, clipped middle-class tones. He increased speed and applied full helm in order to execute the nautical equivalent of a handbrake turn. In the choppy sea, this manoeuvre would have sent anything below decks that was not already lashed down or stowed crashing to the deck, including those men emerging from their hammocks as 'call the hands' was piped at 0630.

As the ship completed its hard turn and closed on her stricken sister ship, Johnson ordered all seamen to the boat deck and 'away all boats'. Boat crews raced to the davits lined along the upper deck that deployed the ship's diminished fleet of boats, which ranged from a whaler to a large steam-powered pinnace.

Down below in every mess deck, grunting and snoring sailors and marines in their hammocks, still swinging in perfect synchronicity with the pitching and rolling of the ship, were shaken awake and told the news. 'I was called out of bed in sick bay – the first thing I saw was the *Aboukir* in a sinking condition,' Able Seaman William John Dolbear told the *Dover Express*.[3]

Johnson ordered a second hard turn to port and neatly brought *Cressy* to a stop, about 2 cables (approximately 400m) off *Aboukir*'s port beam, on a similar heading. By then, all the boat crews were closed up and ready.

Now only a few hundred metres away from the catastrophe, the bridge personnel and boat crews could survey the disastrous scene at close quarters, as could the other members of the ship's company, who had instinctively made their way to the upper deck. Officers and men on the bridge of *Cressy* must have struggled to retain their phlegmatic calm as they watched in abject horror as the ship's company of their sister ship, many of whom would have been well known to them, could be observed frantically trying to launch boats, stripping off their clothes and flinging themselves naked into the frigid swell of water.

In his cabin near the wardroom flat, Temporary Surgeon Dr Gerald Noel Martin was woken by his friend, Chaplain George Collier. The *Sheffield Daily Telegraph* published his account on 26 September 1914. Martin was a doctor practising in Eastbourne but with family connections to Yorkshire and had joined *Cressy* as volunteer surgeon, in the early hours of 7 August, having volunteered for war service at sea. 'About 6.30am I was awoken by the Chaplain and asked him the time. He told me the *Aboukir* was sinking,' said Martin.

'Going on deck I found that the *Aboukir* was sinking down. The weather was fine and clear but the sea was choppy, the waves being about ten feet high,' he said, and others remembered the sight many years later. 'I can remember the scene as though it was only yesterday as it was my first sight of men struggling for their lives,' wrote Herewood Hook, then a Midshipman on *Hogue*, in an account published in 1919:

> The bilge keel and part of the ship's bottom were exposed to view, with hundreds of men's heads bobbing about in the water close by, while a continuous stream of very scantily clad men appeared from the upper deck and started tobogganing down the ship's side, stopping suddenly when they came to the bilge keel, climbing over it and continuing their slide until they reached the water with a splash.[4]

According to the account of Chief Engine Room Artificer William John Taylor of *Cressy*, who had been employed in a workshop on the upper deck, a messenger ordered all engine room artificers and chiefs down below to their stations. In his witness statement to the subsequent Court of Inquiry, Taylor explained he was working in the workshop from 0400 but had gone to obtain a file from the ship's store when he saw steam coming from the *Aboukir* as he returned along the upper deck. 'The Engineer Lieutenant (Stacey Wise) gave orders for all planks of wood to be passed up from the engine room, which we did,' said Taylor.

Around this time, Commander Bertram William Lothian Nicholson arrived on the bridge. Nicholson was the second in command of *Cressy* but was of little tactical help to Johnson. Nicholson (not to be confused with Captain Wilmot Nicholson of *Hogue*) later admitted to the Court of Inquiry that he had never received any training or instruction in how to deal with submarine attacks. Despite his vast experience at sea, his role on board was more administrative than operational. Commanders of cruisers ran the ship's routine, husbandry and discipline, and were more focused on spit and polish than war.

'A Commander's promotion had come to depend on the prettiness of the ship he ran both inside and out,' wrote Peter Padfield in his account of naval life at sea at the turn of the twentieth century.[5] The gleaming brasswork, immaculate paintwork and spotlessly clean teak decks would be of no help to *Cressy* now.

Both *Hogue* and *Cressy* had closed on the senior ship; *Hogue* was ahead of the *Aboukir*, and *Cressy* was on her port beam, all on a similar heading. 'As soon as it was seen that the *Aboukir* was in danger of sinking, all the boats were sent away from the *Cressy*, and a picket boat was hoisted out without steam up,' stated Commander Nicholson in his official report, which included a rough pencil drawing indicating the relative position of the three ships.

In the cramped confines of the conning tower of *U-9*, Weddigen could hardly believe his good fortune. 'The English were playing my game, for I had scarcely to move out of my position, which was a great aid, since it helped to keep me from detection,' reported the U-boat commander, now flushed with success from his first kill of the war. 'On board my little boat the spirit of the German Navy was to be seen in its best form. With enthusiasm every man held himself in check and gave attention to the work in hand,' he stated.

Oblivious to the presence of *U-9*, the officers of *Cressy* and *Hogue*, anxious to rescue sailors from the choppy cold sea, were hampered by a boat shortage. The full list of boats was quite comprehensive: one 36ft sailing pinnace, one 42ft sailing launch, two 30ft gigs, one 56ft steam pinnace, one 40ft steam pinnace, one 30ft cutter, one 26ft cutter, one 27ft whaler, two 32ft cutters, one 13ft balsa catamaran and one 16ft dinghy.

The primary purpose of these boats was not to save lives in an emergency. They were designed to take liberty men ashore, for amphibious assaults and to transport officers to diplomatic functions and cocktail parties. Unfortunately, most of these boats had been landed at Chatham at the advent of war. The logic was that there would be few port calls and jolly receptions during the First World War, but these boats were also the only lifeboats available to the ship. Most of them were sitting idle in Chatham dockyard when they were required urgently.

Johnson ordered the engine telegraphs to half-astern and *Cressy* slowly came to a halt, in order to deploy what boats she had left. It was common for officers under training to be coxswains or crew in sea boats to gain valuable experience handling small vessels. Several of the thirteen teenage cadets from Britannia Royal Naval College Dartmouth were designated as boat crew and it meant they survived the day.

Cressy and *Hogue* had to be slowed to near stop in the water to deploy boats into the choppy swell by the veteran reservist sailors with admirable calm and expertise. One of the whalers was taken charge of by 16-year-old Midshipman William S. Cazalet, who co-ordinated a frantic operation to rescue stricken sailors from the water, including his best friend from Dartmouth, Midshipman A.G. Elliot, who was serving in *Aboukir*.

According to the account given by Able Seaman Rowden to *The Whitstable Times*, two cutters were deployed and he and his mate, Able Seaman Alfred Stroud, plus one other reserve man, volunteered to man the 17ft whaler, the only other boat available.[6] Martin, the surgeon, stated that four boats were deployed from *Cressy*, the fourth being the steam pinnace. That would put Rowden and Stroud in the same whaler as Midshipman Cazalet and they would have been assisting him in his rescue operation.

HMS *Hogue* had done likewise, and men were being frantically recovered by the small boats and brought back to the two remaining ships to get warm and receive medical attention as necessary. Small boats and cutters frantically shuttled back and forth across the cold sea, scattered with bodies and floating debris.

'Her [*Aboukir*'s] crew were brave, and even with death staring them in the face, kept to their posts, ready to handle their useless guns, for I submerged at once. But I had stayed on top long enough to see the other cruisers, which I learned were the *Cressy* and the *Hogue*, turn and steam full speed to their dying sister, whose plight they could not understand, unless it had been due to an accident,' wrote Weddigen.[7] 'The ships came on a mission of inquiry and rescue, for many of the *Aboukir*'s crew were now in the water, the order having been given, "Each man for himself",' he added.

When *Aboukir* was struck, Petty Officer Telegraphist George E. Durrant of *Cressy* went to his station at the wireless office to monitor the radio frequency, known as 'X tune guard', and started his wireless telegraphy machines.

Lieutenant Richard Harrison was still in his cabin, having stood the first watch (2000–2359) on the bridge. He reported that he was awoken by the sound of travelling feet and orders to close all watertight doors, deadlights and scuttles.[8]

Lieutenant Jeremiah McCarthy, a former Warrant Officer Boatswain and now aged 51, was awoken by the half-deck sentry. Donning clothes, he headed for the bridge. On reaching the boat deck he saw *Aboukir* wallowing in the water with a heavy list to port. In his official report to the subsequent Court of Inquiry he described *Aboukir* as about 300 yards off *Cressy*'s starboard beam and *Hogue* about 200 yards ahead of *Aboukir*.[9]

On joining the bridge team, McCarthy heard Captain Johnson ask his second in command, Commander Nicholson, to confirm that all watertight doors were shut properly and the Nicholson reply was, 'Yes sir.' Watertight integrity is a vital factor for any ship's stability. On patrol, Royal Navy warships were required to keep all watertight doors closed to prevent any flood from spreading from compartment to compartment. This can ultimately cause a ship to capsize and/or sink.

The MS *Herald of Free Enterprise* disaster in Zeebrugge, Belgium, in March 1987, when the car ferry capsized due to the bow door being left open on leaving harbour, is possibly the best-known modern-day example of the devastating impact of free surfaces. The free surface of water left to swill across the open car deck was enough to make the large ship unstable and capsize in relatively calm seas. Containing any free surface with watertight doors and bulkheads is essential to a ship's survival.

Captain Johnson asked Gabbett if there was a buoy ready for dropping as the *Aboukir*'s list was increasing rapidly. Gabbett then asked McCarthy to find out if a buoy was ready aft. A 5cwt sinker and mooring buoy were kept on the quarterdeck, so McCarthy headed aft and ordered men to get hold of ropes and make knots in them and deploy them over the side in order to rescue survivors.

It was a long climb for a tired and cold man from the sea up the ship's side to the quarterdeck of *Cressy*, even if he was hoisted and assisted by the men on the upper deck. McCarthy, a Specialist Lieutenant Seaman Officer, also ordered men to fling over any wood and started to rig the accommodation ladder as a line of floating survivors from *Aboukir* started swimming desperately towards *Cressy*. He was working with the First Lieutenant, Lieutenant Commander Harvey, who was stationed in the after bridge, and with Lieutenant William Williams-Mason, who was also in the after section of the ship.

'After about half an hour she [*Aboukir*] turned turtle,' wrote Martin.[10] 'I could see her keel above the water before she sank. There was no noise of any explosion, her magazines being intact. If the boilers exploded underwater after, I heard no sound to indicate anything of that kind had happened,' he added. It was a surreal and haunting spectacle. Three identical 12,000-

ton armoured warships stopped and wallowed in the open sea. Then, one of them floated bottom up and keeled over with its giant propellers airborne.

Stopped in the water, not making way and rolling awkwardly in a swell is never a comfortable feeling for any warship's commanding officer, unless perhaps it is for 'hands to bathe' in a warm tropical ocean in peacetime. At around 0655, just as Johnson must have allowed himself to believe that the situation might be coming gradually under control, and he might enjoy a brief breakfast, the situation suddenly took a turn for the worse.

After successfully torpedoing *Aboukir*, and diving to 15m, *U-9* circled round the ship's bows and reloaded tube one with the reserve torpedo. Desperate to maintain the boat's trim and avoid detection, part of the crew was deployed 'all forward' or 'all aft', racing back and forth through the narrow pressure casing en masse to adjust the horizontal trim with their body weight. Meanwhile, the chief quartermaster battled desperately with the hand-operated horizontal rudders. 'If we came out of the water now, we were finished,' recalled Spiess.[11]

It was an unconventional move by Weddigen as most U-boats passed under the stern of their victims as a matter of course, but *Aboukir* was obviously fatally crippled. He was rewarded for his unorthodox approach because, most conveniently, *U-9* met *Hogue*, which was closing in to aid *Aboukir*.

By the time the tube was reloaded, Weddigen was ready for his second strike and this time the range was even shorter at 300 yards. It was only an eighteen-second journey for the two bow torpedoes he unleashed at the unsuspecting *Hogue* while it was stopped in the water deploying boats.

In fact, *Hogue* was a little too close for comfort and after firing two torpedoes at five-second intervals from the replenished forward tubes, Weddigen temporarily lost control of the boat's buoyancy and had to go astern during its dive to avoid colliding with the incoming cruiser. The turning circle of *U-9* was not tight, and Spiess recalls they brushed the hull of their victim with their periscope as they made a hard turn away.

Fortunately for Weddigen, *Hogue* was momentarily stopped to avoid running down her two cutters, which were proceeding to the assistance of the *Aboukir*. Both torpedoes took effect in the engine room, and the explosions were extremely violent.

In theory, if during a standard approach with the bow torpedo tubes the commander saw that he had approached too close to the target, he could switch to a gyro-angled attack. Weddigen could have ordered a 90 degrees (starboard or port respectively) gyro setting at a distance of 200m from the target and changed the U-boat's course to be parallel to the target. When the target had got to the traverse line of the U-boat, the torpedo was launched.

Weddigen was so close to *Hogue* he may have considered a gyro-angled attack but most commanders preferred the less error-prone standard attack. And with *Hogue* stopped in the water or making very little way, the firing position would have been easy to assume.

Without warning, *Hogue* erupted in an enormous, violent explosion as two torpedoes hit her amidships on the port side and cut it open. 'The whole ship seemed to jump out of the water – number three funnel suddenly collapsed like a house of cards,' wrote Midshipman Herewood Hook, who was on watch on the bridge of *Hogue* at the time.

The German U-boat *U-9* had scored its second direct hit of the morning and the violent blast forced deck plates, coal, rigging and men to be catapulted violently into the air by the blast – a rain of falling debris and human body parts fell about the stricken ship in a ghastly scene of destruction.

Some reports indicated the torpedoes detonated the 9.2in magazine but the official history states the violent explosion occurred in the engine rooms of the ship.[12] In addition to the intense physical shock was now the sudden and irrefutable realisation in *Cressy* that the dramatic destruction was not due to a mine. This was evidently a submarine attack, and a highly effective one at that.

Captain Wilmot Nicholson, the commanding officer of HMS *Hogue*, had warned *Cressy* to beware of submarines as they approached *Aboukir* and knew almost instantly the game was up for his ship. 'After ordering the men to provide themselves with wood, hammocks, etc., and to get into the boats on the booms and take off their clothes, I went, by Captain Nicholson's direction, to ascertain the damage done in the engine room. The artificer engineer informed me that the water was over the engine room gratings,' stated Commander Reginald A. Norton of *Hogue* in his official report.[13]

Watertight doors on *Hogue* had not been fully secured while on patrol. Most significantly, the stokehold doors that contained the ships supplies of coal had been left partially open to enable stokers to deliver coal to the furnaces more easily. Seawater gushed into the engine room compartments, blacking out the ship, removing all power and creating a free surface of water in the lower decks and machinery spaces of the ship within seconds. This made it dangerously unstable and ready to capsize at any moment.

'While endeavouring to return to the bridge, the water burst open the starboard entry port doors and the ship heeled rapidly. I told the men in the port battery to jump overboard, as the launch was close alongside, and soon afterwards the ship lurched heavily to starboard. I clung to a ringbolt for some time, but eventually was dropped on to the deck, and a huge wave washed me away. I climbed up the ship's side and again was washed off,' reported Norton.[14]

Those like Norton who did make it to the upper deck had no lifejackets or survival gear. Ships of that era were fitted with the Kisbie Lifebuoy, a simple wooden circular float that was designed for a single man overboard incident, not a mass abandon ship. No more than a dozen or so would have been fitted along the upper deck and bridge. The men frantically ripped their clothes off for fear of being weighed down in the water and leapt into the sea naked or in their underwear, hoping to find a discarded raft or a piece of wooden furniture to hang on to. Men from *Cressy* now lined the upper deck and desperately held out lifelines or flung every item of timber that was not screwed down into the sea to assist the struggling men, many of whom could not swim a stroke.

Captain Nicholson was the last to leave his ship, cheered by his own men as he stood defiantly on the hull of the capsized vessel before finally being swept into the sea by an irresistible surge of sea water.

It took an estimated seven minutes from the initial impact to the sinking of *Hogue* and the short time meant that many working in the boiler rooms, engine rooms, stokeholds and machinery spaces had little chance of escape. Many of *Hogue*'s on-watch stokers and engine room artificers were taken to the bottom of the Broad Fourteens with her.

To add to the sense of alarm, just as the noise of the explosion from *Hogue* was witnessed, a periscope was sighted off the port bow of *Cressy* at a range of about 300m. *Cressy*'s small 12-pounder guns opened fire frantically and Johnson ordered both engines full ahead with the intention of ramming the submarine. Warrant Officer Gunner Albert J. Dougherty aimed one of the 12-pounders and a huge plume of water erupted, causing men on the upper deck to cheer and shout, believing that a hit had been scored, but it was more likely just floating wreckage and timber that had been hit. *U-9* sustained no damage during her exquisitely executed attack, but Weddigen did admit to briefly breaking surface involuntarily after the successful attack on *Hogue*.

According to the official account,[15] Dougherty's target was probably just a piece of wreckage, for *U-9* was a mile or more distant at the time the engines were put to full ahead. When *Cressy* opened fire at the object sighted, it was merely an acute case of 'periscopitis'. 'The sea was littered with all kinds of tackle that would float and men were struggling in the water,' Petty Officer Stoker Phill of *Cressy* later told the *Birmingham Gazette*.[16] As the stokeholds of the stricken ships, each capable of storing up to 1,600 tons of coal, released their contents into the North Sea, the water turned inky black for as far as the eye could see.

While there was now no doubt in anyone's mind that this was a submarine attack, most thought wrongly that it must be a co-ordinated multiple submarine attack.

Weddigen ordered the second reserve torpedo to be loaded into the bow tube and the crew sweated and contorted themselves in the stale and oxygen-starved air to reload the tube again. The chief engineer advised Weddigen that the boat was now low on battery power and the commander knew only too well that he required at least 800 amperes, enough to surface and restart the Körting kerosene engines. Despite the obvious risk, Weddigen had no intention of aborting his attack while he still had three torpedoes at his disposal.

Realising the magnitude of the situation, Johnson ordered all upper-deck hatches to be closed and for an urgent signal to be sent to all ships at Harwich, reporting the two cruisers sunk by submarines and requesting urgent assistance. 'The message was sent "*Aboukir* sunk, *Hogue* sinking by submarines". We coded the necessary words and it was sent on S tune [a different radio frequency]. We then shifted to D tune and sent it in emergency code to the destroyers,' reported Durrant.[17]

Johnson now had to quickly assess his few remaining options. It was now obvious he was under submarine attack, but he was also responsible for rescuing hundreds of desperate sailors struggling in the freezing water, many calling for assistance or howling in agony from their untreated wounds. He could have elected to depart the area at full steam and leave the men in the water to their fate. However, fleeing the enemy while hundreds of sailors needed his urgent assistance would smack of cowardice.

Johnson had received nothing in the way of guidance or orders from the Admiralty on how to proceed in such circumstances. He had received no intelligence reports about the likelihood of the presence of submarines either. Johnson had to rely entirely on his instincts and experience, and his first instinct was that of every professional mariner – to attempt to save the lives of his fellow seamen and comrades. It was at least a noble one, if not a tactically astute one.

Captain Drummond of *Aboukir* reported that, when Johnson ordered full ahead both engines to ram the non-existent submarine reported on his port bow shortly after the explosion on *Hogue*, he immediately cancelled the order and was heard to say: 'No, I won't leave these men – I will take my chance.' The story was corroborated by *Cressy*'s temporary surgeon, Dr Gerald Noel Martin, but neither were on the bridge of *Cressy* at the time. The accounts demonstrated the agonising moral conflict faced by Johnson.

The commanding officer of *Cressy* must have pinned his hopes desperately on the fact that, with the apparent improvement in the weather, destroyers from the Harwich Force might already be en route at full speed to their patrol area and would be close by. Johnson could not know that, in the absence of any signal from Admiral Christian for a destroyer screen to return to the Broad Fourteens and rendezvous with the three cruisers, there was no great urgency for them to return to their station until his own emergency signal had been received.

Fortunately, the ever-zealous Commodore Tyrwhitt had taken the initiative anyway. As the weather appeared to be easing in Harwich, he led out a force of eight destroyers and light cruisers bound for the Broad Fourteens at 0500 (some reports indicate they left at 0445) and they were en route to the stricken cruisers.

Tyrwhitt later testified at the Court of Inquiry that, when *Cressy*'s signal was received at 0707, they were still 50 nautical miles from the scene. Harwich is approximately 92 nautical miles directly west of the position reported by the stricken cruisers. His flagship was capable of a top speed of 28 knots but achieving this speed may have been impossible in heavy seas. If, as Tyrwhitt testified, he still had 50 nautical miles to run at 0707, he had covered about 42 nautical miles in a little over two hours, suggesting an average speed of approximately 21 knots. This does not allow for the slow-speed manoeuvring required to make the short passage out of the shallow

Stour Estuary and exit the port of Harwich into the open sea. Tyrwhitt was not dawdling, even though until he had received the signal at 0707, he had had no inkling of the dire urgency of the situation.

Even at full speed, Tyrwhitt was still almost two hours away and, as the destroyers raced to the scene, a bad case of 'periscopitis' had broken out in *Cressy*. In almost every eyewitness account, multiple submarines were reported emphatically. 'Altogether, I counted eight of them but there may have been more,' Stoker William Wake told the *Sunderland Daily Echo*.[18] 'I think there must have been at least half a dozen,' Able Seaman Edward Clarke told *The Times*, published on 24 September.[19]

The gun crews were already closed up and the small 12-pounders were fired in almost every direction at real and phantom targets. 'I noticed the guns were firing in three directions: Green 20 degrees (starboard bow), Red 45 degrees (port bow) and somewhere off the starboard beam,' stated Lieutenant McCarthy.[20]

Even Weddigen made comment about the random firing from the ship's 12-pounders. 'I had come to the surface for a view and saw how wildly the fire was being sent from the ship. Small wonder that was when they did not know where to shoot, although one shot went unpleasantly near us,' he admitted. So maybe the ebullient Dougherty did come close to making a hit on *U-9*, even if it was due to little more than the law of averages.[21]

Only the Captain of the Royal Marines, Harold Ozanne, who was stationed on the after bridge where he would have had an advantageous view, admitted that he never saw any submarines.[22]

The entire ship's company of *Cressy*, plus those survivors from *Aboukir* and *Hogue* who were sheltering on board, knew exactly what their fate would be if their Captain did not take immediate and decisive evasive action. According to all accounts, officers and men were calm, philosophical and stoical in the face of imminent death.

About five minutes after the first false sighting of the periscope, another was sighted, this time about 500m off the starboard quarter of the *Cressy* as she lay wallowing in the short swell while engaged in dragging cold, wet survivors aboard.

Weddigen had proceeded around the eastern side of the site of the sinking *Aboukir* and then south towards *Cressy*, intending to use the two torpedoes in the stern tubes to make his third kill. Ordering tubes three and four to be made ready, he turned 180 degrees to offer his stern tubes at the stationary beam of *Cressy*. Spiess unscrewed the protective cover of the firing button for tubes three and four and waited for the order from Weddigen, gripping the handles of the Zeiss periscope.

'But this time, the third cruiser knew of course that the enemy was upon her and she sought as best she could to defend herself,' wrote Weddigen, adding that *Cressy* 'stood her ground as if more anxious to help the many sailors who were in the water than to save herself'.[23] The U-boat commander must have been astounded that the cruiser remained wallowing in the water rescuing survivors from the two sister ships.

On board *Cressy*, Stoker Edward Barber (known locally as Ted Lingard) was on the crowded upper deck just after *Hogue* was struck. Like many not on watch, Barber was tending a rescue line offered to the men from the *Hogue* and *Aboukir*, still struggling for their lives in the coal-blackened sea.

'"It's our turn next", was heard on every side,' he said.[24]

5

LIVERPOOL, RATS AND SINKING SHIPS

The Monday evening before the attack by *U-9* in the southern North Sea, Churchill was on dry land in Liverpool.

As the Asquith government gradually realised that a quick war decided at sea was looking increasingly unlikely and, as Churchill had long predicted, a protracted land war now looked more likely, Army recruitment became the priority. Churchill was dispatched to deliver a rousing speech in the port city of Liverpool – a place with an enormous vested interest in the progress of the war at sea. If anything could restore faith in the war effort and inspire patriotic fervour, it was the oratory prowess of Churchill.

This followed his stirring call to arms at Chatham on 16 September and another at the Royal Opera House in London, the previous Friday, 11 September, both of which were widely reported in the regional press.

In London, Churchill soberly warned of the long struggle ahead. 'The war gentlemen will be long and sombre,' he told the full house in London's Covent Garden, urging them to 'plough over obstacles of all kinds, and to continue to the end of the furrow, whatever toil and suffering may be'.[1] At the same event he gave a more sanguine and upbeat account of the Navy's achievements to date and assured his audience that Britain was building on 'sound foundations'. 'We searched the so-called German Ocean without discovering the German flag,' he concluded.

He used the same 'vanished flag' theme in other recruitment rallies to justify the apparent lack of notable naval victories. Churchill was desperate for a major naval initiative that might influence the outcome of the war and redress a series of recent naval blunders reported in August and September.

Any notable event that featured Churchill, be it his wedding, a policy announcement in Parliament or his presence at a public meeting, invariably made front-page headlines and his Liverpool speech was no exception. The event was described by the *Liverpool Echo* as 'Mr Churchill's Great Speech in Liverpool'.[2] 'Liverpool will always remember the gigantic meeting which signalled Mr Churchill's official call to arms,' sang the report and estimated that 12,000 to 15,000 people were crammed into the city's Tournament Hall, with many others spilled outside in the streets. Churchill could be relied on to pull in the crowds, particularly when the subject at hand was war. 'Inside and out there were scenes of enthusiasm that will live in the memory,' reported the *Liverpool Echo*.[3]

The First Lord was accompanied by his close friend and Conservative Member of Parliament F.E. Smith, who had recently resigned as head of the government's Press Bureau in order to join the Army and serve at the front. He was also accompanied by the journalist and veteran MP, T.P. O'Connor. Lord Derby, the ultra-wealthy aristocratic landowner, known as the King of Lancashire and the self-appointed recruiting sergeant for the war, sent apologies for his absence due to illness.

Churchill was in typical bellicose, tub-thumping form as he outlined the possibility of recruiting twenty-five Army corps of 1 million men to fight in Europe. 'I have only one song to sing,' he told the assembled citizens of Liverpool packed tightly into the smoke-filled auditorium:

> These are days of action rather than speech. You have no need to be anxious about the results. God has blessed our arms with unexpected good fortune. For myself, having studied the matter with some attention, I could not have hoped that at this stage of the war circumstances would have been so favourable to the allied cause.

His comments were greeted by loud cheering, but Churchill was probably guilty of being disingenuous in the interests of further warming the already heated patriotic fervour in the hall and aiding the much-needed recruitment drive.

Characterised by blunders and mishaps, the unfortunate truth was that the war at sea was not going well for Britain. A war plan had been carefully prepared by the new professional War Staff, instigated by Churchill in 1912, and the critical first few days of the conflict had proceeded like clockwork. However, any period for self-congratulation was short-lived.

After a brief honeymoon, there had been several setbacks during the months of August and September 1914 that had started to erode public confidence in Churchill and the Royal Navy – something that would have been unimaginable two months earlier. 'There was our little Army fighting for its life and playing to British eyes almost as large a part as all the armies of France and meanwhile our great Navy, the strongest in the world, lay apparently in an inertia diversified only by occasional mishap,' he wrote later.[4]

Perhaps the single most damaging fiasco was the Navy's failure to capture or sink the German battlecruiser SMS *Goeben* in the Mediterranean Sea during the opening days of war in early August. It was certainly more than a mishap. This embarrassing incident 'jarred the confidence of the country in the Navy', as Marder put it.[5]

As soon as war had been declared on Germany, once the deadline for responding to Britain's ultimatum of midnight on 5 August had passed, the Admiralty was acutely concerned about the whereabouts of the *Goeben*, thought to be the fastest and most powerful warship in the region. Together with the modern light cruiser SMS *Breslau*, the two ships constituted the German naval presence in the Mediterranean Sea. Orders were sent by the Admiralty to Commander-in-Chief, Mediterranean, Admiral Archibald Berkeley Milne, known throughout the Navy as 'Arky Barky', to shadow the crossing of French troops from North Africa but to avoid a direct engagement with a superior force. It was a bizarre instruction at the advent of war and succeeded in confusing the commanders on the front line.

The *Goeben* and the *Breslau* left the Sicilian Port of Messina as war with Britain was declared. The two ships could easily have been bottled up in the Strait of Messina by an imaginative deployment of the big capital ships of the Mediterranean fleet, forcing the German flag officer in charge, Admiral Souchon, to choose between being interned by neutral Italy or fighting his way out. Instead, due to a crippling combination of lack of initiative, confusion over the series of (often contradictory) Admiralty instructions, a mistaken belief that *Goeben* would head west (not east) to exit the Mediterranean via the Strait of Gibraltar and an over-sensitivity on the part of Milne for respecting Italian neutrality by remaining well clear of Italian territorial waters, the opportunity was lost.

Inexplicably, when Souchon exited the southern end of the Strait of Messina, the two modern British battlecruisers most capable of sinking her, HMS *Indomitable* and HMS *Indefatigable*, were 100 miles away, while a third, HMS *Inflexible*, was coaling in Bizerte, Tunisia. The only British naval force in Souchon's way was the 1st Cruiser Squadron, which consisted of the four armoured cruisers HMS *Defence*, *Black Prince*, *Duke of Edinburgh* and *Warrior*, under the command of Rear Admiral Ernest Troubridge.

Even worse, when Admiral Troubridge had the opportunity to come within striking distance of the *Goeben* in daytime, in clear visibility, he elected instead to turn his four ships away from the German cruiser, allowing it to head unimpeded for the safety of Turkey. Troubridge, who was highly regarded by his peers, reluctantly calculated that to engage a much faster and more heavily armed enemy ship in broad daylight would not only be suicidal, it would also be disobeying orders from Milne based on his Admiralty instructions not to engage a superior force.

Though tracked doggedly by the light cruiser HMS *Gloucester*, the two German warships eventually completed their passage to Constantinople (now Istanbul) on 16 August and were sold to Turkey, who joined the war on the side of Germany twelve days later, on 28 August 1914.

It was bad news and, perhaps influenced by the need to create some positive momentum, Churchill enthusiastically endorsed the plans of Commodore Roger Tyrwhitt for the Battle of Heligoland Bight on 28 August. This bold action had been consistently opposed by Jellicoe and his senior flag officers, so the Harwich Force designed it themselves and it came perilously close to being another bungled operation.

Commodores Tyrwhitt and Keyes, the architects of the raid, were not informed that they were being supported by the ships of Captain William Edmund Goodenough and the 1st Light Cruiser Squadron, which had been dispatched by Admiral Beatty from Scapa Flow. Hence, the Harwich Force that led the attack very nearly opened fire on Goodenough's squadron.

It could be said that the only reason this misconceived and clumsily executed raid was successful was that the German High Seas Fleet could not believe that their foe would be so inept as to make a raid on their forward-most naval base without having the might of the Grand Fleet waiting in reserve. The German High Command wrongly thought it was a trap to lure out their big ships. Instead, it was simply poor planning on the British part.

The public knew nothing of the tactical and communications errors that meant Heligoland Bight was almost a disaster. Instead, the final score was that several German warships had been sunk or damaged to no serious losses on the British side. Germany lost the light cruisers SMS *Mainz*, *Caln* and *Ariadne* and the destroyer *V-187*. The light cruisers SMS *Frauenlob*, *Strassburg* and *Stettin* had been damaged and returned to base with casualties.

That was more than enough for Churchill. Desperate for some good news about the progress of the war at sea to report to Parliament and the country, he met Tyrwhitt on the quayside in Sheerness. According to an account by the Commodore, Churchill practically 'slobbered all over me', such was the First Lord's relief.[6] Meanwhile, the *Goeben* fiasco lingered like a bad smell in the corridors of the Admiralty buildings in Whitehall for several months.

A Court of Inquiry was convened to investigate the blunder on 21 September. It was headed by Admiral Sir George Callaghan and Admiral Sir Hedworth Meux, who tried to get to the bottom of the ignominious failure to intercept and engage the only two major German warships in the Mediterranean Sea when their location was known. The inquiry concluded that Troubridge's actions were 'deplorable and contrary to the tradition of the British Navy'. Senior seagoing naval officers like Beatty were outraged that a respected Admiral was having his courage questioned for what they saw as faithfully executing very confusing orders from the Admiralty. Beatty worried about the impact this would have on morale at a critical time in the war.

It was still not the end of the matter. Troubridge was subsequently court-martialled on HMS *Bulwark* on 5–9 November 1914. Troubridge was one of only three Royal Navy flag officers to have been tried by court martial in the preceding forty years and the only flag officer to be court-martialled in wartime. It was hardly inspiring for public confidence in the supposedly invincible senior service. There was even talk of trying Troubridge for cowardice, but this was later reduced to lesser charges. Troubridge was acquitted, mostly by citing the instructions he received from the Admiralty via Milne about not engaging a superior force.

The escape of the *Goeben* and the subsequent recriminations were not the only embarrassments for Churchill and the Admiralty in August and September 1914. On 7 August Churchill was forced to answer questions in the House of Commons about the loss of the 3,390-ton, modern *Active*-class scout cruiser HMS *Amphion*.[7]

Part of the destroyer force from Harwich that included HMS *Lance*, which had pursued and damaged the German minelayer SS *Königin Luise*, forcing the ship to be scuttled, *Amphion* had continued her patrol. Having rescued German survivors from the sea, *Amphion* then struck one of the mines it had witnessed being laid in the Thames Estuary and sank with the loss of 132 lives. The German prisoners on board who were rescued from the scuttled minelayer must have had mixed feelings at the time, having been sunk twice in forty-eight hours, and once due to a mine that they had laid.

Two days later, HMS *Birmingham* managed to ram the U-boat *U-15* while it was undertaking emergency repairs on the surface in the North Sea, and on 27 August, Churchill was able to report to Parliament that a German auxiliary cruiser hand been sunk by HMS *Highflyer*.[8]

'The Admiralty have just received intelligence that the German armoured merchant cruiser *Kaiser Wilhelm der Grosse*, of 14,000 tons and armed, according to our information, with ten guns of approximately four-inch calibre, has been sunk by His Majesty's Ship *Highflyer* off the Ouro River on the West African coast,' reported the First Lord in an official statement.[9] The distant coast of Saharan Africa was hardly the front line of Britain's war at sea but, in terms of stirring victories capable of stoking patriotic fervour, that minor victory combined with Heligoland Bight was about it. Matters deteriorated further in September.

There was another mine fiasco when three minesweepers including HMS *Speedy* were lost over the course of the two days of 2 and 3 September while attempting to clear a minefield laid in the River Humber, on England's east coast. *Speedy* was lowering boats to rescue the survivors from the drifter *Lindsell*, which had also struck a mine, when another mine struck it, killing one crew member. The Press Bureau issued a statement on 4 September, which was widely reported in the press.

The next day, 5 September, marked another naval disaster. The light cruiser HMS *Pathfinder* became the first Royal Navy ship to be sunk by a torpedo fired from a submarine when it was hit by *U-21* while patrolling slowly and in a straight course off St Abb's Head off the eastern coast of Scotland. It was initially reported incorrectly by the Admiralty as another mine incident. Later, when one Scottish newspaper defied the censorship protocols and reported it as a submarine attack, the government's Press Bureau set up by Churchill to deal with the issuing of all official information relating to the war had to issue a humiliating correction to the press. Bemused readers must have wondered why the Royal Navy could not work out what had caused the sudden sinking of one of their own warships.

On 20 September 1914, the *Pelorus*-class cruiser HMS *Pegasus*, which had returned to Zanzibar in East Africa to carry out machinery repairs, was attacked by the fast German light cruiser SMS *Königsberg*. *Pegasus*'s engines were shut down to allow the repairs, so without power and with no means of moving or retaliating, the British ship was completely incapacitated within eight minutes. The commanding officer, Commander Ingle, struck the colours and surrendered his ship to avoid further bloodshed. It was doubtless the correct decision, but it was another embarrassing wartime incident that hardly covered the Royal Navy in glory.

And if that wasn't bad enough to dent British public confidence in wartime, there were the interminable heroic exploits of the German Navy's *Dresden*-class light cruiser SMS *Emden*, which became known as the 'Kaiser's pirate ship'. Under the command of the gallant Captain Friedrich von Müller, the *Emden* became the most famous warship of the opening 100 days of the First World War. The ship had earned widespread admiration from the expatriate community in the British colony of Hong Kong in southern China, where the *Emden* had been a frequent and popular visitor, from its base at the German concession in Tsingtao, prior to the outbreak of hostilities.

Relations between the German and British merchant classes in the colony were so cordial that the governor, Sir Francis Henry May, offered his written condolences to the head of the German community at the announcement of hostilities between the two countries and initially German firms carried on trading as normal. News of the *Emden* was eagerly awaited in Hong Kong, as were the latest updates from the Western Front. *Emden* was known as Hong Kong's favourite foreign warship.[10]

Successfully evading the ships of the Royal Navy's China station and its allies, refuelling from captured British colliers bound for British ports, and seizing and sinking numerous merchant ships, all with chivalrous style, von Müller became the focus of the world's press attention.

On 22 September, the day that Gabbett stood his last watch on the bridge of *Cressy* in the Broad Fourteens, SMS *Emden* sailed unchallenged into the British commercial stronghold of Madras (modern-day Chennai, on India's east coast), which was, according to von Müller's report, 'lit up like a Christmas tree'. *Emden* promptly dispatched 130 shells into the oil storage depot, causing an inferno and widespread panic but, in typically chivalrous style, he took care to minimise civilian loss of life. *Emden* left the scene unopposed and it caused major embarrassment for Churchill and the Admiralty in London as the attack made front-page headlines in the national and international press.

By the time of the Liverpool speech Churchill was already being held responsible for the litany of disappointments, particularly by those sympathetic to the Conservative Party, which was still keen to exact revenge for Churchill's perceived betrayal when he switched allegiance to the Liberals in 1904. He had his enemies outside Parliament, too, and was widely resented for his overt ambition, brash arrogance and vanity within the British political elite of the day. 'Of course, Winston is intolerable – he is devoured by vanity,' wrote Margot Asquith, wife of the prime minister, in her diary, early the following year.[11]

'In spite of being accustomed to years of abuse, I could not but feel the adverse and hostile currents that flowed about me,' wrote Churchill.[12]

Churchill was already recognised as an extraordinary man but that did not make him universally popular. Supported by Clementine, he hungered for fame and glory and believed it was his fate to be bathed in it. He understood that war offered an opportunity to supply it in vast quantities and his ambition was not inhibited by any reservations about his own capabilities or by any lack of self-belief: 'I have faith in my star that I am intended to do something in the world,' he once wrote to his mother[13] but his star was not yet shining in wartime and not for lack of determined effort or industry on his part. He subjected himself to a punishing work schedule.

In addition to his personal direction of the war at sea, Churchill threw himself into a multitude of other tasks in order to advance the general war effort. Such was the wide range of his responsibilities that, according to one newspaper, he had been inspecting a quick-firing gun mounted on a motorcycle that very morning in Horse Guards Parade in London, before travelling to Liverpool for his much-anticipated speech.[14] For the first few weeks of the war, his scope of intense activity knew no bounds and it widened further as the war progressed.

On 7 August, Churchill announced to Parliament the establishment of a new organisation that would oversee relations with the media in regards to the conduct of the war. He stated:

> We are establishing today a Press bureau, and I am very glad to say that the right hon. and learned Member for the Walton Division of Liverpool (Mr. F.E. Smith) will preside over it. From that bureau a steady stream of trustworthy information supplied both by the War Office and the Admiralty can be given to the Press, which, without endangering military or naval interests, will serve to keep the country properly and truthfully informed from day to day of what can be told, and what is fair and reasonable; and thus, by providing as much truth as possible, exclude the growth of irresponsible rumours.[15]

The Bureau set up with Kitchener was to prove controversial and Churchill's close friend F.E. Smith, who ran it, had already resigned by the time he accompanied him to the Liverpool speech.

In the same month, Churchill had also forced through the establishment of the 63rd Royal Naval Division. These men were civilian volunteers and seamen reservists for whom there were no billets available in ships. On 16 August 1914, two brigades of these surplus civilian sailors were issued with antique rifles and added to an existing brigade of some 2,000 Royal Marines to create a composite Royal Naval Division. It was Churchill's favourite pet project and was regarded with disdain by his staff, who referred to it as the 'First Lord's private army' and 'Churchill's pets'.[16]

On 3 September 1914, Lord Kitchener asked Churchill in Cabinet to take on the role of the aerial defence of Great Britain – Churchill accepted and in so doing appointed himself head of the nation's nascent air force as well as the Navy. This led to sporadic aerial bombing of Zeppelin sheds on the German coast, the procurement of new searchlights, the establishment of a new squadron of aeroplanes established at Hendon Aerodrome and a new forward air base at Dunkirk, from which to patrol the skies within a 100-mile radius. These mobile air bases were to be protected by a new fleet of armoured cars, which were a particular passion of the First Lord.

'I have during the latter part of August and September, issued successive orders for the formation of armoured-car squadrons under the Admiralty and as all this arose out of the aeroplane squadron based at Dunkirk, this formation of the armoured-car squadrons was entrusted to Commodore Suiter,' wrote Churchill,[17] who is widely credited as being the originator of the modern armoured tank. 'The armoured car was the child of the air; and the tank its grandchild,' he wrote, which might have been even more admirable had it not been achieved by the political head of the Navy.

According to documents in The National Archives, in the two weeks before the Liverpool speech, Churchill was drafting a detailed document concerning the land defence of Antwerp in Belgium. This memo included detailed advice on the effectiveness of its 'fortress line' and offered prescriptions on the most suitable type of artillery.[18] Regardless of its efficacy, it was something of highly questionable relevance to the Royal Navy, which was facing an increased threat from submarines and mines.

On 10 September, Churchill made a covert visit to France, visited his new air base at Dunkirk and consulted local officials in Dunkirk and Calais on their defence arrangements, including the provision of fresh water in the event of a siege.

On 16 September, Marshal Joffre telegraphed Earl Kitchener requesting a brigade of marines to help defend Dunkirk. Kitchener asked Churchill for assistance and he readily agreed on the condition that Kitchener would also send a brigade of yeomanry and that he took personal charge of the operation.

This was all in addition to his daily War Room duties, Cabinet meetings and attendance in Parliament for key debates. 'I was thus led into accepting a series of minor responsibilities of a very direct and personal kind which made inroads both on my time and thought and might well – though I claim they did not – have obscured my general view,' wrote Churchill.[19] Even his wife, Clementine, asked him why he could not just content himself with running the Admiralty.[20]

On 17 September, Churchill visited the Grand Fleet at the fuelling base at Loch Ewe on the north-west coast of Scotland and held a series of meetings with the Commander-in-Chief, Admiral Jellicoe. Churchill was accompanied by the Chief of War Staff (Sturdee), Director of Intelligence (Rear Admiral Henry Oliver) and Commodore S and Commodore T (Keyes and Tyrwhitt).

One of the key subjects on the agenda was the bombardment and capture of the German base at Heligoland that had been the scene of the slightly fortunate British victory on 16 August. Jellicoe and his entire staff objected to the plan because, according to him, the 'arguments against the operation were overwhelmingly strong' but the idea remained live for some weeks afterwards. Jellicoe also recalls discussion of offensive actions in the Baltic Sea and the capture of the island of Borkum, another hobby horse of Churchill's, being discussed and firmly rejected.

Jellicoe did not report any discussion of the three *Cressy*-class cruisers, and it would have been unusual if he had because they were under direct Admiralty orders and therefore not his direct responsibility. However, according to Churchill, it was during the time of this meeting at Loch Ewe that Keyes and Tyhritt made the case for the three cruisers to be withdrawn from the advanced patrol in the Broad Fourteens because they were unsuited to the task and could achieve very little. Perhaps the discussion took place during the 86-mile drive to Loch Ewe that Keyes undertook in a 'ramshackle old motor', as he described it, crammed on the back seat with Tyrwhitt and Churchill.

'As you know, I often fall under his charm! And he was at his best. T (Tyrwhitt) and I gave him our views on a good many things,' wrote Keyes in a letter, written later the same month,[21] but he did not mention any specific discussion with Churchill about Cruiser Force C or the Broad Fourteens patrol, to which Keyes was vehemently opposed.

Keyes records that he had already made several requests to the Admiralty in August and September to cease the Cruiser Force C patrols. Twice during visits to the Admiralty, he 'protested strongly' about the deployment of the *Cressy*-class cruisers to Sturdee and Leveson. Keyes claimed that on one occasion his pressure led to the ships being redeployed to a patrol off Dungeness. If that is true, and there is no reason to doubt it, the Admiralty War Staff were fully aware of the acute danger and futility of this patrol from early August. 'I begged the War Staff, Sturdee and Leveson, to believe that they were a gift to a submarine,' wrote Keyes, describing the Broad Fourteens patrol as a 'ridiculous parade'.

On 8 August, Cruiser Force C was sent from the Broad Fourteens through the Straits of Dover to take up a patrol off Dungeness while the British Expeditionary Force was crossing. This patrol was from Dungeness to Vergoyer Shoal, some 10 miles south-west of Boulogne.

According to Churchill's account, it was only at the meetings with Jellicoe on 17 September that he overheard an officer use the expression 'the Live Bait Squadron' and demanded to know to what he was referring.

When Churchill was told it was Cruiser Force C, he 'reviewed the whole position in this area' and discussed the situation with Keyes and Tyrwhitt. This persuaded him to draft a crucial memo the following morning (18 September). This neat, two-page, typewritten minute on Admiralty-headed notepaper was addressed to the First Sea Lord, Prince Louis Battenberg. Among other matters, it included Churchill's view on the current deployment of Cruiser Force C on the Broad Fourteens patrol: 'The *Bacchantes* [the ships' class] ought not to continue on this beat,' wrote Churchill.[22]

'The risk to such ships is not justified by any services they can render. The narrow seas, being the nearest point to the enemy, should be kept by a good number of good modern ships,' he continued, suggesting the cruisers should instead be dispatched to the western approaches of the English Channel. This document proved to be crucial for Churchill. In the later investigations and recriminations into the Broad Fourteens attack by *U-9*, this memo clearly demonstrated that Churchill had expressed his firmly held view that the ships should be withdrawn from that patrol, only four days before the incident.

'Prince Louis immediately agreed [with the memo of 18 September] and gave directions to the COS [Chief of Staff, Sturdee] to make the necessary redistribution of forces. With this I was content, and I dismissed the matter from my mind, being sure that the orders given would be complied with at the earliest moment, before they could take effect, disaster occurred,' he wrote.[23]

The following day (19 September), the Admiralty once again ordered Admiral Christian to take Cruiser Force C to the Broad Fourteens but Churchill did not register any surprise that the three cruisers were still on the beat he had insisted they vacate the day before. 'This routine message did not of course come before me,' wrote Churchill, which seems unlikely, but in any case, he had his mind on other matters – lots of other matters.

Churchill had a great deal on his plate in September 1914 and it must be said that much of the workload had little, or nothing, to do with the safety or fighting efficiency of the fleet at sea. On 20 September, the landing of a marine brigade from Dover to Dunkirk, as agreed with Kitchener, was undertaken and Churchill was, as a result, personally overseeing a major amphibious operation on the continent of Europe in wartime, on behalf of the Army. This expedition, widely known as his 'Dunkirk Circus', achieved very little. It did however, have a cosy family connection because his brother, Jack, and cousin, Sunny, were serving with the Oxfordshire Hussars, the reserve regiment offered by Kitchener to support the Royal Marines detachment.

As Churchill delivered his address in Liverpool on 21 September, and as the three cruisers unwittingly progressed towards their fatal rendezvous with *U-9*, the First Lord had no reason to believe the ships might be in any particular danger and had plenty of other matters with which to occupy his mind.

'I could with perfect proprietary indeed with unanswerable reasons, have in every one of these cases left the burden to others,' he admitted but Churchill genuinely believed that only he was armed with the 'special knowledge which I possessed and the great and flexible authority which I wielded at this time'.[24]

It was as though Churchill had created a one-man fiefdom at the Admiralty ready for urgent action and then his fertile mind and hyper-energetic nature simply became distracted when the war at sea appeared to be in stalemate.

His vulnerability to distraction, however noble the motivation, caused an acute problem at the Admiralty, which had grown dependent on Churchill's complete focus and personal supervision since he took the reins in October 1911. Since war had been declared, there seemed no limit to the tasks he was willing to undertake – regardless of his qualifications for doing them or their relevance to his principal responsibilities as First Lord of the Admiralty. 'No one department, hardly one war, was enough for him,' commented his friend F.E. Smith.[25]

Churchill would also have been aware that the day of his high-profile speech in Liverpool was the same day that the Court of Inquiry into the conduct of Admiral Troubridge was convened to investigate his culpability for the *Goeben* blunder and the day after the sinking of HMS *Pegasus* in Zanzibar. It was also the evening before *Emden* bombarded Madras unopposed. Churchill had little choice, given the circumstances, but to put a brave face on things.

Churchill told the febrile audience in Liverpool how he and the Royal Navy craved a major set-piece engagement with the enemy:

> So far as the Navy was concerned, we could not fight while the enemy remained in port. We hoped a decision at sea would be a feature of this war. Our men who are spending a tireless vigil hoped they would have a chance to settle the question with the German Fleet and if they did not come out and fight, they would be dug out like rats in a hole.

The brilliant Churchillian rhetoric had the desired effect and the hall erupted in cheers and laughter but the First Lord was soon to bitterly regret his lurid hyperbole.

As a former journalist and war correspondent, no one understood the damaging impact of embarrassing press reports better than Churchill. It created a negative impression that threatened public morale in wartime and it offered ammunition to the nation's enemies and the First Lord's political foes. The last thing the Admiralty or Churchill needed was any more bad news.

6

THE FINAL TOUCH

As Captain Johnson stood on the bridge with Gabbett and Nicholson surveying the scene of mass destruction, he had no illusions about his prospects.

His most instinctive action, to fight back, was impossible because Johnson had no anti-submarine weapons with which to retaliate. 'In the twelve years which had elapsed since Britain had had submarines, no effective methods of attacking them had been devised,' wrote Rear Admiral William Jameson.[1] Up until 1912, all Royal Navy submarines engaged in exercises at sea were required to be accompanied by a surface vessel flying a red warning flag. *U-9* was unlikely to oblige Johnson with the same courtesy.

The only option for warships engaged in anti-submarine warfare was to locate the target on the surface, catch up with it before it submerged and then attempt to ram it. The light cruiser HMS *Birmingham* had managed to ram and sink *U-15* while it was surfaced undertaking mechanical repairs on 9 August 1914. Johnson could have elected to go charging off after each reported sighting of the submarine in an attempt to ram it, but he would have risked mowing down the hundreds of men struggling in the water.

Neither was it possible to order action stations in response to the submarine attack. An examination of the ship's Watch and Station Bill reveals this was not a feasible option because so many sailors had already been ordered for boat duty, either as crew members or for manning the davits.[2]

There was no contingency or precedent in the Royal Navy for a warship going into action with all its boats deployed, picking up survivors. This was

Johnson's last chance to run for safety but he stayed put. *Cressy* was still busily engaged in assisting survivors of the two sunken sister ships with her remaining boats and with lines hanging over the ship's side.

It was undoubtedly the wrong decision on Johnson's part. *U-9* did not have sufficient speed to pursue *Cressy* if the ship fled at full speed. *U-9* was operating independently and Weddigen only had sufficient battery power to remain submerged for a little longer. Of course, Johnson did not know that. As Stoker Wake told the *Sunderland Echo*, 'The *Hogue* had now gone down in eight minutes from being struck and we were alone. We had crowds of survivors from the other two ships with us, having picked them up from the water.'[3]

The acute 'periscopitis' continued with the small 12-pounder guns firing in all directions at imaginary submarines. If nothing else, it was at least moral encouragement for the men struggling to survive in the water. The last ship in Cruiser Force C was at least making a fight of it, though in terms of effective anti-submarine warfare, it was futile. Many on board were convinced that *Cressy* had destroyed at least one German U-boat, if not more.

The ship's gunner, Warrant Officer Albert J. Dougherty, manning one of the 12-pounder guns, took aim at one apparent periscope on the port beam, claiming to have scored a direct hit. Nicholson later reported at the Court of Inquiry that an officer who was standing alongside the gunner thought that the shell struck only floating timber, which was in abundance. Another account says that the midshipmen on deck were jesting that the enthusiastic gunner was shooting at shadows. Dougherty told the *Yorkshire Telegraph and Star*:

> Someone shouted to me 'look out sir, there's a submarine on our port beam'. I saw her, she was about 400 yards away and only her periscope showed above the waves. I took careful aim at her with a 12-pounder … I fired again and hit the periscope and she disappeared. Up she came again and this time, part of her conning tower was visible. So, I fired my third shot and smashed into the top of her conning tower.

'Altogether, I personally observed five submarines and although our guns pegged away at them, only one was hit as far as we know,' he added in the same newspaper report.

Dougherty was interviewed and photographed by several newspapers, and appeared as a witness at the subsequent Court of Inquiry. He was a loquacious eyewitness, never short of lurid personal accounts.

In fact, *U-9* was never positioned on the port side of *Cressy*. The enemy submarine did not suffer any more than a scratch that day and not everyone was convinced by Dougherty's exploits. 'More cackle than a cow's got cunt,' was one crude yet popular lower-deck epithet of the time that might well have been uttered in relation to Gunner Dougherty.

Many of the eyewitness accounts include what they believed to be a certain hit on the U-boat. The subsequent report in *The Whitstable Times* stated that Able Seaman Rowden was certain that Dougherty hit the forward part of the conning tower and added that another Whitstable man, Able Seaman Phillips, was part of Dougherty's gun crew. When Able Seaman Stroud was asked by the same newspaper if any German submarines had been sunk, he replied, 'Oh yes, the *Cressy* sank one, for afterwards a tremendous quantity of oil was seen on the waves.'[4] Another witness claimed to have seen two floating bodies from a U-boat nearby but if he did they were not those of the crew of *U-9*.

Stoker Wake was convinced he saw eight submarines in his detailed account for the *Sunderland Echo*:

> Then we saw the backs of the submarines. Altogether I counted eight of them but there may have been more. There were two on our bow and we let blaze at them with the 9.2-inch guns from the forecastle head. I saw from one of them a volume of blue smoke and saw the bodies of two men come up so we must have done it in quick.[5]

Stokers are rarely the best authority on matters of gunnery but the sighting of the two bodies of German submariners appeared in a number of other accounts. In reality, the 9.2in gun elevation could not be depressed low enough to be of any use in this close-range fight.

Surgeon Martin was no naval warfare expert either, but his more measured account was given to the *Sheffield Daily Telegraph*.[6] 'Owing to the state of the sea it was difficult for the practised eye and impossible for the unpractised eye to discern the periscope of a submarine,' he said. However, it was evidently the impression of the many men now gathered on the upper deck of *Cressy* that the submarine had been hit and they all 'cheered and clapped heartily', according to another eyewitness report.

Despite the jubilation from the upper deck at Dougherty's apparent success, as Stoker Barber told *The Derbyshire Courier*, the ship's company, like their captain, were not fools and were fully aware of their likely fate. 'But we knew what was in store for us,' he said.[7] 'About five minutes later, another periscope was seen on our starboard quarter and fire was opened,' Barber continued. This time it was not another case of 'periscopitis', not another phantom submarine nor another object of Gunner Dougherty's over-fertile imagination. It was *U-9*.

Lieutenant Philip Kell RNR co-ordinated fire for the 12-pounder guns on the starboard side at *U-9* as Weddigen took up a firing position for a stern tube attack from about 1,000m. Weddigen now felt supremely confident about sinking his third target of the day, and with good reason.

'Now the third one came on,' recalled Spiess.[8]

The final reserve torpedo was loaded into the forward tube as the crew realised they were very low on battery power. 'We will have to stop soon as the batteries are nearly discharged,' warned *U-9*'s chief engineer[9] but Weddigen pressed on to his firing position, submerged under the mass of bodies littering that small section of the southern North Sea. It was a distressing spectacle even for those with the steely resolve of the German submariners. Spiess recalled:

> We in the conning tower sought, by cursing the English who had incited the Japanese and all Europe against us, to dispel the humane [*sic*] and gruesome impression made on us by the drowning and struggling men who were in the midst of the mass of floating wreckage and clinging to overturned lifeboats.[10]

At 0700 (GMT) two stern tube torpedoes hissed away on the orders of Weddigen, leaving only the final reserve torpedo now loaded in the forward tube. This was a long shot but the journey of the two torpedoes fired at five-second intervals, travelling at more than 30 knots, would take a little over a minute. The sound of any impact would then have to travel back to the submarine at about 1,500m per second. It was less than sixty-five seconds in total, but it felt like hours within the cramped and increasingly humid and malodorous confines of the U-boat. 'A long interval passed without anything occurring and we asked each other, depressed, missed?' wrote Spiess.[11]

The distinctive wakes caused by the foamy bubbles of the compressed air were clearly visible to the lookouts in *Cressy* as the two fish cut a path through the mass of bodies in the water en route to their intended target. Men struggling for survival in the cold sea could only look on in helpless horror as the deadly torpedoes fizzed past them and closed on *Cressy*.

'The track of the torpedo she fired at a range of 500 to 600 yards was plainly visible,' reported Nicholson, though he seems to have underestimated the true range. A seaman of Nicholson's experience would be well practised at accurately estimating ranges at sea, so we can safely assume that the torpedo was first sighted on board *Cressy* when it was already halfway to its target. That left Captain Johnson about thirty-three seconds to take effective evasive action in order to save his ship and more than 1,000 men now on board.

With no time to consult Nicholson or Gabbett standing with him, Johnson ordered 'full ahead both engines', and the telegraphs rang out. Time must have frozen as hundreds of sailors on the starboard side of *Cressy* aiding men from *Aboukir* and *Hogue* metaphorically held their breath as the lumbering 12,000-ton armoured cruiser gradually attempted to gather way to avoid the rapidly approaching torpedoes.

Chief Engine Room Artificer William Taylor was in the starboard engine room when the order came from the bridge via the telegraph for full speed ahead. Captains of warships do not order 'full ahead' or 'full astern' without very good reason. Though they could see nothing of the outside world above them, the highly experienced team of perspiring artificers and stokers in the starboard engine room, knowing their two sister ships were already sunk, would instinctively have sensed the acute urgency of the situation. 'I myself was in the starboard engine room. The engines had hardly worked up to 60 or 70 revolutions before we were struck by a torpedo on the starboard side. The electric light went out and the starboard engine eased up and finally stopped,' reported Taylor.[12]

After the first torpedo struck, all the lights went out and the generator stopped for the fire control and gun circuits. Taylor knew instantly that it was a grave situation in terms of damage control. 'We were steaming with 14 boilers – A group and D group. We took our steam from 1 and 4 on the starboard side and 2 and 4 down the port side and cross connected by a steam pipe on the centre-line bulkhead – the steam pipe had blown away in the blast,' he told the Court of Inquiry.

According to Chief Stoker Frederick James Edwards, there were men of *Aboukir* still clambering over the side of the *Cressy* when the first torpedo struck. 'I assisted them into the engine room casing to warm them as the ship was steady and we did not seem to be going any further down. I asked the engineer commander permission to get some towelling to wrap round them,' he reported.[13]

As the two giant propellers churned to propel the ship forward, those in the whalers and cutters, trying to get survivors to safety, found themselves nearly swamped in the resultant wake.

Midshipman Herewood Hook had managed to escape from *Hogue* and was approaching *Cressy* in one of the rescue boats at the moment the first torpedo struck. 'Our launch was just approaching her from astern, intending to go alongside the port quarter, when the *Cressy* must have seen the torpedo coming at her and suddenly went full speed ahead washing us well astern with her propeller wash and shortly afterwards the torpedo struck her on the starboard side,' he recalled.[14]

Able Seaman Rowden, crewing for Midshipman Cazalet in *Cressy*'s whaler, told *The Whitstable Times* he saw his fellow oysterman Fred Wootton tending a line over the ship's side as survivors were disembarked from boats. It was the last time he saw the shipmate with whom he had joined up.

On impact, the entire ship shook and shuddered violently, while debris and coal dust were sent into the air. By now it was shortly after 0700. The morning watch still had nearly an hour left before eight bells could be struck.

Lieutenant McCarthy, working to get the accommodation ladder rigged from the quarterdeck to aid survivors, stated that the first torpedo that struck *Cressy* caused the ship to give a lift and immediately to list heavily towards the starboard side.

Surgeon Martin was providing medical attention to the wounded survivors that filled the sick bay and littered the upper decks of *Cressy*. 'The effect was similar to that which would have been produced by the vessel running against a huge rock. I was rendered unsteady on my feet for a moment but I did not fall,' he recalled.

The torpedo struck in the starboard engine room aft of the boilers, and while power was lost to the starboard propeller, the ship could still float, move and fight.

All the mess stools and table shores, and all available timber below and on deck, had previously been thrown over the side for the saving of life. The ship listed about 10 degrees but appeared to hold steady.

'Our first recollection of the attack on the *Cressy* is that of a tremendous shock. We saw a cloud caused by the explosion rise as high as the mast,' Able Seaman Edward Clarke told *The Times*.[15]

In Able Seaman Dolbear's account given to the *Dover Express*, he stated that after being called out of sick bay to see the *Aboukir* sinking, 'I was walking along the deck with some of the men picked up from the other ships when we got hit in the starboard waist.'[16]

Five seconds after the first torpedo struck, there followed an almost audible collective sigh of relief as the second fired by *U-9* fizzed harmlessly past the ship, missing the stern by about 20ft (6.1m). Chaplain Collier, Leading Seaman Potter and even the less devout members of the ship's company must have uttered a short prayer of thanksgiving under their breath.

Cressy had a distinctive advantage over her two unfortunate sister ships. Knowing there was a submarine attack in progress, Johnson had ordered the shutting of all watertight doors and later all the upper-deck hatches, too. He had sent signals to Harwich informing them of the grave situation. And by immediately ordering full ahead both engines, it had just been enough to cause the second torpedo to pass safely astern. In doing so, Johnson had saved his ship – at least for now.

After an initial lurch to starboard, *Cressy* stubbornly remained steady. 'We should however have been all alright if we had only been struck once. We were smoking at the time and taking it very coolly,' Able Seaman Edward Clarke told *The Times*.[17] 'I was under the impression that *Cressy* would have remained afloat in this condition,' reported McCarthy.[18]

The watertight doors were closed and more men came up from below. It seemed likely that the ship would remain afloat and the work of saving the crews of the other two ships continued.

At this point it appears from several reports that Johnson must have left the bridge and briefly walked the decks reassuring his men. If he felt any self-doubt, fear or uncertainty, no one detected it. 'Our Captain was a perfect gentleman – he chatted to the men and took all the precautions to prevent a panic,' Petty Officer Stoker Phill remembered in his extensive account, published by the *Birmingham Gazette*.[19] 'It's alright men – don't jump overboard yet – we could float for another four hours,' Johnson reassured his ship's company.[20]

Petty Officer Durrant was still in the wireless office having transmitted the signal warning of the sinking of *Aboukir* and *Hogue*. When the torpedo struck, Durrant reported that all the lights went out and he was shortly joined in the wireless office by the first lieutenant, Lieutenant Commander Bernard Harvey. 'We then tied all the wireless books together, except one we could not find, and I went to throw the books over the side but the ship seemed to right itself a little and Lieutenant Commander Harvey told me to "hang on a little while",' he reported.[21]

Harvey was ensuring that signals were being sent alerting Harwich command of the attack and anticipating the ship's fate; he was also eager to undertake the essential duty of securing the ship's confidential code books and cryptography.

In *U-9*, secret codes were the last thing on Weddigen's mind at this critical moment. He had missed his target for the first time in his short wartime career and now had a crucial decision to make. Though no one on board *Cressy* knew it, Weddigen had one torpedo (his sixth) left. If the sixth torpedo hit home, the last of the three ships would be sunk and any remaining survivors left to die of hypothermia or drowning in the cold water. If *U-9* missed, the torpedo malfunctioned or if *U-9* surfaced to recharge or Weddigen decided to withdraw, it would be an entirely different outcome. The men still in the water would be recovered by *Cressy* and the ship would probably remain afloat until relief arrived in the form of the destroyer flotillas now en route at full speed from Harwich.

This was the ultimate roll of the dice and the luck was all with Weddigen.

'The final touch, however, came quickly afterwards,'[22] was how Able Seaman Charles E. Champion succinctly put it and, when it came, it did so in highly dramatic fashion.

In *U-9*, there were spontaneous cries of 'Hurrah' from throughout the boat and they did not even trouble to dive to 15m for safety, feeling confident enough to observe the stricken *Cressy* from periscope depth. 'Weddigen then decided to fire our last torpedo at the damaged ship in order to make sure of the sinking,' recalled Spiess and the boat closed to its ideal range.[23]

U-9 was spotted again – about 500m off the starboard beam of *Cressy*. Once again, fire from the 12-pounder guns commenced to no avail. It is not clear at this stage if the gunnery officer, Lieutenant Commander Walter Bousfield Watkins-Grubb, was directing operations but his primary responsibility would have been the firing of the main 9.2in guns, which were useless to him in this action. 'I noticed the track of a torpedo about 200 yards off coming towards us,' stated Lieutenant Harrison.[24]

Johnson was by now back on the bridge to oversee the rescue operation and his stomach must have churned as he gave his futile order to go 'full ahead both engines' when he only had one operational. The order had hardly even been acknowledged when the torpedo struck.

It was 0717 when *U-9*'s final torpedo struck the ship's starboard beam near the number five boiler room, abreast of number three funnel, and when the 122.6kg of TNT exploded, the entire ship gave a huge heave and lurched over in a heavy list to starboard. At the Court of Inquiry, Lieutenant Richard Harrison RNR from Penarth near Cardiff, in Wales, who stood the first bridge watch (2000–2359) told the court what he had witnessed:

> I noticed the track of a torpedo coming towards us. The time was 0717. The Captain gave the order 'full speed ahead both', but before the ship could gather way, the torpedo struck us. The ship gave a violent heave and started to heel over to starboard.[25]

It caused carnage and chaos in the machinery spaces on the starboard side. Power was lost immediately and a huge explosion sent everything into the air. Sailors were temporarily blinded by the thick coal dust and steel deck plates were ripped off like paper tissues and flung into the air by the blast like confetti.

Able Seaman Joseph John Chidwick later told his son that he was ordered to man one of the 12-pounder guns as *U-9* made its approach. 'I remember we got off a couple of rounds and then we were hit. I managed to get out of the gun turret door. As I did so, the ship began to keel over and I saw the turret door slam on to one of the other gun crew – it almost chopped him in half,' he recalled.[26]

'I could not help him as *Cressy* was listing steeply. The "abandon ship" was sounding and I just slid into the sea,' added Chidwick.

Spiess reported how the final torpedo struck the broadside of the *Cressy*, 'bringing forth a large black cloud and then a gigantic white fountain'. 'It was well hit and now a lively scene was enacted in the tragedy before our eyes,' he added.[27]

As the Royal Navy's first armoured cruiser, *Cressy* was fitted with a 6in-thick armoured steel belt along both sides of her hull that stretched 230ft (70m) and extended from 5ft below the waterline to 6½ft above it. It was closed fore and aft by 5in steel bulkheads but it made no difference in this case. Either the torpedo fired from *U-9* was set at a depth below 5ft (1.5m) or it just punctured the armoured plate like a hot knife through butter. A depth setting of 9ft (2.75m) was a common preference for U-boat captains.

'Coal, machinery and water were sent up into the air to a terrible height and the whole surface of the sea for miles was covered with wreckage and coal dust,' Stoker Phill told the *Birmingham Gazette*, as sailors mentally prepared themselves to be plunged into the icy waters of the North Sea.

In the interview published in the *Sunderland Echo*, Stoker Wake continued:

> I was standing amidships waiting to get relieved to go below when it happened. The torpedo struck amidships near where I was standing and it is wonderful, I am not dead.[28]
>
> There was a terrible noise and a great burst up like a boiler explosion. The deck plates and woodwork and everything were sent flying up in the air with a great pillar of water. I covered my head but luckily wasn't touched by any of the falling stuff.

According to Lieutenant McCarthy, still supervising the rescue of survivors on the quarterdeck, the explosion was 'tremendous, sending a column of water high in the air' and filling inboard compartments with black smoke. 'It was now quite evident the ship would not remain long afloat,' he stated.[29]

It was now about 0730 and as damage reports reached him, Johnson must have realised with a very heavy heart that his options were now severely limited. His decision to continue the rescue operation after the sinking of *Hogue* had been the wrong one. As the ship listed further to starboard, he ordered that every man was now responsible for his own safety. 'After the second torpedo struck, Captain Johnson ordered every man for himself,' reported Martin.[30]

In the telegraph office, Petty Officer Durrant never had the chance to throw the code books over the side. After the second torpedo struck, causing the violent list to starboard, all the bags of books that he and the first lieutenant had prepared just slid down the steep incline off the deck and into the sea. He never saw Lieutenant Commander Harvey again.

Several men who had been forced to swim for it from *Aboukir* an hour earlier and had headed for the *Hogue*, only to be torpedoed for the second time, now found themselves preparing to be immersed in the forbidding waters of the North Sea for the third time that morning.

Midshipman Kit Wykeham-Musgrave of *Aboukir* attained celebrity status for becoming the only Royal Naval officer in history to survive being torpedoed three times in one morning. He had ascended the ship's side of *Cressy* by rope and was getting warm in the sick bay when the first torpedo struck. He recalled the experience:

> I then swam to the *Cressy* where I was hauled up the side by a rope. I went down into the sick bay where I had a cup of cocoa, but directly I had finished she was struck also and we were forced to go up on deck again. We sat on the forecastle and we saw a submarine come as close as 200 or 300 yards and we formed all the guns at her until we sank. I jumped off again and got clear and after swimming about for a long time found a plank to hang on to …[31]

And it was even worse for those 'saints down below', as Midshipman Scrimgeour had described the stokers and artificers working in machinery spaces who were caught by the blast.[32] It was particularly terrifying for anyone near boiler room number five, which took the full impact of the second torpedo as it struck the ship's starboard side. Chief Engine Room Artificer William Taylor recalled:

> We were all in the engine rooms at the time, and when the ship was torpedoed, I got a blow on the head. Something hit me and struck me flat. It was not a serious blow, however. We were all ordered to the engine room when the other ships were struck. All our boats, as well as tables and stools, were gone for the *Aboukir*, so when our turn came, we had nothing. That was why we suffered so.[33]

One man caught down below was Stoker First Class David Spindler, who came from the same small village in Suffolk as Leading Seaman Potter. Aged 39, Spindler was another 'old salt' who had nine children. His youngest daughter was only 3 years old when *Cressy* was hit.

All accounts indicate there was no sign of panic or excitement as men made their way to the upper deck, many gripping rolled-up hammocks in lieu of lifejackets as *Cressy* heeled more sharply.

Gunner Dougherty also had stories to tell of the final moments of the ship, as *Cressy* began to turn over after the second torpedo had struck. 'The men acted like British sailors and those who died, died as Britons should,' asserted Dougherty in an interview published in the *Harwich and Dovercourt Standard* on 26 September 1914. 'Our Captain was on the bridge. "Keep cool my lads, keep cool," he said to the crew in a steady voice.'

'"Pick up a spar my lads and put it under your arm. That'll help you keep afloat until the destroyers pick you up." That was the last I saw of Captain Johnson. He was one of the best,' said Dougherty in typical histrionic style.[34]

His account might have been embellished, as were Dougherty's other colourful and often inaccurate reports, but the general sentiment of respect and admiration for *Cressy*'s commanding officer is not a matter of doubt.

Spiess wrote of *Cressy*'s final moments: 'The giant with four stacks fell slowly but surely over to port, and like ants, the crew crawled first over the side and then onto the broad flat keel, until they disappeared under the waves.'[35]

McCarthy recalled, 'It was deadly quiet and tense, the only shouts coming from the water.'[36]

The gun crews continued to fire gamely to starboard even though the angle of the heel reduced any chance of success to zero.

'The *Cressy*'s gunners were about the gamest men that ever lived. They kept up firing until she had about forty degrees of list and the shells were simply going up into the air,' reported one unnamed survivor from *Aboukir*.[37] 'They died gamely did those fellows,' he added.

'The conduct of the crew was excellent throughout,' confirmed Nicholson.[38]

'There was no panic on the cruiser. The men were as calm as at drill and they behaved splendidly,' Harrison told *The Times*.[39]

The ship heeled rapidly and capsized in a few minutes, remaining with her keel above water for some twenty minutes before disappearing to the bottom of the Broad Fourteens at 0755 GMT.

'A tragic sight for seamen,' wrote Spiess magnanimously.[40]

The challenge was now no longer about naval combat but one of human survival for the ships' companies of *Cressy* and the other two cruisers. As Commander Nicholson explained to the Court of Inquiry, they all now had an additional problem as they abandoned ship to leave themselves at the mercy of the cold and forbidding North Sea: 'All our gear had been thrown over the side after the first torpedo struck – we had no boats left at all.'

What made the German victory even sweeter for Weddigen and Spiess was that *U-9* was not even one of the German Navy's most advanced diesel-powered, long-range U-boats. As Rear Admiral Albert Gayer suggested, it was quite surprising that Weddigen and *U-9* had made it to the Broad Fourteens at all. 'These boats experienced a great number of breakdowns due to ignition troubles. During daylight these boats gave their position away due to their thick exhaust smoke clouds: during darkness the engines misfired and the resulting exhaust fumes and noise indicated their position,' he wrote.[41]

U-9 was not even fitted with an alarm bell to indicate diving stations. Word had to be passed manually throughout the boat crew, creating unnecessary delays that could have been fatal. 'My luck was with me again, for the enemy was made useless and at once began sinking by her head. Then she careened far over, but all the while her men stayed at the guns looking for their invisible foe. They were brave and true to their country's sea traditions,' recalled Weddigen. 'With her keel uppermost, she floated until the air got out from under her and then she sank with a loud sound, as if from a creature in pain,' he wrote.[42]

Having observed the scene of destruction, Weddigen made his way north and remained submerged for another eighty minutes before blowing tanks and surfacing to a beautiful clear day in the North Sea. The horizon was completely clear of warships of any type. 'I knew the wireless of the three cruisers had been calling for aid. I was still quite able to defend myself, but I knew that news of the disaster would call many English submarines and torpedo boat destroyers, so, having done my appointed work, I set my course for home,' recalled Weddigen.

'My surmise was right, for before I got very far some British cruisers and destroyers were on the spot, and the destroyers took up the chase. I kept underwater most of the way, but managed to get off a wireless [signal] to the German fleet that I was heading homeward and being pursued,' he added.[43]

The morning watch was finally over. Three large and highly prized Royal Navy armoured cruisers were on the bottom of the North Sea. Some 2,000 men were struggling to survive in the coal black water of the North Sea and hundreds were already dead.

'It was all over in an hour. We had to do the best we could and that is all that can be said about it,' Lieutenant Harrison told newspaper reporters.

7

THE COAL BLACK SEA

They clung to wreckage, huddled naked in the few overcrowded ships' boats, hung on to lifelines and many slipped beneath the waves, often with a brief and dignified goodbye.

The three cruisers had a combined ship's company of more than 2,250 men and by the end of the morning watch on 22 September most of them were attempting to survive in the choppy water. 'There were dozens of heads bobbing about in the sea and the men were quite cheerful as if they were on dry land. Some of them were on rafts and singing popular songs while others were singing the National Anthem and Near My God To Thee,' said Able Seaman Charles E. Champion.

Champion was a policeman/fireman in Nottingham before he joined up and was interviewed by his local newspaper.[1] He recalled how he supported himself in the water on an empty cocoa box and that many of the men had been joking about the prospects of getting a 'wet shirt'.

The same newspaper published an interview with Stoker First Class Edward Barber (also known as Ted Lingard). 'It was a sight to see the gold coins that rolled out their pockets as they threw their clothes down,' recalled Barber.

According to Petty Officer Stoker Oliver Phill, some of the ship's company were reluctant to enter the uninviting North Sea, preferring to stay with their ship to the last. 'As she heeled over, there would be about one hundred men left on deck. They walked right over with the boat and stood on the keel as she came upwards. It was a remarkable sight to see these hundred men standing on the keel and then the sea washed over and took away half of the men, who were lost,' Phill told the *Birmingham Gazette* in an account published on 29 September 1914.

Just before Able Seaman Hubert Penn, known as 'Bert', the eldest of the three brothers from Deal in Kent serving on *Cressy*, launched himself into the sea, he recognised a familiar face. He wrote his account in a letter to his anxious mother, the contents of which were published in the *Dover Express*:

> I was just going to jump when I saw dear brother Alfred on the deck which was then all awash. The ship was sinking rapidly, but we lingered for a moment, shook hands and bade each other that whoever was saved, to tell dear mother that our last thoughts were of her. We then kissed, wished each other 'goodbye', and dived into the sea together, and we never saw each other again, nor did we see any sign of brother Louis.[2]

'It was a sight I shall never forget. The sea was literally alive with men, struggling and grasping for anything to save themselves,' wrote Penn.

After *Aboukir* was torpedoed, Able Seaman W. Fagg from Hull entered the water and swam for *Hogue*, only to witness it exploding in front of his eyes. Then, after about an hour he was hauled aboard *Cressy* but, after only three minutes on board, *Cressy* was struck, so Fagg dived over the bow as the ship capsized. 'A lot of the wreckage thrown over from the Hogue and the Cressy [to aid the survivors in the water] had drifted away and some of the chaps went down very soon,' he stated.[3]

In one of his many accounts, the much-quoted Gunner Dougherty recalled that men in the water were singing the popular wartime song 'It's a Long Way to Tipperary' when one wag replied, 'It bloody well is, when you're swimming mate.'

Any stirring songs and defiant humour were silenced rapidly by the numbing effects of the shock of the cold water and the onset of hypothermia. Barber described the water as 'very cold while the sea was very rough' and he and his mate managed to get clear of the ship to avoid the suction and clung to a 'nice round piece of wood'. 'The sight of the men floating in the water was awful,' he continued. 'We should watch a man for a short time until he would suddenly throw up his arms and disappear. Others would be seen leaving a weak piece of wood for a stronger piece, while some were pulled under and drowned by their helpless mates.'[4]

Once the men entering the water overcame cold shock response, they had to contend with the symptoms of hypothermia. The condition caused muscles to get weak and victims quickly lost co-ordination and strength. 'One raft passed with fifteen to eighteen men holding on but shortly afterwards I saw that only three or four remained – the others probably dropped off through exposure or exhaustion,' Champion recalled.[5]

Stoker Wake described his experience:

> I waited a while and a volume of smoke and steam came up from below and then I jumped clear. I struck out strongly away from the ship, and by good luck I found a mess table floating with which I was able to keep above water.[6]

On 22 September 1914, after a northerly gale, the surface water temperature was probably close to 12°C. Anyone immersed in water at that temperature would probably experience loss of dexterity and co-ordination within ten to twelve minutes and loss of consciousness within one to two hours. The maximum survival time would have been between two and six hours.

The temporary surgeon and friend of Chaplain Collier, Noel Martin, was also in the cold water. He knew as much about hypothermia and exposure as anyone on board, but he too defied modern guidelines for sea survival and stripped before entering the water, joining the throng of floating bodies. He stated:

> After I had been hanging on to the plank for a quarter of an hour, some of the men were giving out and began to sit on the wood, forcing it under the water. Leaving the plank, I struck out on my own and swam on for some time till I came across a man who beckoned to me. I got to him and found he had a table under one arm and a piece of wood under the other. He gave up the table to me. The top was fifteen inches square, and the legs were very stout.[7]

Those still conscious witnessed the final moments of *Cressy*. 'She was heeling over and volumes of steam were hanging about her. All over the sea were lumps of wood, wreckage and all sorts of things – and men. It was awful. I can't tell you what I did see really. Because it was too awful and I want to forget it,' said Stoker Wake.[8]

The shock and trauma of their experience, the physical injury from the blasts, and the sudden immersion in cold water while wearing little or no clothing proved to be a deadly combination for hundreds of men. 'Sometimes I saw men swimming about looking for something to rest on. They were hurt by falling wreckage some of them, not very strong after it, just put their heads down, stopped struggling – and sank,' said Wake.

'I saw poor old Will Lowery, another stoker who lived at Ryhope, go down, poor chap,' he added.[9] Stoker William Lowery was also an RFR stoker and his home at Ryhope is a coastal village along the southern boundary of the city of Sunderland. The two men were mates and joined up together. Wake recalled:

> I hung on to the table with another man who had got there, a man from South London, I believe, and we watched our ship go down. She heeled over slowly so that the Captain [Johnson] could walk on to the very end of the bridge. I watched him as he walked up and down the bridge quite calm and cool and a lot of the other chaps watched him too. He walked about till the poor old *Cressy* heeled right over and he stood up to his neck in water. We cheered him, all of us cheered him, till he sank out of sight with his ship and we saw him no more.

However, somehow Johnson had made it into the water alive and joined his men bobbing and splashing in the blackened sea. One Royal Marine, who was with him, described the scene of floating humanity for his local newspaper as being 'like a flock of seagulls'.[10] 'As they went, nearly everyone gave a final shout,' added Wake.

Commander Nicholson described the last moment of *Cressy* as witnessed from sea level in his official report. He had made it to the ship's small cutter crammed full of shivering and exhausted men. He recalled:

> The *Cressy* I watched heel over from the cutter. She heeled over to starboard very slowly, dense black smoke issuing from her when she attained an angle of about ninety degrees, and she took a long time from this angle till she floated bottom up with the starboard screw slightly out of water.

> I consider it was thirty-five to forty-five minutes from the time she was struck till she was bottom up.[11]

Beneath the brittle veneer of patriotic heroism and steely stoicism, these experienced mariners were suffering terribly, naked in the cold water with no lifesaving equipment and few boats. 'No one can have any conception of the horrible scenes in the water. Men were crying for help and struggling, clutching at each other and dragging them underneath,' said Petty Officer Phill.[12] Some were competent swimmers but many of the older hands were not.

In the private papers of Commander Herewood Hook, who was at the time a Midshipman on *Hogue*, he states that he deplored the loss of life, which 'may certainly be attributed to the undoubted fact that the real old-time seaman just simply scorned to learn how to swim'.[13]

Lieutenant McCarthy, who had been supervising the rescue of survivors and rigging of the accommodation ladder from the quarterdeck of *Cressy*, went in over the stern when it became awash. 'I swam towards Petty Officer [Tom] Matthews who I noticed had a six-inch cartridge case and joined him on that – later we found a chair, later a piece of deck plank with which we remained afloat until rescued by a boat,' he recalled.[14]

In the absence of life rafts or flotation devices, the range of flotsam that survivors clung to was quite extraordinary. Sailors called the action of flinging an object into the sea a 'float test' and this must have been the biggest float test in modern naval history. One newspaper report stated that one sailor had only survived by clinging to an empty biscuit tin.

According to Commander Nicholson's report, many men were saved by the casting adrift of the Pattern Three gunnery target. He added that *Cressy*'s steam pinnace had floated off her crutches but filled with water and sank.[15]

According to one report in the *Daily Mail*, Midshipman Cazalet saved eighty-six lives from the ship's whaler, deftly assisted by Able Seaman Rowden, one of the Whitstable 'oystermen' who worked on the fishing smacks in the Swale Estuary on the north Kent coast before the war. Cazalet was later mentioned in dispatches for his exploits and, according to his account, 'The poor fellows were holding on to floorboards, hammocks and mess stools'.[16]

Some, like Ordinary Seaman Frederick George Mills from Dover, were lucky enough to locate one of the few Kisbie lifebuoys. Once in the water, he found he had to fight off other men eager to obtain his precious possession.

His account, included in a letter home to his parents, was published in the local Dover newspaper. 'I had hold of a lifebuoy when the *Cressy* was sunk and dived overboard with it and I swam from the ship as fast as I could for, I was afraid of being drawn down with her.'[17] He continued:

> Then I saw four more swimming and they were very exhausted and I asked them to come to the buoy and that made five of us and then everything went wrong.
>
> They pushed me away from it and they were drowning each other and then two of them sank and I went on again, then another went down and that left two, then there was more hope for me. The other fellow was a jolly nice chap and his name was Mills [too] and I believe it was him who made me pull through for he was praying to God to help us and He did.[18]

While Fred Mills survived, the three other men of *Cressy* who were all named Mills were not so fortunate. It was unlikely to have been the boy servant Charles D. Mills who was encouraging his namesake. More likely, it was Royal Marine Private Mark Mills or perhaps Able Seaman William Mills, both RFR men.

In the same newspaper article, Able Seaman Dolbear also from Dover, who had been roused from the sickbay to witness the sinking of *Aboukir*, recalled his first moments swimming in the cold North Sea. 'I got to a table with six of the *Hogue* and *Aboukir* men. I clung to that for about a half an hour until I found another table which I got on and remained there until picked up by Mr Davis of Westbury Road, about two and a half hours after the sinking of the Cressy,' he said.[19] He was referring to his shipmate, Able Seaman Charles Henry Davis, another RFR seaman from Dover.

Able Seaman Edward Joseph Clarke described how he came across the 16-year-old Royal Marines Light Infantry drummer boy, from the RMLI detachment in *Aboukir*, floating on the ship's rum tub. When the senior RFR man, Able Seaman Clarke, offered the young man assistance, it was declined. 'No thanks old cockey,' replied the marine.[20]

Lieutenant Harrison's watch stopped when it first became immersed in the water. It was 0750. Harrison told *The Times* that he had managed to grab a deckchair in the water and witnessed what might be termed a minor miracle, featuring the chaplain, Rev. George Collier. 'One of the most remarkable escapes in our ship was that of the parson. He could not swim an inch and became unconscious as soon as he was in the water. He was still unconscious when he was picked up but otherwise not the worse for his immersion,' reported Harrison.[21]

Hypothermia was to claim many more lives than any of *U-9*'s well-aimed torpedoes, but the loss of life could have been even greater if not for the actions of four nearby vessels.

Captain Thomas Nelson Phillips was calmly gutting fish on his Lowestoft trawler LT-151, known as the *Coriander*, when the experienced fisherman sensed something was not quite as it should be. The level sandy seabed of the Broad Fourteens made good hunting ground for Lowestoft sailing trawlers and his was one of two working the area that morning. War did not stop the fishing industry but it made it a dangerous profession. One estimate is that 117 fishermen from the important east coast fishing port of Lowestoft were killed, and more than 170 fishing boats lost, during the First World War.[22]

When Phillips saw the first cruiser hit, he wrongly assumed it had 'burst a tank' but when he saw the second vessel, *Hogue*, turn turtle with its propellers clear out of the water, he ordered his mate to recover his trawl gear so they could offer assistance. It took about twenty minutes to do this and shortly afterwards they saw *Hogue* explode. 'I saw the water go up and felt the jar in my own vessel,' he recalled.[23]

He put out his boat and pulled over to one of the cruiser's whalers, which they saw had about forty men on board and was so overloaded that it only had about 3in of freeboard (the vertical distance between the sea surface and the top of the gunwale) remaining. 'They were bailing out with a couple of boots. The men were all naked,' he reported.

Phillips carefully got the boat alongside the whaler in the lumpy sea and instructed the survivors to keep calm and cross into the sea boat one at a time. It was a significant act of bravery on the part of Phillips because, with big warships sinking around him, Phillips had no idea if he was operating in a minefield or if a submarine might invest a torpedo on his modest 46-ton timber sailing smack.

One of the sailors saved by *Coriander* was Able Seaman Champion. 'After being in the water for one and a half to two hours I was picked up by the *Coriander*, a boat which did great rescue work,' he stated.[24] He added that he had pulled off his cap ribbon and placed it around his neck in order to help with his identification in case he had not been so fortunate as to be picked up in a conscious condition. Presumably, he had stencilled his name on the inside of the cap ribbon.

Commander Nicholson reserved praise for *Coriander* in his official report. 'I have already remarked on the bravery displayed by Capt. Phillips and his crew, who picked up 156 officers and men,' he testified.

Tragically, Captain Phillip's beloved vessel, built by J. Chambers of Lowestoft in 1908, was sunk by a U-boat the following year. On 30 July 1915, *U-10*, commanded by Otto Steinbrink, ordered the crew of *Coriander* into boats and scuttled her about 20 nautical miles south-east of her home port. It was not only warships that were vulnerable to U-boat attack in the North Sea during the First World War, and the risks for fishing boats and merchant vessels would only increase as the war progressed.

There was another small fishing vessel from Lowestoft close to the scene of devastation. LT-639, a gaff-rigged, three-masted sailing smack with a low freeboard, was known as *J-G-C* and was skippered by George Jacobs. It was probably even closer than *Coriander*. Jacobs estimated he was only about half a nautical mile from the three cruisers when they were attacked by *U-9*.

At about 0700, his third hand reported that one of the warships was heeling over. 'I let the nets go and threw my boat out to save what I could.'[25] Trawling gear is extremely expensive to replace and fit and is highly prized by trawler captains; it is vital for the livelihoods of him and his crew. It was a noble gesture.

After lowering his boat, Jacobs ran his vessel to leeward (downwind) of the scene of the attack under sail and turned his bow into the wind. The men in the water were then drifting down in his direction. He intercepted a launch with about 250 survivors on board and these were transferred to *J-G-C* so that more men could be rescued from the sea. 'We stripped ourselves of clothing [to give to the freezing survivors] and got them some hot tea and food all round,' reported Jacobs.

Those fishing vessels were a very welcome sight to the shivering men. Those that were picked up by the two trawlers got out of the cold water first, but their immersion was still more than an hour from the time of the attack on *Aboukir*.

Another of the men from *Cressy* rescued by the trawler was Surgeon Martin. 'As I got nearer to the smack, I shouted for all I was worth. I would shout, swim a hundred yards, and shout again. At last, the crew spotted me and sent their small boat, which picked me up,' he said.[26] A little later, two other vessels in the vicinity also came to the rescue of the mariners, and by doing so greatly reduced the total death tally.

English newspapers published an interview with the captain of the Dutch steamer SS *Titan*, Captain Joop Berkhout, who rescued some 114 sailors from the sea that morning. The *Titan* was on passage from Leith in Scotland to Rotterdam in the Netherlands. As a Dutch-flagged ship, it was a neutral vessel as far as the war at sea was concerned, unless seeking to transport contraband to the enemy that might assist in the war effort.

Titan had left Leith the previous Sunday evening and was about 30 miles off the Dutch coast when Berkhout stated he saw three British cruisers far away on the horizon. A little later he noticed that one had disappeared but took little notice of this, assuming it had just sailed out of sight. 'Then I happened to look again and noticed that heavy smoke was bursting from another of the cruisers and at the same time I heard the far away sound of an explosion – I knew at once that something was wrong and altered my course to go to their aid,' said Berkhout.[27]

While he steamed towards the three cruisers, the third ship, *Cressy*, was struck, and he stated he saw the two remaining cruisers roll over on their sides and then disappear. 'When I arrived at the spot, I found that two cutters were there saving men struggling in the water. All the men were naked as they had been in the water so long, they had been compelled to discard their clothing in order to save themselves,' recalled Berkhout.[28]

'There was one sloop afloat absolutely full of men and there were other sailors nearly exhausted from their long immersion in the cold sea. Some were clinging to wreckage and others were clinging round a floating table,' said Berkhout, and the captain fell into the water himself in his anxiety to get the men on board.

One of those saved was Commander Sells of *Hogue*. They took him on deck and, like most of the other men recovered from the sea, he collapsed almost immediately from sheer exhaustion. 'I gave him wine and in ten minutes he came round,' said Berkhout. The first thing Sells said when he opened his eyes and smiled was: 'That was a long swim.' This statement was reported in other newspapers as Sells saying 'that was rather a protracted swimming party', which tallies better with English middle-class understatement of the era. Sells told Berkhout that he had been in the water for about three hours and the watch on the commander's wrist had stopped at 0705. Then *Titan* saved 114 men, of whom 5 later died.

Having hung on to a plank with Petty Officer Matthews, Lieutenant Jeremiah McCarthy found himself in one of the cruiser's cutters before he was also 'flung onto the steamer Titan'. He reported that he had been in the water for two and a half hours and his watch had stopped at 0750.[29]

In the same report, Berkhout also related the tale of Midshipman Kit Wykeham-Musgrave, the first naval officer to be torpedoed three times in one morning, who was also recovered by the *Titan*'s crew. 'He was pleased when we got him aboard,' stated Berkhout. 'I wanted to bring him to Holland but he would not come. "I would rather get back to England," he said and so I put him on board a torpedo boat and I hope he is safe at home now.'

Another Dutch steamer, the *Flora*, was also in the area. It was making the reverse passage from Rotterdam to Leith when its skipper saw the three cruisers some 8 nautical miles away.

Captain Roelof Pieter Voorman of the steamship *Flora* told newspaper reporters that at about 0800 European time on Tuesday, 22 September, 'I saw a warship about eight miles off. By 0930 she had heeled over and broken in two.' 'Thenceforward I had only one thought – to save what there was to save.'[30]

As one of the cruiser's sea boats came tentatively towards the *Flora*, there was still quite a heavy sea running so that Voorman feared running the boat down and dispatching a boatload of weak and freezing survivors back into the North Sea. 'While I remained on the bridge, my men endeavoured to get the shipwrecked men on board,' Voorman told *The Times*. It was easier said than done as the sea state was still quite high and the ship was rolling heavily.

'Most of those I took on board were naked having had no time to procure clothing,' he recalled.

Flora, which steamed to the rescue, regardless of danger, rescued 28 officers and 258 men. Those unfortunate souls who were missed by the trawlers or could not be accommodated on board had to wait for the destroyer flotilla to arrive from Harwich and some, like Stoker Wake, were in the cold water for more than four hours.

Stoker First Class George Ambrose, from Long Melford in Suffolk, told his local newspaper that he found himself swimming 'amidst a crowd of men and wreckage'. He first clung on to a plank and later discarded this for a tin box, which he shared with a mess mate. After some two hours of buffeting by the waves, his mess mate could no longer tolerate it and went down. Ambrose was later picked up by HMS *Lowestoft* after some four hours and taken to Harwich. 'His hands, arms and body were badly scored and bruised, and bear eloquent testimony to the grueling [*sic*] he received,' reported the newspaper.[31]

Able Seaman Fagg, from Hull, claimed to have been in the water for about six hours. 'I thought life was too sweet to give up without a struggle, so I went for it, swimming towards a steamer I saw. I had lost consciousness however before reaching her,' he stated.[32]

Fagg was more fortunate than his commanding officer. One local newspaper revealed the story of heroic Captain Johnson as told by Coxswain E.W. Hull, from Croydon. According to Hull, Captain Johnson appeared to have been struck by wreckage and, like most of his ship's company, was desperately trying to remain afloat by holding on to some discarded pieces of wood. '"Hang on to these," he exclaimed, pushing the wood to a sailor in difficulties and then sank for the last time,' reported Hull.[33]

At the Court of Inquiry, Signal Yeoman Webb, who was on the bridge close to Captain Johnson during the early part of the morning watch, gave his own detailed account of the fate of his commanding officer. Webb testified he was sharing a griping spar (a long spar with fenders, shipped between the davits, to which a boat is secured) with Captain Johnson, who 'slipped away after about seventy-five minutes'.[34]

'I was on the same piece of wood as he was,' stated Webb, who explained he and his commanding officer shared it with a signalman (named Nelson), an Able Seaman, a gunner's mate and three or four engine room ratings. 'One I know for certain was saved,' he said, probably referring to Signalman George Henderson Nelson of *Cressy*, who was listed as a survivor.

'After being in the water about one, to one and a half hours during which the Captain was giving us instructions to keep our mouths closed and to breathe through the nose and not to expose too much of our bodies above the water but just our heads,' stated Webb, 'he also mentioned he had made a signal for the destroyers to come out and they would probably be out by 10 o'clock. Soon after that I heard noise like choking and shortly after he floated away.'

Private William Stevens RM, aged 37, stated he saw Captain Johnson deliberately let go of the timber after about ninety minutes, when he realised it was not enough to support all the men desperately clinging to it.

'Proper old father to us – everyone on the ship thought the world of him,' said Stevens.[35]

According to one unnamed surviving officer, quoted in Johnson's official obituary published in the De Ruvigny's roll of honour, 'Our commander, Captain Johnson, died like a hero; he had his confidential books lashed to his arm when he went down. He deserved ten Victoria crosses for he stopped on board until the last moment.'[36]

In common with many of his ship's company, Johnson left a widow and young family. His three children were Algernon Paley, John Paley and Elisabeth Freda, whose first birthday he had been forced to miss eleven days earlier. It was both common practice and good form to make a tribute to a captain who had lost his life in action. However, it is evident from the many affectionate comments from members of his ship's company and from fellow officers that Johnson was extremely highly respected and warmly admired by his subordinates and contemporaries.

Commodore Tyrwhitt and the destroyer flotilla eventually arrived. By 1030 they were on the scene and began to assist in the work of rescue, when HMS *Lennox*, *Lucifer* and *Lance* all reported submarines in sight. It was another case of 'periscopitis' because Weddigen and *U-9* were at least 20 nautical miles to the north-east and there were no other U-boats in the area.

Tyrwhitt soon realised this but still took the precaution of ordering four destroyers to steam round the *Lowestoft* while the survivors were trans-shipped from the boats and trawlers. According to his report, by 1345, all survivors in the vicinity having been recovered, the flotilla was formed in line abreast, a mile apart, and the surrounding area was searched for any stragglers. 'A number of boats were seen and some wreckage but no sign of the ships themselves or the men were seen,' he reported.[37]

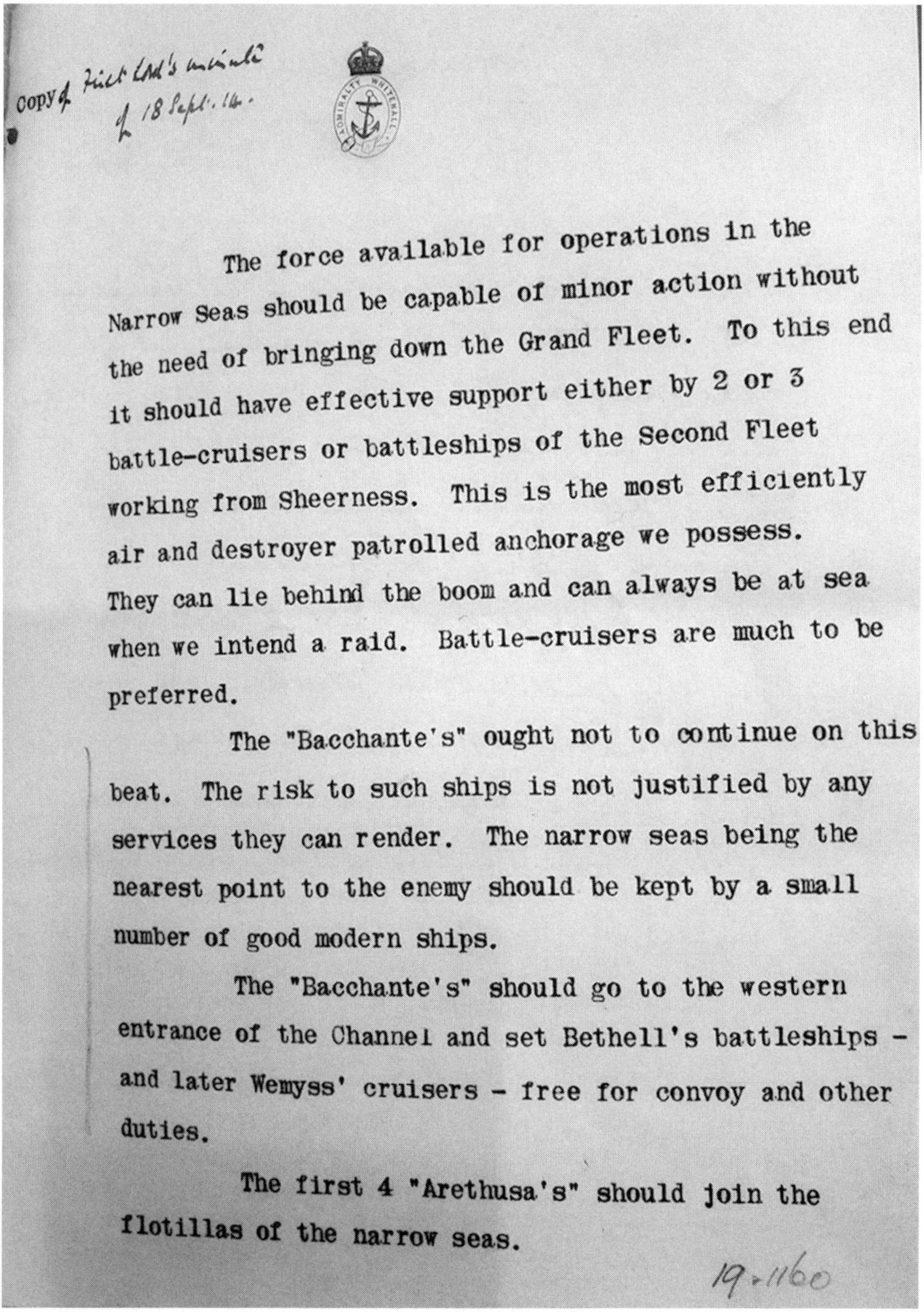

Copy of First Ld's minute of 18 Sept. 14.

ADMIRALTY WHITEHALL

The force available for operations in the Narrow Seas should be capable of minor action without the need of bringing down the Grand Fleet. To this end it should have effective support either by 2 or 3 battle-cruisers or battleships of the Second Fleet working from Sheerness. This is the most efficiently air and destroyer patrolled anchorage we possess. They can lie behind the boom and can always be at sea when we intend a raid. Battle-cruisers are much to be preferred.

The "Bacchante's" ought not to continue on this beat. The risk to such ships is not justified by any services they can render. The narrow seas being the nearest point to the enemy should be kept by a small number of good modern ships.

The "Bacchante's" should go to the western entrance of the Channel and set Bethell's battleships - and later Wemyss' cruisers - free for convoy and other duties.

The first 4 "Arethusa's" should join the flotillas of the narrow seas.

19-1160

Churchill's minute of 18 September 1914 with a key paragraph marked by a line on the left, probably by Churchill himself. (The National Archives)

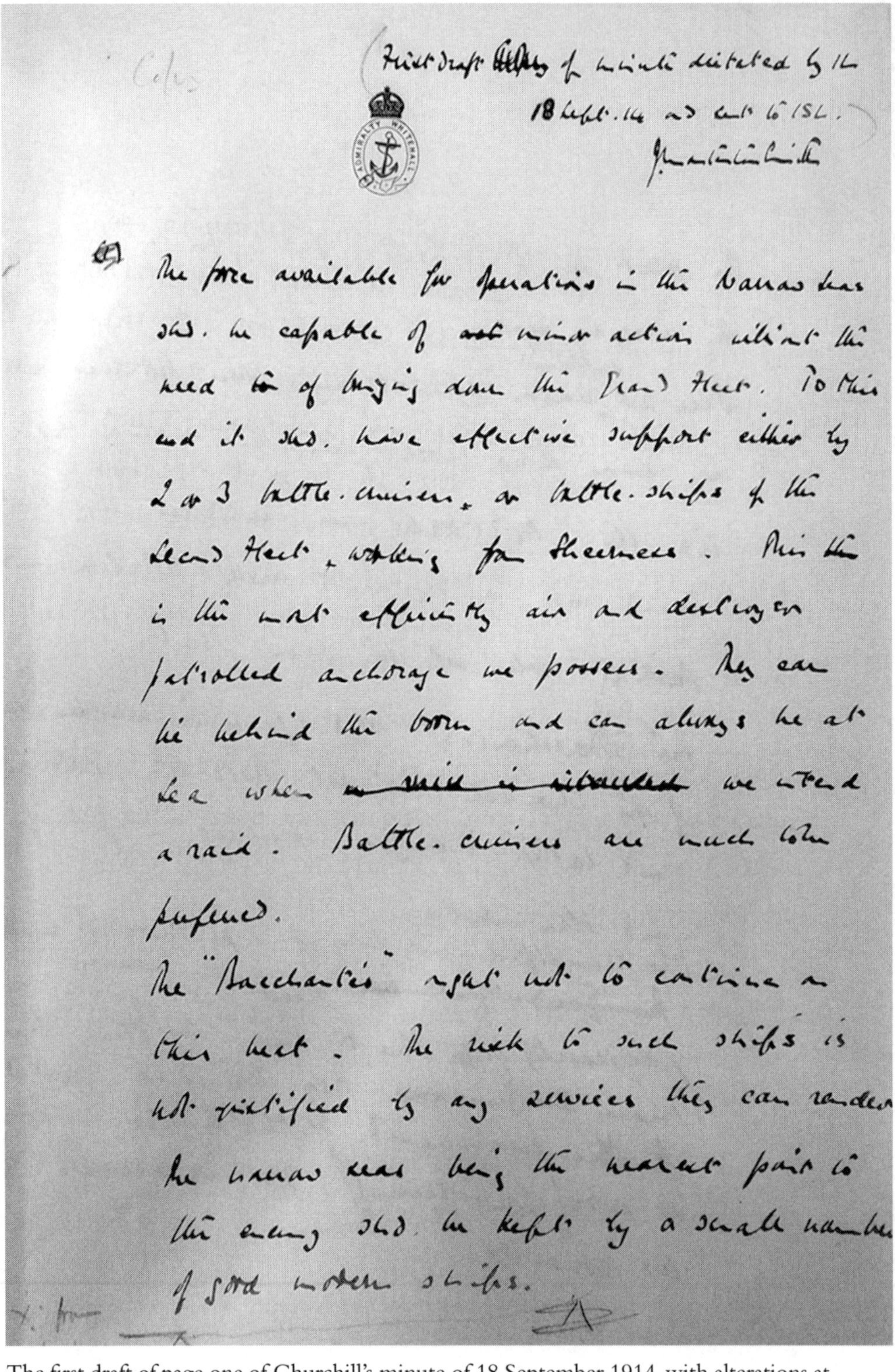
(First draft ~~copy~~ of minute dictated by the 18 Sept. 14 and sent to 1SL.)
Winston S. Churchill

The force available for operations in the Narrow Seas should be capable of ~~not~~ minor action without the need ~~to~~ of bringing down the Grand Fleet. To this end it should have effective support either by 2 or 3 battle-cruisers, or battle-ships of the Second Fleet, working from Sheerness. This ~~the~~ is the most efficiently air and destroyer patrolled anchorage we possess. They can lie behind the boom and can always be at sea when ~~a raid is attempted~~ we intend a raid. Battle-cruisers are much to be preferred.

The "Bacchantes" ought not to continue on this beat. The risk to such ships is not justified by any services they can render. The narrow seas being the nearest point to the enemy should be kept by a small number of good modern ships.

The first draft of page one of Churchill's minute of 18 September 1914, with alterations at heading. (The National Archives)

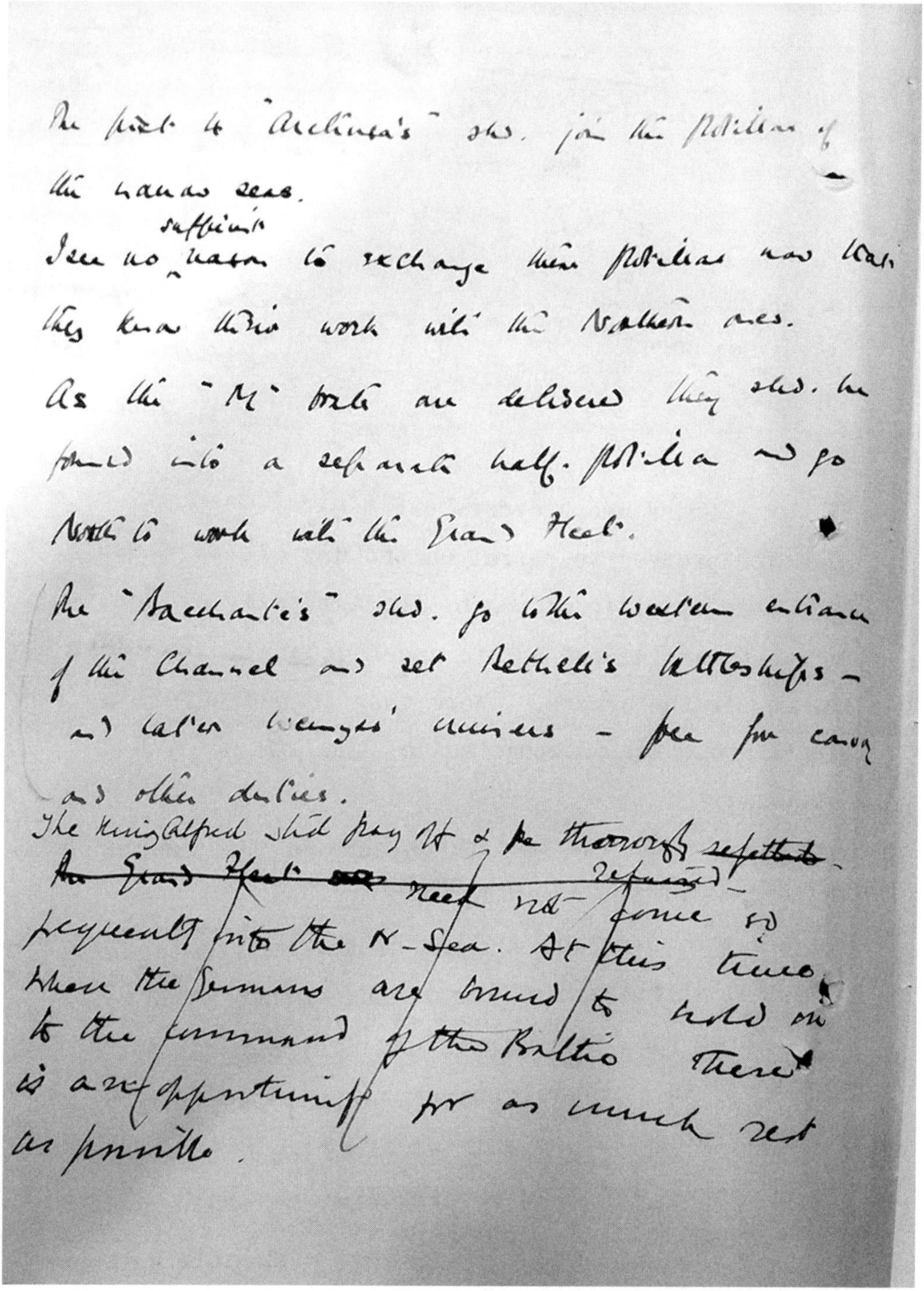

The first 4 "Arethusa's" shd. join the flotillas of the narrow seas.
I see no sufficient reason to exchange their flotillas now that they know their work with the Northern ones.
As the "M" boats are delivered they shd. be formed into a separate half-flotilla and go North to work with the Grand Fleet.
The "Bacchante's" shd. go to the Western entrance of the Channel and set Bethell's battleships – and later Wemyss' cruisers – free for convoy and other duties.
The King Alfred shd pay off & be thoroughly ~~refitted~~ ~~the Grand Fleet~~ refurnished –
Fleet need not come so frequently into the N-Sea. At this time when the Germans are bound to hold on to the command of the Baltic there is an opportunity for as much rest as possible.

The first draft of page two of Churchill's minute of 18 September 1914, with scratchings out. (The National Archives)

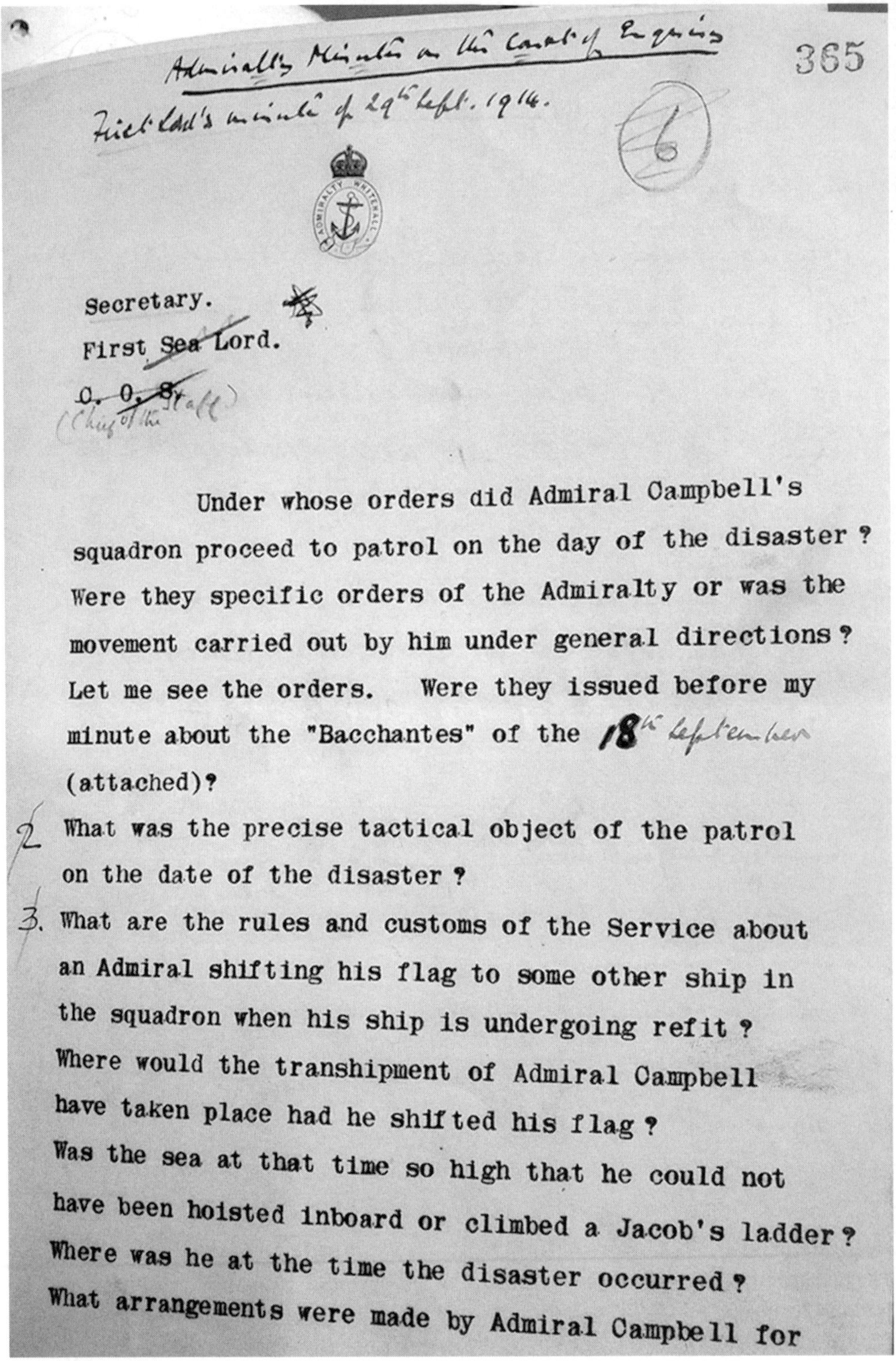

Admiralty Minutes on the Court of Enquiry

First Lord's minute of 29th Sept. 1914.

365

(6)

Secretary.

First ~~Sea~~ Lord.

~~C. O. S.~~ (Chief of the Staff)

Under whose orders did Admiral Campbell's squadron proceed to patrol on the day of the disaster ? Were they specific orders of the Admiralty or was the movement carried out by him under general directions ? Let me see the orders. Were they issued before my minute about the "Bacchantes" of the 18th September (attached)?

2 What was the precise tactical object of the patrol on the date of the disaster ?

3. What are the rules and customs of the Service about an Admiral shifting his flag to some other ship in the squadron when his ship is undergoing refit ? Where would the transhipment of Admiral Campbell have taken place had he shifted his flag ? Was the sea at that time so high that he could not have been hoisted inboard or climbed a Jacob's ladder ? Where was he at the time the disaster occurred ? What arrangements were made by Admiral Campbell for

Churchill's minute of 29 September 1914 with an apparent date change. (The National Archives)

A watercolour of HMS *Cressy* and the Broad Fourteens disaster, produced in 1920. (Courtesy of Chatham Historic Dockyard)

Model of HMS *Cressy* at Chatham Historic Dockyard on loan from the Imperial War Museum. (Courtesy of Chatham Historic Dockyard)

Seaman George James Keam (RNR) added into a photograph of his family taken after his death. (Courtesy of Violet Maidment)

Heath
LIEUT.-COM. E. P. GABBETT
H.M.S. Cressy, *missing.*

Image of Lieutenant Commander Gabbett from *The Illustrated London News*, 3 October 1914. (© Illustrated London News Ltd/Mary Evans Picture Library)

Captain R.W. Johnson (RN).

Leading Seaman William John Potter (RFR). (Courtesy of David Heaver)

Chatham Naval Memorial featuring the name of Captain Johnson of Cressy. (Stuart Heaver)

Chatham Naval Memorial. (Stuart Heaver)

THE DAILY MIRROR, Wednesday, September 23, 1914.

THREE BRITISH CRUISERS SUNK BY GERMAN SUBMARINES

The Daily Mirror

LATEST CERTIFIED CIRCULATION MORE THAN 1,000,000 COPIES PER DAY

No. 3,406. Registered at the G.P.O. as a Newspaper. WEDNESDAY, SEPTEMBER 23, 1914 One Halfpenny.

BRITISH NAVAL LOSS IN THE NORTH SEA: THREE SISTER CRUISERS SUNK BY GERMAN SUBMARINES.

Captain Wilmot S. Nicholson, of H.M.S. Hogue.

H.M.S. Aboukir. All three vessels were of a comparatively old type, having been built fourteen years ago.

Lieutenant A. Tyrer, of the Hogue.

Captain Cuthbert Williams, of the Hogue.

Lieutenant L. C. Ingham, of the Hogue.

Engineer Commander W. R. Lawton (Aboukir).

Lieutenant Commander J. S. Parker (Aboukir).

H.M.S. Cressy. The three sunken vessels were sister ships.

H.M.S. Hogue. The cost of each vessel was about £800,000.

Three British cruisers—the Aboukir, the Hogue and the Cressy—have been sunk in the North Sea by German submarines. The first-named vessel was torpedoed, and while the other two were standing by to save the crew they suffered the same fate. The loss of many of our brave sailors is deeply to be deplored, but, though the news is bad, there is no cause for depression. Great Britain has a great preponderance of cruisers over Germany, and we are bound to lose a certain number of ships. The portraits of the officers on this page are given in the September Navy List as serving in the lost cruisers.—(Russell, Swaine, Heath and Stephen Cribb.)

The front page of *The Daily Mirror*, 23 September 1914. (© John Frost Newspapers/Mary Evans Picture Library)

DAILY SKETCH, FRIDAY, SEPTEMBER 25, 1914

PHOTOGRAPH OF BATTLE OF THE AISNE TAKEN UNDER FIRE.

DAILY SKETCH.

No. 1,731. LONDON, FRIDAY, SEPTEMBER 25, 1914. (Registered as a Newspaper.) ONE HALFPENNY.

"THE CRESSY WAS FIRING AS SHE SANK."

Gunner Dougherty, photographed yesterday at his home.

Some of the North Sea survivors who were amused at their new rig-out.

The men of the lost Aboukir, Cressy and Hogue photographed at Shotley Barracks yesterday.

Hitching up their new trousers.

Mr. Albert Dougherty, the chief gunner of H.M.S. Cressy, was the man who kept the guns booming when his vessel was torpedoed. He sent one of the enemy's submarines to the bottom, set fire to a German boat in disguise that was directing the attack, and kept pegging away at four other submarines until the Cressy heeled over and broke in halves. While he was clasping a spar in the water a seaman called to him "It's a long way to Tipperary this way!" and the gunner cheerily replied "It is, if you're going to swim!" The men floated about for four hours before they were picked up.

Daily Sketch front page of 25 September 1914 with image of Gunner Albert J. Dougherty (top left). (John Frost Newspapers/Alamy Stock Photo)

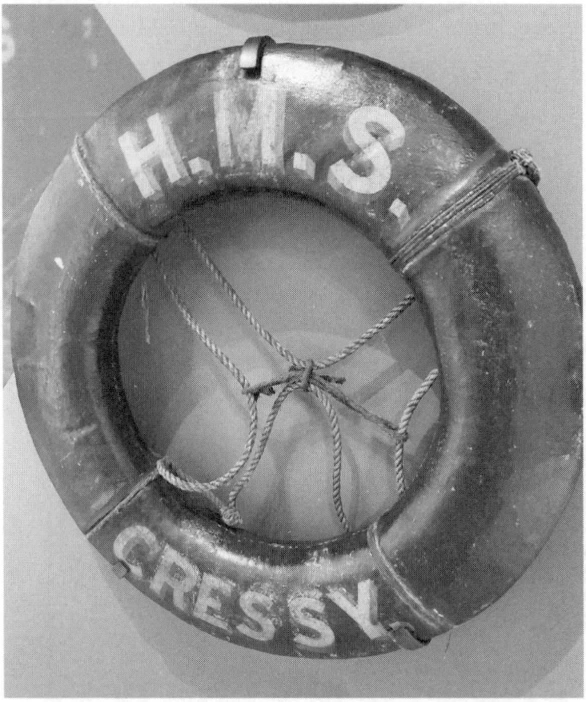

Kisbie design lifebuoy from HMS *Cressy*. (Courtesy of Chatham Historic Dockyard)

Lieutenant Commander Otto Weddigen wearing the Iron Cross, 1915. (George Grantham Bain Collection, US Library of Congress)

Churchill at the start of his political career, *c*. 1900. (US Library of Congress)

Churchill in 1911, the year he was appointed as First Lord of the Admiralty. (GRANGER/Alamy Stock Photo)

Mr. Winston Churchill, the First Lord of the Admiralty, learns that the cruisers Aboukir, Cressy and Hogue have been sunk by the Germans.

Cartoon of Churchill from *The Daily Mirror*, 14 October 1914.

Charles William de la Poer Beresford (1846–1919), who was a British Admiral and Member of Parliament. (George Grantham Bain Collection, US Library of Congress)

Lieutenant Commander Weddigen (seated, third from left) with the crew of *U-9*. (George Grantham Bain Collection, US Library of Congress)

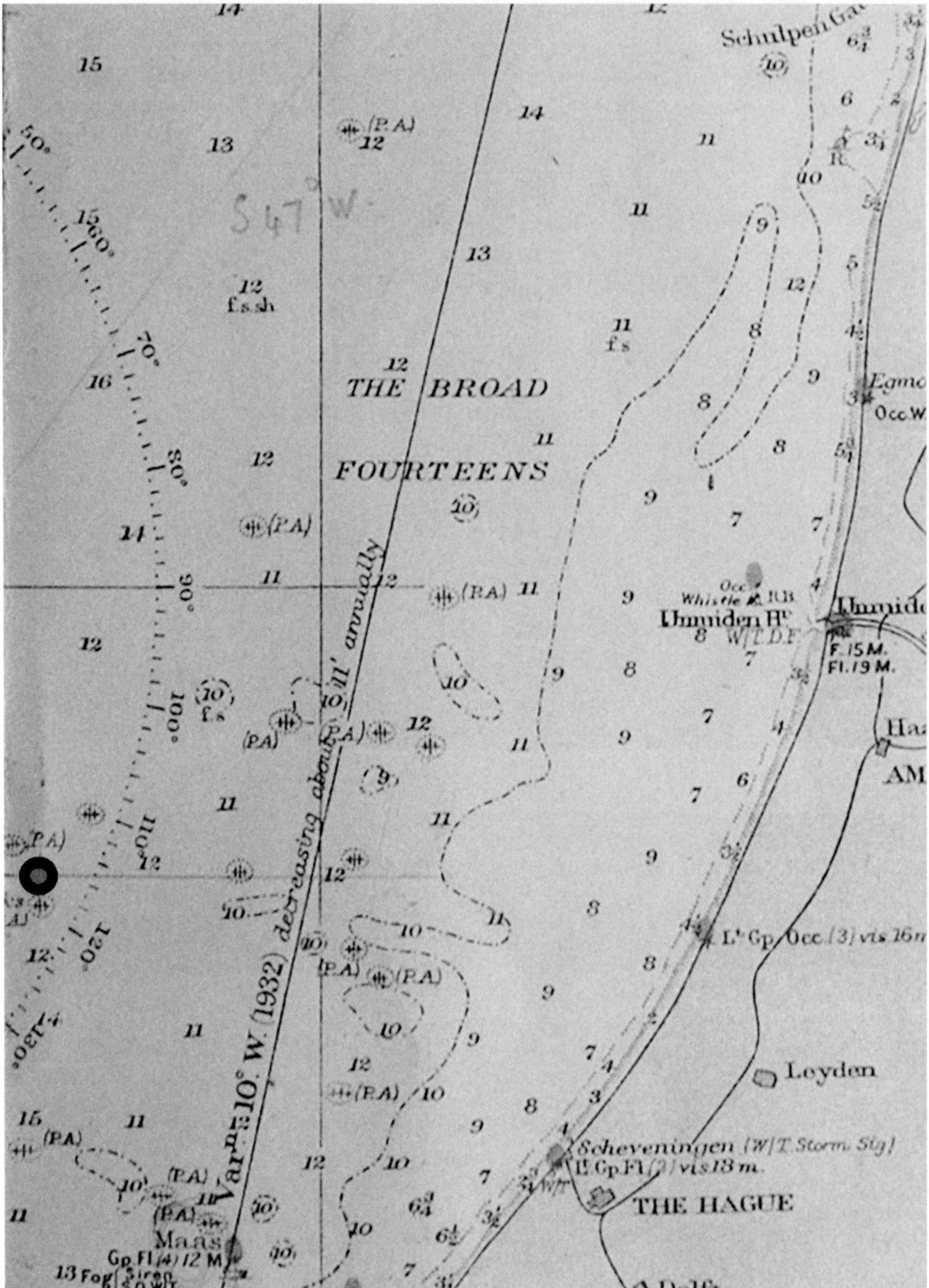

Admiralty Chart 2182 of Broad Fourteens with the location of *U-9* attack marked by the target on the left.

8

A NEUTRAL COUNTRY

Shivering uncontrollably, dazed and hugely relieved, some of those survivors fortunate enough to be safely below decks on the two Dutch steamers, *Flora* and *Titan*, were taken to the neutral Netherlands.

As Britain reeled in shock at the news of the naval disaster, these men, wrapped in borrowed clothing, rags, flags and blankets, accepted their destiny with customary naval stoicism. Some were unconscious, some were gravely ill and five in SS *Titan* never made it to the Dutch coast. One of the five dead bodies landed by *Titan* was that of Colour Sergeant Horace Farmer, Royal Marine Light Infantry (RMLI), from Chatham, who served in *Cressy*. Farmer was another RFR man and the senior non-commissioned officer in the RMLI detachment. He had lived with his wife in Herbert Road, Chatham, the ship's home port.

'I lost consciousness, and when I woke up, I was on a steamer called the *Titan* and they were kind to us, for they gave us all their clothes, and they took us to Holland,' Able Seaman Fred Mills told his parents in a letter published in the *Dover Express*.[1]

A few, like Midshipman Wykeham-Musgrave, the young officer who had been sunk three times before breakfast, had expressed his desire to return to Britain as soon as possible to avoid the prospect of internment in the Netherlands for the remainder of the war. He, with Commander Sells and most of the others on board, were transferred from *Titan* to one of the arriving British destroyers from Harwich.

Captain Berkhout of the *Titan* originally had 114 survivors on board. While the majority were transferred with Commander Sells and Midshipman Wykeham-Musgrave to British warships and taken to Harwich, several, including Able Seamen Mills and Clarke, were not. They later stated they were too 'battered and bruised' to contemplate a transfer to the warship. Whether the remaining twenty surviving men in *Titan* were too badly injured to be transferred, or simply too well concealed, is a matter for conjecture. 'This torpedo boat took most of the men I picked up and the rest I took to Holland and landed them at the fortress at the Hook,' reported Captain Berkhout of the *Titan*.[2]

Such was his determination to return home, Stoker First Class Clifford Dingley from Dudley claimed that, after being picked up by *Titan*, he 'swam to the *Lucifer*'. HMS *Lucifer* was one of the first destroyers from the Third Destroyer Flotilla from the Harwich Force to arrive at the scene and take casualties from *Titan*.

'I shall be glad to have an opportunity of being in the engagement in which we shall get our own back,' Dingley told the *Birmingham Gazette* in suitably stirring fashion.[3] Others were more ambivalent about the prospect of rejoining the war at sea and just grateful to be alive. It is more likely they were just looking forward to celebrating their survival by 'getting as drunk as a fiddler's bitch', to use a popular lower-deck expression of the period.[4]

All expressed their gratitude to the captains of the two Dutch ships for risking their vessels to save the lives of them and their shipmates. 'I can't speak too highly of the Dutch people. Their kindness to us was great,' Stoker Wake told the *Sunderland Echo*.[5]

After *Titan* had landed her cargo of survivors by the fortress at Hook of Holland that evening, it continued on its scheduled passage from Leith to Rotterdam as though it was business as usual. Another of those rescued by *Titan* was Able Seaman Fagg, who related his experience of landing in the Netherlands to the *Hull Daily Mail* in a report published on 30 September 1914. According to Fagg, twenty survivors were landed at the Hook but five had died before their arrival. Eight of them were taken to a soldiers' hospital attached to the fort. The following day they were taken under armed guard to the waiting room at the railway station to await orders. They did not know whether they were prisoners of war or not.

An enterprising special correspondent from *The Times* proceeded from Rotterdam to the Hook on 23 September and managed to obtain permission from the commander of the fort to interview some of the British survivors. In the report published on 24 September, Edward Clarke told *The Times* that most of the men had been rescued from the water by *Cressy* by the time the fatal sixth torpedo from *U-9* struck.[6]

Lying in the bunk next to Clarke was Fred Mills, writing the letter to his parents in Dover that was later published in the *Dover Express and East Kent News* on 2 October. 'Nothing could have been kinder, the men said, than the treatment they received from the crew of the *Titan*,' reported *The Times*.[7] The same report stated that of the twenty-five not transferred from *Titan* to the British destroyers, five had died, one was injured and four were suffering from illness, 'while fifteen are all right except for shock and bruises'.

According to *The Manchester Guardian*, published on 23 September, the *Flora* landed 287 men some 65km further up the coast at Ijmuiden in the Netherlands. It had arrived earlier in the day and the newspaper reported that some of the survivors were wounded. One of those on board *Flora* was Able Seaman Dolbear from Dover, who was called out of *Cressy*'s sick bay to witness the sinking of the *Aboukir*. According to his account, he was pulled on board *Flora* by another Dover resident, Able Seaman Charles Henry Davis of Westbury Road. 'We were taken to Ijmuiden in the Dutch steamer, *Flora* where we were treated well, everyone wanting to do something for us,' said Dolbear.

One of the survivors from *Flora* subsequently lost his life shortly after rescue and was buried at Ijmuiden. According to a Reuters report: 'At noon yesterday [24 September] the remains of a British sailor named P. Green [Seaman Percy E. Green RNR of *Aboukir*] were interred here with military honours, the Reverend Mr Chambers, British chaplain at Amsterdam, conducted the funeral service.'[8]

The senior surviving officer on board the two Dutch vessels was Captain Wilmot Nicholson. The former commanding officer of *Hogue* was reduced to just another naked and shivering human being, huddled down below decks in SS *Flora*. In his report, Nicholson said that the Dutch authorities put them on a train to Heerenveen, a town about 80 miles to the north of Ijmuiden, which arrived at 1615 having 'made good the pressing deficiencies in clothing', as Nicholson politely put it.

Sympathetic locals, seeing the sorry state of the sodden British survivors wrapped in sacks and flags, had taken pity on them and donated food and clothes. Uniforms from the Dutch military were also made available.

'The men were first fitted out with Naval clothing by the Dutch Navy. The Dutch army supplied Great Coats,' stated Dolbear.[9]

Those survivors fit to travel took a second short train journey to Sint Nicolaasga, and were then required to march the final 23km to the Gaasterland military camp, where they were provided with a hot meal and sent to very basic accommodation in tents. 'The men arrived at the camp cheerful and in good order at 9pm though suffering considerably with footsoreness,' reported Nicholson.[10] The sore feet were largely attributable to the recent Dutch issue of new boots, most of which did not fit properly.

Between them the two Dutch ships had saved more than 400 lives, including those transferred at the scene to the recently arrived Harwich-based British destroyers. Such was the gratitude of the British nation that the crews of the two vessels were later awarded £10 per head. According to a consular report dated January 1915, receipts were obtained from thirty-one crew members of the two vessels, and Captain Berkhout and Captain Voorman were both presented with commemorative silver cups by British officials at a formal ceremony.

According to an official announcement: 'The King has been pleased, on the recommendation of the President of the Board of Trade, to award the silver medal for gallantry in saving life at sea' to the commanding officers of the two Dutch steamers and the skippers of the two Lowestoft trawlers. This was 'in recognition of their services in rescuing survivors of His Majesty's ships *Aboukir*, *Cressy* and *Hogue* which were sunk by torpedoes in the North Sea on September 22'.[11]

In accordance with the Peace Treaty of The Hague signed on 18 October 1907, the neutral nation of the Netherlands was obliged to disarm and intern all military personnel until the cessation of hostilities. It was already proving quite a burden and a logistical challenge.

In the first days of war, 52 Belgian and 179 German military men had crossed the border and the Belgians were soon transferred to Camp Gaasterland. They were still there to greet the arriving British sailors and marines, and according to some reports a goodwill international football fixture was organised between the British and the Belgian personnel. There is no record of the final score.

The officers of the three sunken cruisers were treated rather differently from the rest of the men, of course. It meant they had to march a further 5km but had the relative luxury of dinner at a hotel at Rijs before being billeted in a large farmhouse. Nicholson visited the camp with the chaplain of the *Hogue* and Kolonel E.A. Teding van Berkhout on 24 September to check on the men's well-being and, from all accounts, he was more than satisfied with their treatment. Most were frantically scribbling notes on postcards to be posted to their families and loved ones back in Britain, assuring them of their safety.[12]

Some men were accommodated at the Duin en Kruidberg estate in Santpoort. The owner of the palatial manor house was Jacob Theodor Creer, a former Cabinet minister and Dutch ambassador to Washington DC. 'A Dutch gentleman took a number of the men who were suffering from the effects of their immersion to his house,' said Dolbear.

The Dutch authorities were under the impression that they were obliged by international law to intern the British sailors until the cessation of hostilities as they had the German and Belgian Army personnel in the previous six weeks of the war. However, Britain saw things very differently and, while the survivors were recovering in Camp Gaasterland, a covert diplomatic row was brewing behind the scenes.

A letter written by Foreign Secretary Lord Grey (the long-serving British Cabinet minister who hated travel and preferred to conduct diplomacy via overseas ambassadors in London or, even better, on the telephone) explained that he had protested by telephone to the Dutch Foreign Minister, John Loudon, the day after the attack. In reply, Grey was told by Loudon that it would be necessary to interview the captains of the two Dutch steamers to ensure that they had not encountered German submarines or warships that may have ordered them to a Dutch port. If they had, and the sailors were subsequently released, it would represent a serious violation of the principles of neutrality.[13] The Dutch pleaded with the British not to issue a protest because Loudon felt confident that, after the required interviews with the two steamer captains, the British sailors would be released anyway.

In the same letter dated 28 September, Grey says that Loudon made it clear that the Dutch wanted to release the British sailors of their own free will and not as a result of a protest or other diplomatic device to exert pressure on them. It suggests that, from a German perspective at least, the Dutch were probably a little less neutral than they might have been. 'It is stated on good authority that there is uncertainty in Government circles whether the rescued British sailors can be returned. The resolution agreed at the second peace conference with regard to Naval warfare contain no provision in this particular case,' reported *The Times* on 24 September.

The relevant portion of the Convention for the Adaptation of the Principles of the Geneva Convention to Maritime War was agreed at The Hague on 18 October 1907. Evidence suggests that the Dutch Government had interpreted the convention as only applying to belligerent persons landed by their captors. It was ready to release the survivors of its own free will without the necessity of any request or protest being made by Lord Grey.[14]

As the survivors continued their rehabilitation and the diplomacy continued in the background, the local press in the Netherlands was avidly reporting every development of the sailors' stay there. Pictures appeared of Royal Navy bluejackets dressed in Dutch artillery uniforms or in ill-fitting civilian clothes.

Eventually, the men left the tents of Camp Gaasterland and followed the same path as their hastily written postcards and letters home. They were transported back to Sheerness and Folkestone via Flushing on the mail packet on 26 September. From Folkestone and Sheerness, the survivors travelled to Chatham and then were granted ten days' leave, with most proceeding to their hometowns. This gave local newspapers the opportunity to interview survivors and publish their harrowing eyewitness accounts.

While those survivors were returning home on 26 September, the bodies of many of their shipmates were still arriving on the beaches of the Netherlands during the month of October. Across a wide expanse of Dutch coastline, members of the public, soldiers on patrol and local fishermen reported finding the bloated and distorted, naked and semi-naked corpses of young men washed up on desolate windswept beaches. Nearly as many members of the ship's companies of HMS *Aboukir*, *Hogue* and *Cressy* washed up in the Netherlands as had arrived on the two Dutch steamers. The combined effect of tide and the northerly wind had steadily transported these bodies to their penultimate resting place.

According to official report number 438, filed by British Consul Ernest Maxse, based at the British Consulate General in Rotterdam, and dated 17 November 1914, there was a total of 161 bodies of British sailors and marines recorded by local police and officials. Each body is recorded with the town or village where it was found.[15]

At the seaside town of Gravenzande, about 5km north-east of where *Titan* had landed survivors at the Hook, forty-six bodies were found over the course of two months. Twenty-nine more were found at The Hague, some 12km further north. Twelve bodies were found at Wassenaar, 10km north of The Hague, eight at Katwyk and twenty-seven at Noordwyk, further north still.

Twenty were recovered at the village of Monster near the Hook and eleven at the town of Loosduinen on the western periphery of The Hague. Three were recovered at the town of Oostvoorne, near what is now the modern Europoort container port at Rotterdam. One body was found at the tiny village of Oudenhoorn and three at Rockanje.

A solitary body was recovered from the small seaside village of Renessee on the island of Schouwen-Duiveland. This is some 40km south-west of the Hook, the area where the majority of bodies were washed up by the wind and tide. It's a pretty village, set around a Gothic-style Jacobuskerk church, complete with its fifteenth-century tower. On an overcast and windy autumn day, it feels a long way from Chatham Dockyard.

The body of Able Seaman Henry A. Brown, of *Hogue*, an RFR seaman, was found here. He was discovered on 6 October 1914 and identified by a letter in his pocket that was postmarked Birmingham and dated 11 September 1914. He was probably reading it before the torpedo struck his vessel. No one knows who wrote the sodden 'maily' to him. According to a report sent from the British Consulate, immediate internment was recommended by the Burgomaster of the village due to the decomposed state of his body. He was buried in the local church the next day after a formal funeral service, presided over by the local clergyman.

Across a 75km stretch of coastline from the picturesque and remote village of Ressie in the south-west, to Noordwyk in the north-east, 161 naked corpses of British sailors and marines littered the white sand beaches. These are long flat sandy stretches backing onto grassy dunes. Beautiful in summer and now very popular with kite surfers, they offer visitors attractive stilted coffee shops with impressive views of the North Sea. In the autumn and winter, they can feel windswept, desolate and forbidding. Of those 161 bodies recorded, only 17 were positively identified.

One of the eleven bodies found at the town of Loosduinen was Able Seaman Henry Suttie of HMS *Cressy*. Born on 27 October 1884, Suttie was from North Shields, Northumberland, and was a regular Able Seaman, not a reservist. He was identified by the name written in the blue serge trousers he was still wearing and was buried a few days later at nearby Gravenzande cemetery with full military honours. There is no official record of who discovered the body of Suttie on the beach. Perhaps a family out for a picnic, an old lady walking her dog, schoolchildren playing on the sand or a fisherman returning home.

The sinking of the three cruisers by *U-9* was common knowledge in the Netherlands by now and neither the local police nor Dr H.W. Hong, the Mayor of Loosduinen, would have regarded the discovery of these dead bodies as suspicious. No one feared these were potential crime scenes and their presence was no mystery. The sinking of the three cruisers had merited front-page headlines in most Dutch newspapers, including the local ones.

In a letter written by Dr Hong to the British Consulate in Rotterdam dated 3 October 1914, it was confirmed that Suttie's body was photographed along with the place where he was buried. 'He will be buried on Monday next at 3 o'clock pm in the church yard near the Protestant Hervormde [Dutch Reformed] church in this place.'[16] Hong requested a British flag to be supplied so it could be draped over Suttie's coffin and asked for the presence of a British official or clergyman because Suttie was to receive a formal military funeral. The Netherlands was a neutral nation and formalities had to be strictly observed.

The identification process was vitally important so that anxious and distraught next of kin and families in Britain could be informed by Admiralty telegrams as soon as possible. Suttie's next of kin was his married sister, Ellen Stott, 23, of Front Street, Milbern Place, North Shields. She was informed of his death but had no way of attending his funeral in the Netherlands.

The process of identifying the dead and informing next of kin was undertaken with due diligence. It could be a tricky business, though, as demonstrated by the fascinating case of Crawley's trousers. A terrible error of identification was nearly made with a body discovered in Loosduinen and conscientiously reported by Dr Hong and buried in the same churchyard as Suttie. The body of a Royal Marine was identified by the name and service number sewn into the beltline of his trousers, 'E.A. Cranley 11620'.

The problem was that there was no one called Cranley serving in any of the three cruisers. Neither was the name listed anywhere in the Royal

Navy or Royal Marines. However, a Gunner E.A. Crawley, Royal Marines Artillery (RMA), was listed as serving as part of the ship's company of the *Lion*-class battlecruiser HMS *Princess Royal.*

HMS *Princess Royal* had taken part in the Heligoland Bight offensive on 15 September but was nowhere near the Broad Fourteens when the three cruisers were attacked by *U-9*. The presence of the corpse of Gunner E.A. Crawley on the beach in Loosduinen in the Netherlands, when he should have been alive and well while serving on HMS *Princess Royal*, presented something of a mystery. Consequently, General Sir Herbert Edward Blumberg, Deputy Assistant Adjutant-General at the Royal Marine Forces headquarters, urgently contacted the commanding officer of HMS *Princess Royal* to investigate if Gunner E.A. Crawley was present, and if so, whether he had given his trousers to anyone.

In his report in October 1914, Blumberg solves the mystery:

> It has been ascertained that RMA/11620 Gunner E.A. Crawley RMA, who is at present serving in HMS *Princess Royal*, gave a pair of trousers to RMA/11488 Gunner Ernest George Stephen Collins RMA, who was serving in HMS *Aboukir* when that vessel was sunk and not reported as saved. Gunner Collins was tattooed but no definite description of the man is obtainable.[17]

The authorities in the Netherlands had no way of knowing that the 27-year-old Collins from Bristol had been wrongly identified because he died while wearing someone else's trousers.

The mystery of how and why two young men ended up exchanging trousers was not investigated in an era when sailors might ironically take pride in the Navy's traditional mantra of 'rum, sodomy and the lash', but same-sex love was both a strict taboo and a criminal offence, and would remain so for almost a century.

Collins was buried in his mate's (or possibly his lover's) trousers in the same cemetery as Suttie. His widowed mother, Georgina Collins, who lived at 2 Moreton Street, St Paul's, Bristol, was informed of his death. She could not attend her son's funeral either, but it's doubtful if she could have afforded to make the long journey to the Netherlands even in peacetime. Working-class folk did not generally take overseas trips in the early twentieth century unless they were emigrating.

Evidently, the imprecise process of identification of casualties was a flawed one. The British Army introduced identity tags in 1907. They were produced within each unit and stamped with key information – typically service number, surname and initials, regiment, and sometimes battalion and rank. Religion was also indicated.

The Navy did not follow suit until later and then identity tags were inserted into footwear. This was a futile measure because sailors invariably removed their boots before entering the water to facilitate swimming. Clothing was usually named to avoid it being lost in the laundry or stolen and this was often the key to identifying the dead but, as the Crawley case demonstrated, it was hardly a reliable method. Some men like Able Seaman Champion resorted to writing their names on the inside of their cap ribbons and wearing them around their necks.

Instead, records kept of tattoos were more helpful. Often corpses were identified by officials looking specifically for artistic renditions of sea serpents, poems, lions, unicorns, anchors and roses all inked on the pallid skin of the bodies of the dead. By 1914, tattoos were a firmly established part of naval culture. Even the King of England, George V, known as the Sailor King after his coronation in 1910 because of his naval career and ardent support for the Royal Navy, was tattooed in Yokohama, Japan, in 1881.

According to diaries published recently, the future King of England and his brother were both serving as midshipmen in HMS *Bacchante* (coincidentally, sister ship to the three torpedoed cruisers) when it visited Japan. According to the official diary of the tour, compiled by their tutor, the Rev. John Dalton, both princes had their arms tattooed during their visit. Albert Victor chose a couple of storks and George opted for a dragon and a tiger – one image on each arm to symbolise east and west.

Meticulous lists were made of the tattoos found on the unidentified bodies in the Netherlands in the hope it would aid identification. In the report from Loosduinen dated 10 October, victim number two had a tattoo of Japanese women on his right forearm.

Another report dated 6 October, and included in Consul General Maxse's dispatch of 17 November 1914 from Wassenaar, lists twelve victims. Those without names are numbered. Victim number one had tattoo marks on his right forearm, one a wreath in which a compass surrounded by the words 'light our guide' was inked. He was 1.69m tall. Number three was tattooed with a religious cross with 'father' written below. He was fair haired and had a moustache. Perhaps he was one of the godlier members of the three ships' companies, like Leading Seaman Potter of *Cressy*. Victim number eleven at Wassenaar was E.R.R. Chilman, who was also identified by the name marked in his trousers.

The bodies were conveyed to the cemetery at Wassenaar and examined by Dr Duetz. Most were in such poor condition that an accurate description was impossible and photographs could not be taken. The report is signed by the Burgomaster of Wassenaar.

The three bodies found on 7 October at Rockanje were said to be in an 'unrecognisable state' and were buried with full military honours in a service presided over by Rev. U.J. Witkop of the Dutch Reformed church.

At Oostvorne on 6 October, one man washed ashore who was about 30 years old. The victim had W.E. Greener embroidered on his coat. Able Seaman William E. Greener had served in *Aboukir*. The same day, two more bodies were found. One had a golden ring with a star engraved on it and the other was wearing flannel undershorts, marked CH 8249. This is the service number of Sergeant John Butler RMLI of HMS *Cressy*. The CH abbreviation referred to Chatham, his home port. Two days later, another man washed ashore in the same village according to a report signed by G. van Andel, Burgomaster.

Some of the men had personal items with them. Private Francis W. Holman RMLI of *Cressy* was one of those found at The Hague. He had the remnants of a glove. Able Seaman James Hynes, a Devonport-based coastguard serving in *Cressy*, had a leather purse containing £1. Many of those found had money or gold about them, even those who were partially naked. A sailor took his gold with him to the bitter end, or to use Tennyson's poetic phrase, when it was time for 'crossing the bar'.

Body number twenty at The Hague had £6 in gold. He had a tattooed left arm with a parrot, a pigeon and a swan. Also, a tattoo of a child's head with curly hair. Another body had Britannia tattooed on his right arm complete with a lion and a flag. A woman was tattooed on his left arm with clasped hands and the words 'True love – I love Flo'. One had a signet ring engraved E.H. and some nail clippers, while another had a silver watch by J.G. Graves with the number 168115. J.G. Graves was a well-known watch supplier based in Sheffield and this would have been a pocket watch, not a wristwatch.

Random objects from the three cruisers were also offered up by the North Sea as a gruesome souvenir of the great loss of life and ignominious defeat that had occurred on the distant horizon to the north. Many of the sea chests, mess tables, wardrobes, drawers, hammocks and other sundry floating items that were flung desperately into the sea to offer some sort of buoyancy aid to those floating in the frigid waters were recovered. Many personal effects were also found: dance cards, photographs, items of clothing, cap badges – all mementos of lives cut short by war and the questionable leadership of those in charge of naval strategy within the distant and safe corridors of Whitehall.

Mrs Elizabeth Penn, the widowed mother of the three Penn brothers, Hubert, Alfred and Louis, who lived with her in Customs House Lane, Deal, lost two of her three sons all serving on *Cressy.* Only the eldest son, 28-year-old Hubert, survived the attack by *U-9.* Mrs Penn received a letter from the British Consul in Rotterdam informing her that her youngest son's sea chest or 'ditty box' had been found with his name, Louis, etched on to a metal nameplate on the lid.

A ditty box was a precious item for sailors serving at sea. In cramped and confined conditions sleeping in tightly spaced hammocks in large mess decks and with little in the way of privacy, the small wooden ditty box was the only opportunity for men on board to store personal effects and mementos. While the traditional canvas kit bag was for uniform and bedding, the ditty box was reserved for non 'Pusser' (naval issue) items. Often the box had a metal plaque with the owner's name inscribed on it. It was sacred territory as far as shipmates were concerned, a sailor's private and personal refuge from brutal lives on the lower deck.

Penn's ditty box contained his mother's address, a packet of cigarettes, a silver watch, a brooch, some books and a photo of a young woman without a name. It was all Mrs Penn had left of her youngest son, who was 25 years old when he died.

One report includes details of a small wooden cupboard containing the personal effects of Commander B.W. Lothian Nicholson of *Cressy.* There was writing paper, envelopes and photographs of cricketers. Inside a brown leather wallet were visiting cards with Nicholson's details, confirming the ownership of the cupboard. It also contained a book of a dance party at Admiralty House, Chatham, dated 2 July 1914, some revolver bullets, a key to the captain's cabin and a silver gold holder containing £2 in gold.

There was a book entitled *Public Schools and Universities*, an up-to-date railway guide and two rings, one silver and one gold.

The graves of the 161 victims of the U-boat attack can still be seen in the Netherlands with a number of memorial stones. They are mostly maintained in excellent order. While the dead were being assiduously recorded and buried with due ceremony and dignity in the Netherlands, the dreadful impact of the loss of life and the shocking defeat for the Royal Navy was still resonating around the coastal towns and cities of Britain and Ireland.

9

THE SHOCK ASHORE

In Britain, the grim news of the loss of HMS *Cressy*, *Aboukir* and *Hogue* made an enormous national impact.

The initial sense of shock was not confined to the families of those who served. It was felt by the entire nation, including the monarch. The cruel irony of Churchill's speech in Liverpool the evening before the incident, and particularly the First Lord's comments about 'digging out rats' was not lost on King George V, a former serving naval officer who took an intimate personal interest in naval matters. The king complained to Prime Minister Asquith via his secretary, Lord Stamfordham, that the First Lord's reference to 'rats in a hole' was unfortunate, seeing that the rats came out of their own accord and to Britain's cost, and was 'hardly dignified for a cabinet minister'.[1]

The Royal Navy was also unhappy with Churchill's remarks. Admiral Sir Lewis Bayly, flag officer of the 1st Battle Squadron, complained to the Second Sea Lord, Vice Admiral Sir Frederick Hamilton, about the Liverpool speech. 'We feel we have been dragged down to the level of boasting and breathing bombastic defiance and we hate it,' he wrote.[2]

Churchill was also openly criticised for his remarks in some quarters of the press. The socialist newspaper *Justice* even (wrongly) suggested that Churchill may have provoked the German attack on the cruisers.[3] In retrospect, his remarks proved to be tempting fate, but they were also widely resented for being tasteless. Churchill was widely vilified for them.

He later wrote that his words at the Liverpool speech were 'fastened upon and pilloried'.[4]

The significance of the loss was not lost on the prime minister either. Asquith thought it was the worst news since the start of the war. 'To have lost three good and powerful cruisers of an old but not obsolete type was a blow because the Navy in general was not doing well,' he wrote.[5]

News of the sinking of the three cruisers had reached the naval base at Harwich by the early morning of 22 September and spread extremely rapidly. Harwich was the port where the destroyers returned with survivors, presenting a huge story of national and international significance for the local Essex newspaper, the *Harwich and Dovercourt Standard*. The editor must have been cursing his luck that he was running a weekly title and would have to wait four days to publish his coverage because the newspaper was ideally placed to obtain the first eyewitness accounts from those that had been rescued from the sea and taken to the naval base.

Under the headline 'British Navy sustain a severe loss', the *Standard* explained how, in the early hours of Tuesday morning, 'The Germans inflicted a terrible blow upon the British Navy by sinking three cruisers when about forty miles from the Dutch coast.' This was the general tone of the initial local and national media coverage, as details of the losses emerged and the Essex newspaper gave an enthralling quayside perspective of subsequent events as they unfolded in Harwich.[6]

'Harwich was in a state of great excitement on Tuesday evening (22 September). During the day the harbour was denuded of warships, but at about seven o'clock in the evening one by one, the Harwich vessels of the flotilla began to return and, in some cases, they were flying the flag at half-mast which told its own tale,' reported the newspaper.[7]

Crowds of local people had gathered on Harwich Pier and the adjacent quayside on the southern side of the estuary. Shortly after 2000, the first batch of survivors came ashore at Harwich. The *Harwich and Dovercourt Standard* reported they all appeared to be officers: 'They appeared in odd garments, some wearing large wraps, others a piece of sacking round their loins and for the most part they were bare footed,' read the report, and it estimated that thirty in all came ashore in Harwich. They walked across the road to the Great Eastern Hotel Hospital and 'received every comfort and attention'. The survivors appeared to be 'wet through' as though they had been recovered from the water.

Red Cross boats shuttled the wounded from the returned destroyers to Shotley Pier on the northern side of the Stour Estuary, where they were transferred to the Royal Navy Training Establishment (RNTE), Shotley. It was a large naval training establishment and barracks for boy seamen as young as 15 years of age, and, most importantly, it was home to a fleet medical facility where survivors from the three sunken cruisers could be treated for their injuries and the effects of exposure and hypothermia. RNTE Shotley is better known as HMS *Ganges*, its name from 1927, after the training ship that left the waters of Shotley in July 1906. Thousands of former Shotley Boys, as they were known, served in the First World War and were trained in the arts of seamanship within a tough and harshly disciplined environment.[8]

The newspaper report also included some courageous accounts. 'Many are the tales of heroism told and it is said there was no panic whatsoever,' it added, citing the example of Sick Bay Attendant Johnson of *Cressy*. While the *Cressy* was sinking, the order was given to save those in the sick bay first and Johnson called for a party of volunteers and, according to the newspaper account, personally saw the wounded lowered into waiting boats.

Harwich had been a naval town since the seventeenth century and warships had been constructed for the Navy in its naval yard since 1664. The impact of this incident created a collective sense of unease amongst this small tight-knit coastal community and major British naval base.

The first naval action of the war had involved Harwich-based ships when HMS *Lance*, *Laurel*, *Lark* and *Linnet*, all destroyers assigned to the 3rd Destroyer Flotilla of the Harwich Force, were sent in pursuit of the SS *Königin Luise*, a German minelayer, on 5 August 1914. HMS *Lance* is credited with firing the first British naval gun in anger during the First World War, though some accounts attribute this honour to HMS *Amphion* earlier the same day while pursuing the same minelayer.[9]

The destroyer fired a shell from one of her 4in guns at the German vessel, which attempted to flee before her captain ordered her to be scuttled. *Lance* picked up twenty-eight German survivors. The following day, HMS *Amphion* and 132 lives were lost when the British ship struck one of the German mines laid by *Königin Luise*. Harwich was already accustomed to naval disasters.

'A thrilling story has been told by Mr Albert Dougherty, chief gunner Cressy,' continued the local newspaper report into the sinking of the three cruisers. The personal account of the loquacious Warrant Officer

Dougherty, evidently a man not inhibited by media shyness, was quoted in many local newspapers. He was also to be a key witness at the subsequent Court of Inquiry.[10]

By the time the survivors had arrived at Harwich, the Admiralty had already issued a statement to the press via the Press Bureau, which was drafted by Chief Naval Censor Captain Brownrigg, in close consultation with the Admiralty war group and Churchill. This report, issued at 1615 that day, formed the basis of the front-page headlines in the national press that stunned the British public the following morning (23 September).

The loss of the three cruisers made banner headlines in many editions, the 'splash' in most, and competed with news of British advances in the First Battle of the Aisne in a few local titles. It was the biggest news story since the declaration of hostilities on 4 August 1914, and the Press Bureau announcement of modest British gains at the Battle of the Aisne issued later the same day did little to dilute the negative impact.

The Press Bureau statement was reproduced verbatim by newspapers such as *The Manchester Guardian*:

> The Secretary of the Admiralty communicates the following statement for publication:
>
> HM Ships *Aboukir*, Captain John E Drummond; *Hogue*, Captain Wilmot S Nicholson; and *Cressy*, Captain Robert W Johnson have been sunk by submarines [plural] in the North Sea. The *Aboukir* was torpedoed and whilst the *Hogue* and *Cressy* had closed and were standing by to save the crew they were also torpedoed. A considerable number were saved by HMS *Lowestoft*, Captain Theobald W. B. Kennedy and a division of destroyers, trawlers and boats. The lists of casualties will be published as soon as they are known. The *Cressy*, *Aboukir* and *Hogue* were sister ships, armoured cruisers of a comparatively old type, built fourteen years ago. They were of 12,000 tons and 18 knots speed and carried two 9.2in, and twelve 6in guns.[11]

At 2300 on the same day (22 September), the Admiralty sent out the following signal to all ships:

> The serious lesson to learn from loss of *Cressy* and *Hogue* is that it must henceforth be recognised by all Commanding Officers that if one ship is

torpedoed by submarine or strikes a mine, the disabled ship must be left to her fate, and other large ships clear out of dangerous area, calling up minor vessels to render assistance.

Like many newspapers, the front-page headlines of *The Manchester Guardian* on 23 September reported an attack by five submarines, of which two were believed to have been sunk, reflecting the many eyewitness accounts, including that of Gunner Dougherty, that claimed the attack was carried out by multiple submarines.

It also included a Press Association report from Harwich that thirty officers had been landed unhurt and were being treated at the Great Eastern Hotel on the quayside, which had been converted into a naval hospital. It estimated that 700 souls had been saved. Another Press Association report from Ijmuiden in the Netherlands, where the Dutch steamer *Flora* had arrived, reported that 287 survivors had been landed.

'An estimate of the loss in life cannot be attempted with any confidence,' warned *The Manchester Guardian*, but its report turned out to be surprisingly accurate given the short timescale and lack of official information. The same newspaper warned that there was no value in underestimating the magnitude of the loss: 'Nothing is to be gained by minimising the affair. The German fleet has boldly and skilfully achieved an important success.'[12]

'Although the eldest of the heavy armoured cruisers in the British Navy List, having been launched eleven years ago, the destroyed vessels possessed a fighting power which might have given them a place in the battle line during a vital and desperate naval struggle only a few years ago.' The newspaper also published a list of all officers serving on the three ships.

The Daily Mirror went further and published pictures of five of the ships' officers on its front page, together with images of Captain Wilmot Nicholson and images of the three cruisers, under the banner headline: 'Three British cruisers sunk by German submarines'.[13] 'The loss of many of our brave sailors is deeply to be deplored but, though the news is bad there is no need for depression,' read its report, noting that Britain had a great preponderance of cruisers at its disposal.

That would not have been of immense consolation to those families desperately anxious to hear news of their loved ones, nor was the assurance from the Admiralty that 'the list of casualties will be published as soon as they are known'.

The strain proved too much for some stoical naval families, all too familiar with the dangers of serving at sea, in war and in peacetime. 'My mother and the children were hop picking when they were told of the tragedy. My grandmother of course, collapsed and my mother (Mary Jane) was bereft as she was also very close to her dad,' said Violet Maidment, granddaughter of Seaman George James Keam RNR of *Cressy*, who had worked as an oyster dredger for the Seasalter & Ham Oyster Company in Whitstable, Kent, before being mobilised in 1914.[14]

In this oyster-fishing and shipbuilding town on the Swale Estuary, the uncertainty was hard to take. There were eight local men who worked for the Whitstable Oyster Company or the rival Seasalter & Ham Oyster Company, who were all serving in *Cressy* as RNR seamen at the time of the attack by *U-9*.

On 26 September, *The Whitstable Times* reported that only three men had sent telegrams to their families confirming their well-being and the newspaper expressed its hope the remainder were alive and well in the Netherlands.[15]

Seaman George J. Keam RNR, of 64 Middle Wall; Seaman Henry Phillips RNR, of 22 Waterloo Road; Seaman Frederick W. Down RNR, of 17 Middle Wall; Seaman James 'Fred' Wootton RNR, of 20 Middle Wall; Seaman Jack Baker RNR, of 8 Fountain Street; and Seaman Charles W. Jordan, of 66 Albert Street, were all lost but it took several days for the tragic news to be confirmed.

Of the *Cressy* men, only Able Seaman Alfred Stroud, who lived with his parents in Victoria Street, and Able Seaman James Rowden, a married man from 4 Nelson Road, survived.

Other Kentish ports, fishing harbours and dockyard towns where the companies of Chatham-based ships were traditionally recruited also bore much of the brunt of the shock. 'A painful scene was witnessed, the wives of a couple of the crew of the vessels fainting on reading the news,' stated one account in the *Dover Express*.[16] The women were reacting to the Admiralty telegram displayed in the window of the well-known Kentish brewers Leney & Co., which was based in Dover and Folkestone and had premises in Castle Street, Dover.

As the same Dover-based newspaper reported under its headline 'Loss of the three cruisers', the local impact of the loss in the town was huge. 'It's known that a very considerable number of Dover men were on board the cruisers, a large number of the cross-channel sailors being naval reserve men; and there were also a considerable number of men from the dredger crews.'[17]

Local newspapers became a vital source of information for worried relatives. The *Dover Express* went on to report news from other families in the town about the fate of the Dover men. It reported that Mr W. Dolbear (Able Seaman Dolbear, who was in the sick bay of *Cressy* at the time of the attack, was rescued by SS *Flora* and taken to Ijmuiden in the Netherlands) was a well-known resident at the pier who had participated in election campaigns in that electoral ward. His family had received a telegram from him on Wednesday, 23 September, from Amsterdam. He later sent a postcard saying that four more Dover men were safe. Able Seaman Dolbear later gave the same newspaper his harrowing personal account of escaping from the sick bay of *Cressy* and clinging desperately to a mess table in the freezing water until he was rescued and pulled into SS *Flora* by another Dover man, Able Seaman Charles Henry Davis.

The newspaper also reported that Able Seaman Stephen George Bailey RNR, whose parents lived at 32 St James Street, Dover, was one of the men receiving treatment at Shotley Barracks, near Harwich. Able Seaman Charles Henry Davis of Westbury Road was reported to be safe and well in the Netherlands, probably by Able Seaman Dolbear in the postcard hastily written to his parents from the country.

There was also a list of those from Dover all serving in *Cressy* of whom no news had yet been received. This included Able Seaman William J. Terry RFR, Leading Signalman Willie G.C. Chittenden RFR (who served as Willie Collins), Able Seaman John R. Back RFR and Leading Stoker George Henry Ernest Bull RFR. Of that list of four missing Dover men, only Leading Stoker George Henry Ernest Bull, who had worked at the local coastguard station, made it home safely. The uncertainty was agony for the families of the lost sailors from Dover and elsewhere, who knew all too well that with disasters at sea, no news was very rarely good news.

The waiting was intolerable. The *Hull Daily Mail* reported on 23 September that Yeoman of Signals Joseph Williams was feared missing. His baby daughter had been born after he went away and he had only received one day's leave in August. Williams did not return.

By 25 September, under the headline 'Heroic Seamen', *The Times* was able to report eyewitness accounts from survivors in Hook of Holland landed by the steamer *Titan*. Their intrepid reporter had tracked down survivors in the Netherlands such as Able Seaman Clarke RFR of *Cressy*. These were the first eyewitness accounts of the war at sea and they did not make comfortable reading. Instead of an epic gunnery engagement, the whole action had been over in ninety minutes.[18]

An initial list of surviving officers was published on Thursday, 24 September and showed that sixty had survived but there was no information yet provided for the loved ones of those serving on the lower deck.

At 1318 on Thursday, 24 September, forty survivors (probably the officers) departed by train from Harwich town railway station for Chatham Dockyard, in Kent. Later the same afternoon, about 300 survivors who had been treated at Shotley also left for Chatham on a separate train. 'When interviewed, they spoke as if amazed that they had been saved,' reported the *Harwich and Dovercourt Standard*.

As the 300 surviving sailors and marines arrived at Harwich Pier from Shotley on Thursday, 24 September en route to the railway station, they were cheered by a large crowd of spectators and seemed in good spirits:

> The men were unshaven with towels around their necks and they seemed as merry as if they formed members of a bathing party. They sang lustily as they marched to the station, 'It's a long way to Tipperary' and 'Who's your lady friend?'.[19]

Written and recorded by Harry Fragson, the latter ditty was a risqué song that was enormously popular at the time. Fragson was a popular British music hall singer and comedian. He recorded this song shortly before his untimely death in 1913 (he was murdered by his father), and it was the big music hall hit at the advent of the First World War:

> Hello, hello
> who's your lady friend
> who's the little girly
> by your side
> I've seen you
> with a girl or two
> Oh, Oh, Oh
> I am surprised at you
> Hello, hello

stop your little games
don't you think your ways
you ought to mend

The men were reported to be in a jocular mood, though probably still in shock and just thankful to be alive. They were gratefully accepting gifts of cigarettes and chocolate from members of the public as they were cheered on their way to the station.

Shortly before 0900 the next day (Friday, 25 September), the London and North Western Railway hospital train steamed into Harwich station under the supervision of Surgeon Elder, two naval nursing sisters and forty Red Cross attendants. The train took forty-eight wounded from Shotley Naval Hospital to Chatham for further treatment. This number included eleven survivors from the three stricken cruisers and fourteen German seamen. It is not stated how the Germans had arrived in Harwich, but they were possibly survivors rescued after the scuttling of the German minelayer *Königin Luise* the previous month.

One omission from the comprehensive local newspaper report of 26 September was any detailed assessment of the scale of the deaths and the terrible impact of the loss on the victims' families. Perhaps with the number of casualties still being tallied it was too soon to commence speculation, or more likely the editor was obliged to wait for confirmation from the Press Bureau, but it meant the *Harwich and Dovercourt Standard* missed one powerful local angle in its coverage.

One of those missing was the commanding officer of *Cressy*, who was born in the town. Captain Johnson was born in Dovercourt on 10 May 1868 while his 45-year-old father, John Ormsby Johnson, was serving as a captain of HMS *Pembroke*, a depot ship assigned to coastguard duties and based in Harwich.

Initially, it was very difficult for the Admiralty to confirm who had died. Some survivors had been taken by the two steamers to the Netherlands and some had died en route. If bodies were washed ashore, identification would be required.

It was largely a process of elimination though. If a man was not confirmed as alive, the assumption was he was missing or, more likely, dead. In the meantime, the next of kin of those on board had no choice but to wait anxiously for news of loved ones, either via the press, by official

Admiralty telegram, or via notices posted in town halls and other prominent public places. Some had to wait longer than others to learn the fate of their loved ones.

By late evening on Friday, 25 September, the Admiralty issued a list of survivors from the three ships but without names:

HMS *Aboukir*	381
HMS *Hogue*	254
HMS *Cressy*	202

Each cruiser had a ship's company approaching 800 men, so the terrible implication was immediately evident. More than half the men were still missing. Most loved ones would not be returning home and their patriotic naval service had lasted less than fifty days. And in the case of *Cressy*, which had no boats and little timber left by the time she sank, nearly three-quarters of the ship's company were still unaccounted for.

That same evening, the Press Bureau also issued a full account of the incident that included personal reports by the senior surviving officers.

Immediate reaction to the loss of the three cruisers within the Royal Navy was largely one of anger and grief. Commodore Roger Keyes was furious. In a letter dated 29 September, written from the submarine depot ship HMS *Maidstone* to his friend and fellow officer Rear Admiral John De Robeck, who was in command of the 9th Cruiser Squadron, Keyes lets rip:

> After a week I can't write or think temperately about that appalling and I think, absolutely unnecessary sacrifice – for what? God knows I had the cheek to write twice and ask a dozen times verbally what those *Bacchantes* were supposed to be doing.[20]

Surprisingly, perhaps, there is no specific reference to the incident in Jellicoe's private papers or his letters to Churchill, but he was clearly increasingly nervous about the risk of submarine attack on the Grand Fleet.

Admiral David Beatty, writing to his wife, the glamorous American heiress Ethel Tree, on 23 September 1914, sounded genuinely exasperated:

> It was bound to happen, they (our cruisers) had no conceivable right to be where they were. It is not being wise after the event, but I had

> frequently discussed with others that sooner or later they would surely be caught by submarines or battle cruisers, if they continued to occupy that position.[21]

'I am so sorry for all the poor mothers who had sons, little naval cadets on board, just from Dartmouth,' he added, and Beatty had cause to be emotional. This was his former cruiser squadron and HMS *Aboukir* was his former flagship.

Shock and dismay over the loss of the ships was not confined to senior ranks. The diary entry of Midshipman Scrimgeour for 23 September 1914 reads as follows:

> Loss of the *Hogue* confirmed, also *Cressy*, *Aboukir* uncertain. A great disaster, as they were excellent ships, just older than the *Drake* class. Most of the snotties [Midshipmen] were Granville term [at Dartmouth], a year junior to us. Do not know if they were all killed or not.[22]

While Britain attempted to come to terms with an unexpected and ignominious defeat and Churchill's reputation was tarnished, Germany was milking every last drop of propaganda value from Weddigen's highly successful submarine action.

The reaction to the incident in Germany was the complete opposite to that in Britain. It was hailed as a magnificent victory by Otto Weddigen and his crew. Three front-line British warships had been destroyed by the twenty-three-man crew of *U-9* without any of the surface ships' main guns even being brought into action. It was an unmitigated and glorious naval victory for the German Navy.

Weddigen was hailed a hero for his near-perfect handling of the U-boat in combat conditions. Five of his six torpedoes found their target within ninety minutes of his first engagement of HMS *Aboukir*. Of course, it was made all too easy for him by a series of strategic and tactical errors on the part of the Royal Navy, but the job still needed to be accomplished and he did so with a cold-blooded professional flourish. As one unnamed British survivor conceded, 'the Germans did it on us beautifully'.[23]

The official German version of the incident was published in many British national newspapers and confirmed that the humiliating defeat had been exacted by a single German submarine, *U-9*, not the squadron of three, four, five or six, as reported by most eyewitnesses and in the first official accounts published in the press.

'At the time of the attack, the majority of the British sailors were still in their bunks and not a single shot was fired by any of the cruisers. In recognition of their services, an Iron Cross has been awarded to each member of the U-9,' stated the official German press telegram.

The 32-year-old submarine commander and his crew became celebrities and heroes on their return to Germany. Marder wrote, 'the Emperor was reported to be in seventh heaven over the sinking of the *Cressys*.'[24] Weddigen later wrote an account of the attack and sinking of the three cruisers. He recalled:

> I reached the home port on the afternoon of the 23rd, and on the 24th went to Wilhelmshaven, to find that news of my effort had become public. My wife, dry eyed when I went away, met me with tears. Then I learned that my little vessel and her brave crew had won the plaudit of the Kaiser, who conferred upon each of my co-workers the Iron Cross of the second class and upon me the Iron Cross of the first and second classes.[25]

The German naval command also used the victory to fuel propaganda efforts overseas. In a report from Rome headlined 'Through German Eyes', one London newspaper stated that 'telegrams from Berlin on the subject of the sinking of the three British cruisers in the North Sea made remarkable reading … The consternation and dismay of the whole English people is depicted with vivid colouring – in certain political circles in London it is said the resignation of Mr Winston Churchill is expected.'[26]

Reaction at the Admiralty was curiously tentative – except in the Naval Censor's office, of course, which issued a series of communiqués. The Admiralty signal to all ships instructing them not to stop for stricken sister ships was released into the public domain and became a subject of wide debate. It raised the issue of whether the principal motivation for the signal was the safety of warships at sea or public relations. In Cabinet, the First Lord was uncharacteristically taciturn and only responded to questions by describing the incident as 'very provoking'.[27]

The loss of the three cruisers forced the much-belated recognition of the deadly potential of the submarine, although many of the old school 'gin and bitters brigade', including Admiral Lord Beresford, still thought the capability of the U-boat was exaggerated. Though the sinking of HMS *Pathfinder* was the first example of a successful U-boat torpedo attack on a British warship, it was still possible for conservative naval figures such as Beresford to discount the incident as an anomaly, or some sort of freak incident. Many younger serving officers at the time even refused to believe that HMS *Pathfinder* could have been sunk by a single submarine.

The loss of *Aboukir*, *Hogue* and *Cressy* was irrefutable proof, if any was still needed, that submarine warfare was a reality and a major threat to British dominance of the seas. After years of internal wrangling, vacillation and denial about the potential threat of submarines, the truth was now undeniable. As the classified official historical account confirms: 'There can be little doubt that to many officers the news of the disaster in the Broad Fourteens came as a revelation of the capabilities of submarines.'[28]

Despite this, there appears to have been no immediate emergency reaction to the now apparent submarine threat, even though it was probably Jellicoe's primary concern. Churchill's immediate reaction was to bury himself in other matters as though in some profound state of denial. The day after the worst naval loss for 200 years, when the shock was at its apotheosis, he was issuing detailed instructions to Colonel Ollivant, Director of Air Division, on how to bridge trenches that had been dug by the enemy to block the progress of armoured cars. This message included the recommendation to carry 'planks capable of bridging ten or twelve feet spans quickly and easily' and that they 'should be carried with every ten or twelve machines'.[29]

As Scott wrote, the war was 120 days old before he was summoned to the Admiralty to spearhead an effort to develop anti-submarine weapons. When he arrived, he found that a committee had been at work for some time but 'had evolved nothing'.[30] 'Reproach has been levelled at the Admiralty for not having accurately measured this [submarine] danger before the war and taken proper precautions against it,' wrote Churchill later,[31] but the more justified criticism is that more drastic measures were not taken immediately after the loss of *Hogue*, *Aboukir* and *Cressy*.

Some precautions and changes were implemented but they were timid and ineffective. One precaution was to order the Commander-in-Chief to withdraw the *Duncan* class of battleship from that part of the North Sea where they had been sent to support the patrolling cruisers. In the future, no armoured ships were to patrol that area.

The Admiralty further gave orders that the practice of employing armoured ships to board vessels was to be abandoned, owing to the danger of stopping to lower a boat. There were, however, only two fleet messenger vessels available to accompany the battle squadrons for the purposes of examination, and with the permission of the Admiralty, the older battleships and the armoured cruisers continued to be employed on boarding duties in northern waters. This made them a large and stationary potential target for any passing submarines.

It was intended that the Channel Fleet should move up from Portland to Sheerness on 23 September to provide more proximate support for Admiral Christian's force.[32] The planned transference was postponed on the evening of 22 September as a precautionary measure until the situation arising from the disaster in the Broad Fourteens had been appreciated. Twenty-four hours later, however, the order went out for the move to be carried out as previously arranged, and on 25 September they proceeded up the English Channel.

At 1050 on 26 September 1914, as part of the High Seas Fleet was still in the Baltic, Admiral Burney, off Dungeness, was ordered to return to Portland. The Admiralty had changed its mind again and appeared to be vacillating in a time of crisis.

10

WIVES AND SWEETHEARTS

After the initial shock of the naval disaster was absorbed in late September, realisation of the tragic human cost of the loss of the three cruisers gradually permeated via the press reports, obituaries and memorial services in parishes across the nation.

The brief obituary of Lieutenant Commander Edmund Gabbett, the navigating officer of *Cressy*, was published on 26 September in the same newspaper that had reported his marriage in January the previous year. Entitled 'Officer, formerly of Dursley', it made mention of his wife, Alicia, and their 9-month-old daughter. He left his widow £202 10*s* in his will.[1]

Last seen on the ship's bridge assisting his captain, Gabbett was typical of naval officers in that he married his wife shortly before his promotion to Lieutenant Commander the following March. Within the wardroom, it was frowned upon for a Lieutenant to marry while serving at sea and most officers waited until they achieved the rank of Lieutenant Commander before considering marriage and starting a family. The salary was better, and the chance of extended sea service overseas was lower.

Gabbett had secured an appointment as navigating officer of HMS *Duncan*, the Portsmouth-based gunnery training ship, meaning that no overseas deployments were on the immediate horizon prior to the declaration of war. His wife and baby lived nearby, just outside Portsmouth at Myrtle Cottage in Castle Street, Portchester. The attractive detached house can still be seen and is now a listed building.

The *Walsall Advertiser* told the story of Mrs Beckett of 130 Bath Street, Walsall, who in early October was still waiting for news of her husband, Able Seaman Richard Beckett RFR, a 49-year-old gunner in *Cressy*. There was no shortage of pathos in their report headlined 'The Price of Empire':

> In a little house in Bath Street, Walsall an anxious sad-faced wife was waiting for news of a sailor husband when an Advertiser representative called yesterday. Although hope is not quite given up, the worst is feared but, in any case, many who know Mrs. Beckett will remind her that amid all her sorrow she has cause for great pride on one who bravely did his duty.[2]

A full list of officers lost and believed dead was issued by the Admiralty and published in national newspapers on 25 September 1914 but Mrs Beckett, like many of the sailors' wives and loved ones, was still waiting for news of her husband on 6 October. Beckett was later confirmed dead.

Letters of condolence and pious epithets about patriotic pride and sacrifices made by families for the good of the empire did not put food on the table, and the widows of the dead sailors were left in an even more intolerable situation than distraught parents and siblings.

The *Hull Daily Mail* carried an account of Stoker Frances G. Bursall, typical of many other reports around the UK. Bursall's photograph appeared in the newspaper as a craggy-featured man in uniform with a full moustache and lantern jaw. He was 46 years old and married with one child. He had been employed by the local shipping firm Thomas Wilson and Sons Co., before being called up for the Royal Naval Reserve six weeks earlier. The newspaper reports his widow receiving a letter on 6 October 1914, signed by Churchill and offering his condolences on behalf of the king and queen: 'The King commands me to assure you of the true sympathy of His Majesty and the Queen in your sorrow,' read the message from Churchill.[3] It must have been a sobering duty for the First Lord of the Admiralty to have to sign 1,459 similar messages.

Some of the bereft mothers received comforting personal letters of condolence from officers on board. Commander Nicholson of *Cressy* sent a personal letter of condolence to the mother of Able Seaman Harry Midmer, a former policeman, and another RFR man who, at 6ft 7in, was the tallest serving member of the ship's company and must have been a formidable and well-known character on board. The letter was reproduced in the *Sussex Courier* and the original is held in the Sussex county archive:

Dear Mrs. Midmer
Little I can say I am afraid, can be of any comfort to you to the loss you have already suffered, but I feel I should like just to write you a line to say how much I share your sorrow in the loss of such a fine man as your son. He was, may I say, almost the life of the ship's company, always ready and willing for any job that came to hand continually cheerful and usually doing at least half a dozen men's work as well as his own and assisting everyone. You may rest assured he was doing his duty to the last minute and that no man could have done more for his country and his ship than did your son – Believe me.
Yours sincerely Bertram Nicholson Commander, late HMS *Cressy*.[4]

As the death toll was confirmed, memorial services were held at parish churches around the country. In the small farming village of Hernhill near Faversham, Kent, a memorial service was held at the pretty twelfth-century St Michael's church for two of those lost: Stoker First Class Charles Edgar Arnold RNR, of *Cressy* aged 26, the son of Mr and Mrs Arnold of Oakwell Cottages, and Petty Officer Harvey of *Aboukir.* They died on the same day and are both commemorated on the war memorial in the corner of the churchyard opposite the Red Lion public house. According to the local newspaper report: 'Charles always bore an excellent character and was generally liked and esteemed.' His story is kept in the church archives.[5]

Some of the newspaper accounts of the deaths included touching details of local interest. The survivor from *Cressy*, Able Seaman Rowden, told *The Whitstable Times* that the last time he saw Fred Wootton, his mate, was holding rope over the side of *Cressy* to help survivors scramble on board.[6] The *Shields Daily News* reported how Engineer Lieutenant Fred Richard Monks of *Cressy* was rescued after four hours struggling in the sea but died about five minutes after being rescued.[7]

For many other bereaved families, this was not the only tragic family loss they had to suffer in the opening few weeks of the First World War. The parents of 22-year-old Engineer Lieutenant Stacey Wise, who was last seen ordering timber to be sent up from the engine rooms of *Cressy*, also suffered the loss of his elder brother less than a month later on 24 October.

Lieutenant Edward Selby Wise was killed while serving in HMS *Severn* while leading a shore party near Nieuport in support of armed landings in Belgium. He was 27 years old.

Private Joseph Robert French of the RMLI, aged 34, was another RFR man from Kent who lost his life that day. French, from Lower Rainham, near Chatham, left a wife, Emma, and three young children. According to a family member, Barry Fellowes, his younger brother, Bugler Harry French RMLI, was lost on HMS *Pathfinder* when that ship was torpedoed and sunk by a U-boat on 5 September 1914.[8]

The death of Lieutenant Commander Walter Bousfield Watkins Grubb had an additional tragic twist. Grubb was the brother of the Vicar of Shepherdswell, near Dover in Kent, and was another recently married man. On 22 April 1913, Grubb married the daughter of Dr and Mrs Dunbar from Clapham, south London, and he joined *Cressy* the following March. It seems that his brother, the Rev. Grubb, who was married to a member of the Coutts banking family and was father to three children, must have struggled to cope with the loss of his brother and appeared to die from the grief it caused him.

'His loss was a great shock to the vicar,' said *The Whitstable Times* in a report on the reverend's sudden and untimely death at the age of only 37. 'The sad event has cast quite a gloom over the village.'[9]

Many children were admitted to naval children's homes and many young mothers were obliged to remarry to survive. Alberta Wootton, wife of Seaman Fred Wootton of Whitstable, quickly remarried into the Shilling family, well known in the town. Eventually she bore another son, Albert Shilling. According to family members, Alberta died before she reached 40 years of age from cervical cancer.[10]

When Able Seaman Charles Alfred Larking RFR from Bramford, near Ipswich in Suffolk, died that day he left a pregnant wife, Lily, aged 25, and their baby daughter. Lily remarried her late husband's brother Charles, who also served in the Royal Navy, and they had another daughter together.[11]

The fact that two-thirds of the three ships' companies were reservists meant they were usually older and, more often than not, family men. Many of them were Royal Fleet Reserve ratings who had married after being discharged on completion of their twelve-year engagements. Some, like Bursall, were civilians serving in commercial maritime roles with families ashore and they served part-time in the Royal Naval Reserve. The reservists were easily identified because they were permitted to retain moustaches in the early years of the war, while career sailors had to be clean shaven or sport beards, known as 'full sets'.

It was highly unusual for sailors to marry during their active service due to the financial unfeasibility of supporting a family on such low pay. Then, as now, Britain preferred to defend the realm on the cheap, particularly when it came to personnel. There was also the fact that in 1914 a sailor was more than likely to be dispatched to a ship on a three-year commission to some distant corner of the extensive British Empire. There was no home leave during that period; no naval accommodation provided for the families of married men; no financial support provided for dependants; and no means of communication at sea, except handwritten letters that could take weeks or even months to reach their destination.

For sound economic and practical reasons, most sailors did not marry until they left the service. The familiar phrase 'wives and sweethearts', which remains a traditional naval toast, usually only fully applied to officers and older senior ratings.

The fact that brothers and mates from the same town or village were encouraged to serve in the same ships meant that, over the course of late September and early October 1914, several telegrams were delivered to a number of houses in the same street, often to the same households on the same day. We know that, in one day, not only were multiple telegrams delivered to the same small oyster fishing town of Whitstable, three were delivered in the same street. Middle Wall is a short walk south from the town's shingle beach and shipyards, and connected to the High Street by narrow alleyways. It adjoins Waterloo Road, where a fourth telegram was delivered.

Leading Seaman William Potter and Stoker First Class David Spindler were both from the same small Suffolk village of Westleton. Both their names adorn the war memorial located outside the Crown Inn and both are listed as being lost on 22 September 1914, on *Cressy*. These family men from the same small village also lost their lives on the same ship, on the same day.

Spindler married on 28 June 1896 and he left a wife, Ellen, and nine children, seven of whom were under the age of 14 when he died. According to the 1911 census, their eldest daughter, Emma, worked as a net mender to help make ends meet and his second son, Delgarde, born in 1899, was listed as a 'child unwell'. On receiving news of her husband's death, Ellen Spindler was left with the daunting task of supporting their large family alone.

Curiously, Spindler was not listed at the same address as his wife on that 1911 census, but as living with his brother nearby. His official next of kin, who was informed of his death, was his sister Hannah Gissing, of Flixton, near Lowestoft, in the same county. Perhaps Spindler and his wife were estranged or maybe he just wanted to spare her the shock and distress of receiving a telegram informing her of the death of the family's principal breadwinner.

Potter's widow, Sarah Ann, received her telegram at her house near the dock gates in Hull, where her husband had worked as a dock gate operator prior to being called up. She had moved to Potter's mother's home village of Westleton in Suffolk at the start of war but had returned to Hull. She had to explain his death to their young daughter, Lily Vera May, then 7 years old, whom Potter adored. It's not clear if Potter was the biological father to Lily Vera May because she was 6 years old when he married her mother. No father is listed on her birth certificate but, according to verbal family accounts, Potter treated Lily Vera May as his own. Sarah Ann will have received condolences and spiritual support from the local Salvation Army branch in Hull, where Potter had served as a Sergeant before the war.[12]

It's not clear who informed Potter's mother of his death. Anna Louisa Potter was 54 years old and a hard-working widow who could neither read nor write and could offer little, except her love and devotion, to her children living in the small cottage in Baker's Lane, Westleton. The son she lost was the second of fourteen children born between 1880 and 1906. As well as four adult sons serving in the war, she still had six children under the age of 16 to care for. Her youngest child, Walter Claude Potter, was only 7 years old when she told him of his elder brother's death.

Her 19-year-old son, Arthur Edward, known always as Tosh, was also serving in the Royal Navy, and would later take part in the Battle of Jutland aboard the *Arethusa*-class light cruiser HMS *Phaeton*. Another brother, Ernest Edward, a fisherman, joined the Army on 21 September 1914, just a month before his 22nd birthday.

After twenty-six years of bearing children and having been widowed since 1910, Anna Louisa made ends meet by providing laundry services for officers at an Army garrison stationed nearby and with the help and kindness of neighbours. Never more than a step or two away from physical exhaustion and the workhouse, where her late husband had been born, she was too proud to ever accept charity. When she died in 1920 at the age of 60, the doctor recorded the official cause of death as 'worn out'.[13] Daily life for women like Anna Louisa Potter was a relentlessly challenging and physically wearing daily struggle, which can no longer be fully appreciated.

The First World War was to herald a revolutionary change in the role of women in society. Due to the lack of men, women found themselves in occupations unheard of previously. Munition factory workers, lift attendants, agricultural labourers, postal delivery workers and police constables were all roles undertaken by women for the first time during the years of the war. 'The one thing about which there is no dissension and concerning which there can be no difference of opinion, is the splendid manner in which the women of the Empire have risen to the occasion in this horrible crisis in the affairs of the Empire,' wrote the (male) editor, M. de Beck, in the Foreword of *Women of the Empire in War Time*, a celebratory souvenir pamphlet published in 1916.

In order to assist the war effort, many women called for their own uniformed service and, eventually, the first women's corps of the British Army was founded in December 1916. The Women's Army Auxiliary Corps was renamed the Queen Mary's Army Auxiliary Corps in April 1918 and was joined by the Women's Royal Air Force in April 1918 and the Women's Royal Naval Service (WRENS) in November 1918. More than 100,000 women served in Britain's Armed Forces during the First World War. But while women could serve their country, they could not vote for those who governed it. It was not until February 1918 that women were permitted to vote (if they were over 30 years old) and women were not elected to Parliament for another decade.

While the social role of women was to change drastically during and after the First World War, due largely to the shortage of males, in September 1914, life for the vast majority of working-class women in rural locations around Britain was still much the same as it had been for centuries. And it was tough.

The dominant status of marriage in British society at this time and the widely accepted conventional role of the male as the sole breadwinner was not only restrictive, but it caused great hardship in time of war if he was killed or rendered physically disabled. In an unapologetically patriarchal society, most women were simply not equipped or permitted to earn a living to support their families. If these widows had adult children in employment, they might receive some financial support from them, but if not, many were expected to make a rapid and respectable marriage of convenience. Those who didn't struggled.

During wartime, propaganda made much of mothers sacrificing their sons 'for the cause of justice on sea and land', as the publication *Women of the Empire in War Time* put it. But in 1914 these mothers were not offered any financial support when their sons were killed at sea. Told of her son's death, it is unlikely that Anna Louisa Potter could afford much time for more than a brief private prayer, but there is a tribute to her son from the once-famous Walter Scott Montgomery, the so-called Blind Organ Grinder of Westleton, a copy of which has survived. Perhaps she asked this local celebrity to compose something in her son's honour.

According to the Suffolk county archive, Montgomery was a colourful local character, who having lost his sight and money, was presented with a barrel organ by the residents of Southwold in 1905. Montgomery was well known in the area for his barrel organ performances, and for writing verse on local events and people. Like Leading Seaman Potter, he was also a respected member of the Salvation Army, and this might explain why he dedicated an entire poem to the fellow Suffolk man who lost his life on *Cressy*.

The loss of a son or husband was not only an emotional blow, it was a financial catastrophe for many of these women. The outbreak of the First World War prompted the British Government to introduce a National War Widows' Pension scheme, but this only extended the pension rights of Army wives who were 'on the strength' (those wives officially sanctioned by the regiment) to all the wives of volunteers who fought in the war. All war widows were now eligible for the princely sum of 5*s* (25p) per week plus a dependant's allowance for each child of 1*s* 6*d* (7.5p) per week, up to a maximum of three children. It was wholly inadequate.

These young women were often unable to go to work because they had young children to care for. Even worse, neither was there an effective administration in place to administer the pensions until the Pensions Department was set up in 1916, so even fully eligible women often received nothing at all. According to research undertaken by Dr Janis Lomas, the War Office had little choice but to use the Armed Forces charity Soldiers' and Sailors' Families Association (SSFA, renamed the Soldiers, Sailors and

Airmen Families Association, SSAFA, from 1919) as its agent during 1914 and 1915. The organisation began to administer separation allowances and widows' pensions on behalf of the War Office and Admiralty from 1914.[14]

When Colonel James Gildea founded SSFA in 1885, it was primarily an Army charity and he initially struggled to inspire any interest from senior naval officers in the welfare of the families of their men. The two services had a very different culture when it came to the welfare of families of those serving – and to some extent, they still do.

The Army distinguished between those wives who were 'on the strength' and those who were not. Those 'on the strength' were the wives of men who had been officially granted permission to marry, so were usually the spouses of senior non-commissioned officers (NCOs). These wives travelled with the regiment unless the soldiers were on active service overseas. When their husbands were away, they were entitled to a modest separation allowance and other minor benefits, not least that of being recognised as a legitimate, albeit peripheral, part of regimental life. Many younger soldiers married without permission and these wives were not recognised and were officially entitled to nothing.

The culture of the Royal Navy was quite different and much more dismissive of the status of sailors' wives and their families than their Army counterparts. However popular the romanticised ideal of the loyal, lachrymose wife waiting at home for her brave sailor husband, when the ship sailed, his spouse and family were forsaken, in every sense. A sailor's life ashore was widely regarded as his private business and not a matter of interest for the naval hierarchy unless it became a disciplinary matter.

According to the official history of SSAFA, compiled by Alison Barnes, when Gildea wrote to a distinguished Admiral for information about the procedure for sailors' family welfare and allowances, the Admiral replied that he knew of 'no such useless encumbrance as a sailor's wife'.[15]

At the first Annual General Meeting of SSFA on 8 May 1886, Admiral the Right Honourable Sir Astley Cooper stated, 'At the Admiralty we do not recognise a married sailor, we do not help him with his family, officially,' and he urged the ladies of the SSFA Council to try to influence the Admiralty to look on sailors' families 'with a more favourable eye'.[16] Some twenty-eight years after that meeting, attitudes had not changed significantly in regard to official attitudes to naval wives and families.

For a sailor's wife, the system provided very little. There was no separation allowance and no compulsory deduction from a man's pay as there was for official Army wives. Any pay allotment was voluntary and took even longer to come through with men thousands of miles away at sea or transferring from ship to ship. And while SSFA was well established in garrison towns, it was often less well organised and accessible in the ports of Britain. The first SSFA county network was established in Kent, which was home to many of the families of those lost in the three cruisers.

The inadequate state provision meant SSFA attempted to fill the void and it triggered a national campaign for funds led by Queen Alexandra on behalf of SSFA, and the money raised became part of the National Relief Fund. In the first five months of the war, SSFA paid out more than £1.2 million and its network of voluntary social workers had grown to a force of 50,000, typically respectable married middle-class women wanting to do their bit for the war effort.

Admiration for this huge voluntary effort was far from universal. Despite its essential work, the charity was widely criticised for being parsimonious and for making unwelcome moral judgements on the women and families they were supposed to be helping. The suffragette Sylvia Pankhurst, living and working in the East End of London, noted:

> From all over the country … came complaints that officials of the Soldiers' and Sailors' Families Association were telling the women whose men were at the war to move into one room, and to sell pianos, gramophones, even furniture, before applying anywhere for aid. The notion that the women were entitled to separation allowance as a right, not as a charitable act of grace, seemed difficult for the Association's officials to assimilate.[17]

According to some sources, these moral judgements about the deserving qualities of an applicant even extended to the behaviour of the wives or widows. Not only did a woman have to handle the grief of a recent bereavement and the anxiety of facing an uncertain financial situation, she also had to suffer the indignity of probing questions from a visiting SSFA social worker. In order to feed her children or pay the rent, she also had to fear potential gossip about extra-marital relationships or illegitimate children. Some SSFA representatives assumed the role of prurient and nosy busybodies, scrutinising the client's home for signs of unnecessary extravagance or frivolous excess.

The mass press coverage of the sinking of the three cruisers and the terrible loss of life reignited the long-standing political row over the welfare of service families and pushed it into the political and public spotlight. There was widespread and increasing public disquiet about the financial welfare of war widows and naval widows in particular. It prompted many newspapers to call for improved welfare for widows and children. Shortly after the loss of the three cruisers, the *Framlingham Times* ran a typical opinion piece entitled 'The Wives and Dependents'. It stated that, while it was necessary to economise with national resources in wartime, this should not be done at the expense of the wives and dependents of those who have 'made the greatest of all sacrifices to serve their country'.

'Poverty and hardship have too often been the lot of old soldiers and sailors and their families but we cannot in this century have war on the cheap, when it comes to caring for disabled warriors and the families of those who are fighting their country's battles,' stated the newspaper.[18]

On 9 October 1914, in an article headlined 'Pensions for the Heroes' Widows', the *Vote for Women* suffragette newspaper called for the government to provide adequate war pensions for war widows 'such as exists in most countries where women are enfranchised'. Later that month, the West London Co-operative Society called on the government to accept the Labour Party proposal for a pension of £1 per week to be paid to all war widows, men returning from war who were permanently incapacitated due to the nature of their wounds and to others who were solely dependent on those men who were killed in war.

The view outlined in a letter to *The Globe* newspaper from Mr Frederick Gratton of Huntingdon was typical of public sentiment at the time. It called for the government to make 'full and adequate provision for the widows and fatherless children of those of our heroes who have sacrificed their lives'. He describes the allowance of 5*s* per week as a 'miserable pittance' and he concluded accurately, 'This means poverty'.[19]

For all the stirring patriotic rhetoric about the proud sacrifices made by mothers of the empire, most working-class widows who lost their husbands on *Aboukir*, *Hogue* and *Cressy* felt only hunger, desperation and poverty, and many received only ephemeral pity. The widows of the officers, even those like Alicia Gabbett who had young children, received nothing at all.

They were not entitled to a widow's pension but instead were expected to rely on family funds. Some of the parents of the young midshipmen who died that day continued to receive invoices for their sons' education at Britannia Royal Naval College, Dartmouth, long after their deaths.

In 2014, at the impressive centenary memorial service staged at Chatham Historic Dockyard and organised by Henk van der Linden, an attendee called Chris Rutter explained how the name of his great-grandfather was something of a mystery to him. He and his great-grandmother were not married when she became pregnant and the father died before the baby, a girl, was born. She then married another man quite quickly, as was the custom.

Though hardly exceptional, the situation was something of a social taboo in 1914, so Mr Rutter's great-grandmother kept her original partnership a closely guarded secret and only mentioned it a few years before her death. However, her daughter (Mr Rutter's grandmother) was named Cressida after the ship on which her biological father served.[20] Unfortunately, her birth certificate does not mention her father's name, so Mr Rutter has no way of knowing the identity of his great-grandfather who lost his life on *Cressy* on 22 September 1914.

The widely reported family tragedies contributed to a national sense of unease and they started to have far-reaching political connotations too.

11

SPIN

The mass aggregate of personal tragedy, exposed in vivid detail by local and national newspapers across Britain, created a major public relations challenge for the Admiralty.

It was personally humiliating for Churchill, too. He was already associated with a long series of minor losses, cock-ups and blunders, and his ill-timed comments on the eve of the disaster about rats being dug out from holes had earned him the opprobrium of the king.

The report in *The Manchester Guardian* of 23 September encapsulated the scale of the problem. News of the loss of the three cruisers competed for column inches with a large photograph of the Indian port of Madras (now Chennai) accompanying a report on the German light cruiser SMS *Emden*'s daring attack that had turned a fuel depot into an inferno. It could not have been more embarrassing for the First Lord, who had assured his patriotic audience in Liverpool that the Navy was searching the ocean for the German flag. 'A storm of criticism was directed at the Admiralty, and naturally it was focused on me,' admitted Churchill.[1]

The loss of three large armoured cruisers, only six weeks into the First World War, did not adhere to any public expectation as to how the war at sea would play out – ignominious defeats were not part of the British script.

The timing of these shocking and negative newspaper reports of the sinking of HMS *Aboukir*, *Hogue* and *Cressy*, and the scale of the consequent loss of life, could hardly have been worse as far as the First Lord was concerned. The former war correspondent was uniquely sensitive to the impact of negative press and he had no illusions about the power it offered the nation's enemies – not to mention his own political foes nearer to home. He wrote: 'The loss of the three cruisers marked a turning point in the attitude of those who in the evil time of war are able to monopolize the expression of public opinion. As the expectation of a great sea battle faded, the complaint began to be heard, "What is the Navy doing?"'[2]

Churchill's own public image had been fashioned by lurid newspaper coverage of his daring escape from a prisoner-of-war camp in December 1899, having been captured while reporting on the Boer War. 'Journalist escapes from prison camp in Africa' may not sound like an obvious front-page headline, but the Boer War was going badly for Britain and this was a much-needed story about the pluck and courage of a fearless young Englishman, defying the enemy. It made Churchill a media celebrity and to some extent launched his political career.[3]

The Chief Naval Censor at the Admiralty, Captain Douglas Brownrigg, who held Churchill in high regard, once described his boss as 'a gambler' who would hold on to bad news in the hope that some good news would crop up later to mitigate its impact.[4] Much later in his glittering career as a politician and statesman, Churchill was quoted as saying, 'in wartime, truth is so precious that she should always be attended by a bodyguard of lies'. He was ideally qualified to understand the significance of propaganda or what in modern times, might also be referred to as 'spin'.

Churchill oversaw all naval affairs and the war at sea and, in so doing was required to work closely with the Secretary of State for War and national hero, Lord Kitchener of Khartoum. The relationship between the two supremos of the war effort was not an easy one, partly because they were such contrasting characters.

Kitchener had an instinctive contempt for journalists and a long-standing distrust of Churchill, but together they established the Press Bureau on 5 August 1914. Initially, it was headed by the barrister, Conservative Party Member of Parliament and close friend of Churchill, Frederick Edwin (known as F.E.) Smith, later Lord Birkenhead. Churchill assured Parliament on 7 August 1914 that the move was designed to ensure a steady flow of accurate information from the War Office and Admiralty to the press.[5]

On 17 September 1914, in the week before the loss of the three cruisers in the Broad Fourteens, the offices of the Press Bureau were established at the Royal United Services Institute in London. The Navy room dealt with press cables and newspaper articles dealing with naval matters, while the Chief Naval Censor, Brownrigg, at the Admiralty, retained ultimate authority for what did and what did not appear in newspapers about the Navy. Brownrigg's office was adjacent to that of the First Sea Lord, Prince Louis of Battenberg, and close to the offices of the Chief of Staff, Admiral Frederick Doveton Sturdee and the Director of Operations Admiral Arthur Leveson, who both had their offices on the first floor of Old Admiralty Building.[6]

Soon after being set up, the Press Bureau allowed a report to be published in *The Times* of the British Army's defeat at the Battle of Mons and the news created a public outcry. The government was horrified about the possible 'public demoralisation'. Within a few weeks of its inception, the Press Bureau was widely criticised by newspaper editors and others for concealing and distorting information. However, maintaining public morale and preserving political reputations rapidly became more important than protecting military and naval secrets from the enemy.

A critical letter to *The Globe* dated 7 October 1914 from Mr H.D. Ellis, written from the Conservative Club in London, was typical. 'Due reticence from aught that may convey information to the enemy is commendable, though the [Press] Bureau have been singularly unfortunate in their discrimination between what to publish and what to suppress,' he wrote.

Colonel Charles à Court Repington, the former soldier and distinguished military correspondent for *The Times*, described the Press Bureau as 'the cloak to cover all political, military and naval mistakes'. Lord Northcliffe, the proprietor of *The Times*, was of the view that Churchill was personally responsible for the worst evils of the Bureau.

The control of the media was further strengthened by the Defence of the Realm Act (DORA), which also became law in August 1914. This prohibited the publication of information that 'might be directly or indirectly useful to the enemy' and was the precursor of the Official Secrets Act.[7] While the Navy room of the Press Bureau attempted to take control of Admiralty press communications, it remained firmly in the grip of Brownrigg, who enjoyed open access to Churchill and the Sea Lords, most of whom he knew personally from his previous naval service. No information for public consumption left the Admiralty without the sanction of Brownrigg and Churchill.

As Brownrigg reveals, Churchill often personally penned the press communiqués himself. 'He was of course, a master of language and had a flair for framing communiqués, and I still have some of his which have never been seen in the light and are to my mind, masterpieces,' wrote Brownrigg.[8]

Churchill was also happy to adopt the role of censor when he thought it necessary, as during the disastrous Dardanelles campaign in 1915: 'Mr. Churchill naturally took an interest in the whole proceedings, and he said to me one day, "For this business, I am Chief Censor, not you,"' wrote Brownrigg. He was personally thanked by Churchill when the First Lord left office on 22 May 1915: 'I want to thank you for the wonderful loyal way you have protected my interests and those of the service,' said Churchill, which is a telling reference, as it was hardly the job of Brownrigg to protect the personal reputation of the First Lord.[9]

Early newspaper headlines about the sinking of the three cruisers by *U-9* were unambiguous. The incident was described as a 'defeat' or a 'loss'. Many newspapers ran headlines referring to the 'sinking' of the three cruisers or sister ships. Initially, there was no implication of an accidental disaster of little military significance, or even as some tragic mistake made by those on board, as it was later to be portrayed by the Press Bureau. This was a disastrous and shocking naval defeat in wartime and that was the message initially conveyed by the press in the biggest story since the outbreak of war. Via the Press Bureau, Brownrigg and Churchill issued reassurances to newspaper editors that the Navy was blessed with many more cruisers, so there was no need for public panic as far as the overall war effort was concerned.

Quickly, coverage in British newspapers started to openly question and criticise Churchill and the Admiralty for the events of 22 September in the Broad Fourteens. While most of the early coverage focused on the loss and sinking of the three cruisers and subsequent tragic loss of life, some newspapers also raised some obvious questions. Why were the three cruisers patrolling alone, at slow speed, so close to known German submarine bases? Was this not a very high-risk strategy for no apparent benefit? Why were there no anti-submarine measures available to Royal Navy ships?

The naval correspondent of *The Manchester Guardian* led the inquisition the day after the loss of the three cruisers, before many of the details were known. The article immediately questioned the wisdom of employing older cruisers with limited speed in this role and claimed that the vessels 'could not be a thoroughly effective part of our cruising squadrons':

> No doubt these old cruisers were of some service in the North Sea where the shipping is generally slower than it is on the Atlantic but they and their kind would be of little use against a modern liner and however gallantly fought, they would enter an action against more modern vessels, on the other side of heavy odds.[10]

As September turned into October and the news reports of the victims and their distraught families continued to fill newspaper columns, the criticism showed no sign of abating in an era when naval strategy was regarded as a legitimate and popular subject of public discourse.

The Globe's article headed 'Naval Notes' referred to the lack of anti-submarine measures available to the three ships. 'One of the first principles of naval warfare is the best defence is a vigorous offensive, but the means for taking the offensive against submarines had yet to be discovered,' wrote their naval correspondent.[11]

The same newspaper underlined the historically unprecedented scale of the loss of life. 'Two or three correspondents have called into question the statement made in these notes the other day to the effect that we lost more men in the disaster of September 22 than we did in several great battles of the old wars put together. It will, then be advisable to set out the facts,' which the newspaper's naval correspondent then does:

> At the Glorious First of June (1794) we lost 290 men killed; St Vincent (1797) 73: at the Nile (1798) 215 and at Trafalgar (1805) 449. This makes a total of 1,030 killed in the four greatest battles of the Napoleonic wars. We lost 534 officers and men in the *Aboukir*, 562 in the *Cressy* and 376 in the *Hogue* a total of 1472. In the old days of course, it was exceedingly difficult to sink a ship – a process that had been greatly simplified by the substitution of steel for wood.[12]

The scale of the loss was now taking on historic proportions and even local newspapers started to question the wisdom of the Admiralty's tactics in exposing these older cruisers to such risk and the absence of anti-submarine weapons. By the end of the month, some also started to question the Press Bureau's official narrative.

The *West Sussex Gazette* claimed that the official accounts had left out important details. 'We are not told why the cruisers were steaming slowly enough to give the submarines their chance,' it stated, and asked what special tactics or weapon were used by the enemy 'that took in our gallant chiefs so completely'.[13]

Churchill was also openly criticised in the press for the employment of cadets, some as young as 15 years old, on front-line warships, many of whom had been killed. By November, criticism aimed personally at Churchill extended to Parliament, where questions were asked on the same subject. The case was taken up by William Joynson-Hicks, Conservative MP for Brentford, who wrote a letter to *The Morning Post* in late September specifically questioning Churchill for allowing boys to be sent to the front line:

> Perhaps the Admiralty answer would be that it is desirable to harden boys but if Mr Churchill will only apply to the officers in command of cruisers where these boys are, I think he will be told that they would be better sent back to complete their education at Dartmouth [naval college], and that by so doing they will preserve the supply of officers for the Navy of the future which is seriously endangered by the result of the disasters such as we are bound to expect in the course of a prolonged and difficult war.[14]

Churchill was the focus of widespread press and political criticism: what he called 'the fierce wartime censures of Press and Public'.[15] His flamboyant, sometimes brash, style made him a natural target, of course, but there was more to it than that. The man with the Midas touch appeared to be losing the confidence of the public and those around him.

Under increasing pressure, Churchill felt obliged to try to restore public confidence in him and the Royal Navy. Though he could not change the basic facts of the loss of the three cruisers, which were already in the public domain, he could at least try to play down the significance, adjust the tone and shift the focus of blame. With the support of Brownrigg and the Press Bureau, Churchill sought to change the narrative from ignominious defeat to inconsequential setback for which, crucially, he was not responsible. The First Lord felt compelled to resist the torrent of criticism and negativity, and the former war correspondent and master of prose was well equipped to do so.

There is nothing novel about official communiqués of military incidents being exaggerated, tailored, warped, or even invented, to fit a broader political agenda. Napoleon was not averse to some cynical press manipulation and the Bayeux Tapestry depicting the Battle of Hastings in 1066 has been described by some as an early example of military propaganda. As Marder observed, 'the press and the Admiralty assured the country that the loss was no more than a regrettable incident, it made no appreciable diminution in the Navy's great margin of strength, and consequently there was no need to feel nervous. Criticism of the Admiralty there was, nonetheless, with the brunt of it falling on Churchill.'[16]

The first Admiralty press release issued on 22 September had noted the three cruisers were sister ships of a 'comparatively old type'. This was no doubt a legitimate and sensible measure to reassure the public that the ships were not prime battlecruisers of the First Fleet. However, the theme was gradually developed over time into a narrative that implied these cruisers were obsolete old ships manned by amateur part-timers and young boys, in a blatant example of spin.

On 26 September 1914, the Press Bureau issued the formal accounts of the surviving senior officers, which was very unusual. It naturally deflected attention from Churchill and the Admiralty to those on board the three cruisers at the time. It also meant the narrative conveniently shifted from a naval defeat and loss to acts of individual heroism. Using what is now a well-established government public relations tactic, victims of military blunders are transformed into heroes, so that any third-party criticism or over-zealous investigation into the causes of the disaster implies a disloyalty and a disrespect for those brave souls on the front line.

By late September, *The People* was, obligingly, towing the official Admiralty line:

> Fine ships as they were, among their best in their day, they were going out of date and no longer counted as part of the real British battle line. Their loss signifies less to us than the loss of their three cruisers and two destroyers in the Heligoland Bight did to Germany.

And if there was any doubt that the First Lord was the chief author of the spin, the same report went on to quote Churchill directly:

> And as Mr Churchill has told us, the longer the struggle continues, the stronger shall we be, thanks to our superior shipbuilding programme and arrangements.[17]

There seems little doubt that the press communiqués were the personal creations of Churchill, or at the very least heavily influenced by him. Only a master of prose and sophistry could convert widespread disquiet about lack of success in the war at sea into a strategic advantage for Britain. The longer the situation continued, he assured the public, the better off Britain was. This was in stark contrast to his assurances in Liverpool on 21 September that the German fleet would be 'dug out like rats'.

Any detailed speculation in the press as to why the three cruisers were patrolling in such an exposed location, at slow speed, in a straight line, with no anti-submarine weapons, no life-saving equipment, no instructions or procedures for submarine attack, no flag officer present and inadequate lifeboats were neatly obfuscated by lurid accounts of personal heroism – including those of Gunner Dougherty, of course.

The Daily Mirror included accounts of 'heroism on sinking cruisers', 'a seaman who jumped overboard for his comrades', 'an officer's brave work to the last on boats'; the men who 'obeyed orders even when swimming for life'; and the 'ready self-sacrifice and no panic of any sort'. The same newspaper added some Admiralty-supplied pathos for good measure: 'Very moving and significant is the Admiralty statement that "the lives lost are as usefully, as necessarily and as gloriously devoted to the requirement of the service, as if incurred in a general action"'.[18]

The Admiralty statement reported in *The Daily Mirror* is revealing for several reasons. Firstly, the status of the loss of these three ships in a major submarine action of enormous strategic significance had been automatically minimalised. This was not a naval action at all and it has never been recognised as such by the Royal Navy. Secondly, it revealed the ingrained Admiralty prejudice that submarine warfare was, somehow, not proper naval warfare at all. *The Daily Mirror* continued to quote from the official Admiralty statement: 'The sinking of *Aboukir* was of course a normal hazard of patrolling duty,' but the loss of the other two ships was due entirely to the fact that 'they proceeded to the assistance of their consort'.[19]

In his attempt to deflect responsibility from himself and the Admiralty, Churchill now appeared to be venturing into dangerous territory: 'The natural promptings of humanity have in this case led to heavy losses which would have been avoided by a strict adherence to military considerations.'[20]

In a quite breathtaking act of spin, the humiliating loss of three cruisers and 1,459 men to a single U-boat was turned into a heroic failure on the part of those on board. And just in case anyone should still be in doubt as to whose fault this catastrophe was, another sentence was added to the official statement for good measure, which appeared in many newspapers during this period: 'Modern naval warfare is presenting us with so many new and strange situations that an error of judgement of this character is pardonable.'[21]

In an extraordinary break with long-established naval protocol, the press report not only made comment on the cause of a major loss but attributed blame to individual officers. It was unprecedented to do so in public within a few days of the incident, when all of the facts and mitigating circumstances could not possibly be established. It also contradicted centuries-old naval tradition that only a formal Court of Inquiry or a court martial could establish blame and that any officer accused of serious wrongdoing should have the opportunity to defend his name and his reputation. Captain Nicholson of *Hogue* had received no such opportunity and Captain Johnson of *Cressy* was already dead, so hardly in a position to defend his actions.

There is little specific reference to it but many naval officers, including those serving at the Admiralty, must have been outraged. Certainly, both Keyes and Beatty held the Admiralty responsible for the loss of *Aboukir*, *Hogue* and *Cressy*, not the ships' commanding officers. Perhaps it was no coincidence that several officers moved on or recorded having disagreements with the First Lord around this time.

Churchill's Naval Secretary, Rear Admiral Horace Hood, was suddenly dispatched to a seagoing post in command of the Dover Patrol on 3 October 1914. The Naval Censor, Brownrigg, who had a good working relationship with Churchill, stated in his memoir that he only had one notable 'bust up' with Churchill during his tenure. This was in September 1914 but the cause of it was not disclosed.[22]

If there is any doubt that it was the First Lord of the Admiralty who was the architect of the spin in the press in September and October 1914, in *The World Crisis*, Churchill recreates exactly the same narrative that he crafted for the press in the autumn of 1914, via the Admiralty censor and the Press Bureau. This alternative narrative was based on the notion that can be crudely summarised as 'chivalrous duffers, commanding worthless ships, manned by part-timers'.

'My own position was already to some extent impaired. The loss of the three cruisers had been freely attributed to my personal interference. I was accused of having overridden the advice of the Sea Lords and of having wantonly sent the squadron to its doom,' he wrote and he was desperate for an alternative version of events. Churchill was not trying to conceal any responsibility on his part as First Lord and effectively CEO at the Admiralty for the terrible loss of ships and life – he genuinely believed he was faultless.

'Both her [*Aboukir*'s] consorts had hurried with chivalrous simplicity to the aid of the sinking ship,' he wrote,[23] subtly implying both naïve stupidity and obsolete medieval notions of gallantry:

> The ships themselves were of no great value: they were amongst the oldest cruisers of the Third Fleet and contributed in no appreciable way to our vital margins. But like all Third Fleet ships, they were almost entirely manned by reservists most of whom were married men and they carried also young cadets from Osborne [actually, the cadets were from Dartmouth] posted for safety to ships which it was thought, would not be engaged in great battles.

Churchill, the master of argument and virtuoso of prose, managed to relegate the value of these three warships to little more than scrap, bury the significance of the incident as a trifle and discredit some 2,100 officers and men in the same paragraph.

As many naval officers at the time confirmed, *Aboukir*, *Cressy* and *Hogue* were not obsolete, worthless, expendable, rusting or even particularly old, yet this misinformation made its way into almost every respected naval history of the First World War.

Beatty, who probably knew those ships better than any senior officer in the Royal Navy, did not dismiss the ships as old, obsolete or of limited value. 'That is three fine ships and the greater part of two thousand two hundred men that can ill be spared,' he wrote to his wife on 23 September.[24] Midshipman Scrimgeour described them in his diary on 23 September as 'excellent ships'.[25]

All Third Fleet ships were required by the First Sea Lord to be immediately ready for war and they were not, as Churchill stated, 'almost entirely manned by reservists'. They all had a 40 per cent nucleus crew, which included the commanding officer, all key officers and senior ratings including the navigator, gunnery officer, engineering officers, gunner, bosun and senior engine room artificers and stokers.

The nucleus crew scheme was set up by Admiral Fisher when he was First Sea Lord (1904–10) and he had zero tolerance for obsolete or worthless ships. There is no implication in any testimony at the subsequent Court of Inquiry that these were expendable. *U-9*'s Weddigen was delighted to have destroyed such important British assets.

There were many older Royal Navy warships operating at sea in 1914. HMS *Pegasus*, sunk by SMS *Königsberg* in Zanzibar two days before the three cruisers were lost in the North Sea, was launched in March 1897. *Cressy* was launched in December 1899 and was the first of class. *Aboukir* was launched May 1900 and *Hogue* in August 1900.

The *Diadem*-class armoured cruisers that were also used extensively for patrol duties were of the same vintage as the *Cressys*. One of them, HMS *Argonaut*, launched in 1898, was stationed until 1915 at Cape Finisterre with the 9th Cruiser Squadron and captured the German armed cargo ship *Graecia*. The *Drake*-class cruisers were also built around the same time. HMS *Good Hope*, Admiral Cradock's flagship, was lost with all hands after being deployed by the Admiralty to engage Maximilian von Spee at the Battle of Coronel on 1 November 1914. HMS *Good Hope*, launched only six months after *Hogue*, was described by Churchill as 'a fine old ship from the Third Fleet with a 9.2in gun at either end', or the same principal armament as the *Cressys*.

HMS *Canopus*, the pre-dreadnought battleship that was to be involved in the British revenge for Coronel and the subsequent victory over von Spee at the Battle of the Falklands, was launched in October 1897. *Canopus* was four years older than *Cressy* but was described by Churchill as a 'citadel around which all our cruisers in those waters could find absolute security'.

A 14-year-old warship is not particularly old, even in an era of rapidly advancing technology like the turn of the twentieth century. HMS *Victory* was 40 years old at the Battle of Trafalgar and, in a more recent example, the aircraft carrier HMS *Hermes* was more than 22 years old when deployed to the Falkland Islands in 1982.

Of course, this is not to say the *Cressys* were the most technologically advanced or capable of warships, or that they were suitable for the task the Admiralty assigned them, but they were a typical vintage for ships of the Third Fleet and vital to the war effort. This was acknowledged by Churchill himself when in early August 1914 he sought Cabinet approval for the mobilisation of the Reserve to complete full manning of the Third Fleet before the official declaration of war. When Asquith refused on the grounds that the Third Fleet comprised only the Navy's older ships, Churchill wrote: 'I replied that though this was true we needed the Third Fleet ships, particularly the older cruisers, to fulfil the roles assigned in our war plan.'[26]

The notion of these ships being obsolete was spun by Churchill to downplay the scale of the loss and, it must be added, to minimise the damage to his own reputation. It was something of a red herring but many eminent and respected naval historians bought into it: 'The old armoured cruisers *Cressy*, *Hogue* and *Aboukir*, three of the four crocks in the 7th cruiser squadron (*Bacchante*-class) nicknamed the "live bait squadron" by the Grand Fleet,' is how Marder describes the three ships, reflecting the expert consensus that was largely the legacy of the First Lord's spin.[27]

Corbett, who wrote the official history of the First World War, went even further:

> As for the ships themselves, their loss was a small matter. They were already ripe for being sent to slumber out their obsolescence on the Mother Bank and were but ill adapted for naval warfare in its recent development.[28]

It is difficult to find any subsequent account of the 22 September disaster that does not emphasise the old and obsolete nature of the three cruisers. Given some of the more extreme references to the decrepit nature of the ships and the men who crewed them, it is a wonder they ever made it out to sea, never mind continued to patrol at sea without respite for the first six weeks of war.

The term 'Live Bait Squadron' used by Marder was also used in Churchill's version of events written eight years later after the loss of the three cruisers. Curiously, the phrase formed no part of the press communiqués at the time. Churchill wrote that it was during a visit to the Grand Fleet in Scapa Flow on 17 September 1914 that an officer spoke of the Live Bait Squadron and first brought the matter of the vulnerable cruisers to his attention. He does not mention the earlier letters written by Keyes and others before this meeting drawing his attention to the same issue.

Perhaps an officer did use this phrase but there is no other reference to it in any letter or personal account in September or October 1914. The phrase is not used anywhere in the many testimonies at the Court of Inquiry or in any of the press reports. It's such a memorable phrase and would have made an ideal attention-grabbing newspaper headline. Why was it not used more widely in diaries, private letters and press reports of the time?

There appears to be no sign of this phrase anywhere in the official documents before Churchill quoted it in *The World Crisis*. The only other vague reference to Live Bait Squadron apart from Churchill's was from an account published in 1937,[29] which used the phrase 'suicide squadron', which is probably more apposite. Churchill's phrase attributed to the squadron a mystery mission or secret purpose that deflected from the fact that the ships were simply poorly deployed.

Churchill also made many references to the fact that many of the ship's companies were made up of reservists and to them being 'married men'. In doing so he somehow managed to reduce the public perception of these highly experienced Royal Navy veterans and professional mariners of the RFR and RNR into feeble old civilians, shuffling to their stations in carpet slippers.

The blame game had started in earnest but, unfortunately for Churchill, it was not to be played out only in newspaper accounts supplied with information from him and Brownrigg, via the Press Bureau.

An official Court of Inquiry was called for 29 September 1914 in Chatham. Now the blame game would reach new levels and further light would be shed on the loss of the three armoured cruisers and 1,459 lives and who was responsible.

12

THE BLAME GAME

As pressure mounted on Churchill, the blame game regarding the loss of the three cruisers became increasingly tense as it continued to be played out across three spheres during the autumn of 1914 – in the press, in political circles and within the Royal Navy.

Many newspapers, like *The Daily Mirror*, were content to peddle Churchill's spun version of events. This was based on the premise that the three cruisers were obsolete ships of negligible strategic value and that, while the loss of *Aboukir* was a normal consequence of routine patrol duties, the loss of the warships would have been much less serious but for the errors of the gallant but ultimately incompetent officers who attempted to save lives.

The Tory press, sympathetic to the Conservative Party position, was less compliant and continued to relentlessly question the reason for the patrol and highlight the inexplicable deployment of the Cruiser Force – and the lack of preparedness for submarine warfare. As the official Court of Inquiry convened in Chatham on 29 September 1914, the blame game was also being undertaken more discreetly, as senior naval officers privately articulated their reaction to the incident.

Keyes directed his fury at the Admiralty War Staff in a letter to a colleague dated 29 September: 'I begged the WS [War Staff] Sturdee and Leveson to believe that they were a gift to a submarine, I can't understand why they weren't caught long before,' he wrote.[1] Even worse, Keyes believed that his friend, Captain Johnson, the officer being blamed in the official press communiqués for the losses, knew the perilous situation he was put in by the Admiralty. In the same letter, Keyes states:

> There can be no doubt that this was the work of one submarine, the intervals prove that – and she was well handled but it was all too easy. No one knew better than my gallant old friend Johnson what he was in for and he said so to *White Nick's* brother, his commander after the *Hogue* was struck. [*White Nick's* brother referred to Commander Bertram Nicholson of *Cressy*.]

'They all knew it was only a matter of days before they were bound to be had in the end on such a ridiculous parade,' he added.[2]

Johnson must have remarked privately to Nicholson, the second in command of *Cressy*, that their situation was hopeless, but Nicholson makes no mention of it in his official report. And Beatty, like Keyes, was also in no doubt who was responsible. In his view, it was not Nicholson or Johnson as implied by the Press Bureau: 'It was inevitable and faulty strategy on the part of the Admiralty,' he wrote in a letter to his wife dated 23 September.[3]

Jellicoe made no specific comment on the incident because the three cruisers were under direct Admiralty orders via Admiral Christian and therefore not his concern. Besides, he had enough to worry about and was evidently increasingly nervous about the submarine threat. 'Unfortunately, Germany has got a lead over us in over-sea [*sic*] submarines and consequently the situation in this respect is not very easy,' he wrote, but insisted the fundamental British strategy of the war at sea must not change by risking the major ships of the fleet in waters 'infested by submarines'. In other words, the strategy for the Royal Navy was to continue keeping the capital ships of the Grand Fleet mostly at a safe distance and enforce a distant blockade of Germany's maritime commerce.[4] In his reply, dated 8 October 1914, Churchill was in 'full agreement' with his Commander-in-Chief.

Admiral Christian, who was in charge of the Southern Force at the time of the incident and was alongside in Sheerness, in HMS *Euryalus*, when *U-9* struck, seemed as concerned with his own professional reputation as he was with the men lost or the impact the loss might have on the war at sea. 'I cannot tell you how much I have felt this tragic disaster which was accompanied by such loss of life and ships, and feel that you will have no confidence in me now,' he wrote to Jellicoe on 29 September 1914.[5]

In naval parlance, his letter might be regarded as a clear case of 'clearing his yardarm'. That is, seeking to exonerate himself of any blame before an inquiry could be assembled. In the same obsequious letter, Christian assured his Commander-in-Chief there was nothing he (Christian) could have done to prevent the loss. He heavily implies that it was mostly the fault of the commanding officers of *Hogue* and *Cressy* for not deploying their boats in order to rescue survivors and then departing to stand off from a position of safety.

Christian also attempted to deflect blame on to the Admiralty for not redirecting the Queenborough to Flushing mail ship, which Christian believed was guilty of reporting the location of his warships to German High Command. There is no evidence it was doing any such thing. It later became clear that Weddigen located the three cruisers purely by chance, having diverted in bad weather en route to Ostend in search of Allied transports.

What his letter does attempt to do is outline Christian's personal defence, which was closely aligned with Churchill's explanation for the incident, despite the views to the contrary of senior naval officers and the subsequent findings of the official Court of Inquiry. It also became part of the official interpretation. 'The loss of the *Hogue* and *Cressy* was due to the anxiety of Captains Nicholson and R.W. Johnson, the latter of whom was drowned, to assist in saving the crew of the *Aboukir*.'[6]

In accordance with Admiralty Memorandum No. W 381 U, dated 28 September, a full naval Court of Inquiry assembled at Chatham Naval Barracks. Admiral Christian immediately requested to be present at the inquiry in order to clear his name and reputation. It was a hollow gesture because there was never a possibility he would not have been called, as the absent Admiral in charge.

On 29 September, Admiral Christian formally lodged a letter of complaint about the nature of the inquiry and pointed out that two of the officers on the board were junior to him, and one by some considerable margin. Christian appeared to be as attentive to his status and professional reputation as he was to the loss of his ships and men.

There is also evidence to indicate that some at the Admiralty did not want a full-blown Court of Inquiry at all. In the official archive, there is a reference to the inquiry being upgraded from a 'Depot Enquiry', which would have had a much lower profile. The same document contains a note indicating that it was the intervention of Commodore T ('his letter 0032 of the 26 September') that led to a full-scale Court of Inquiry 'instead of by Depot'. Letter 0032 is not included in the file, but the clear implication is that Commodore Tyrwhitt pushed for the full and formal Naval Court of Inquiry, so that the incident could be properly investigated, any blame properly apportioned and any relevant lessons could be learned. No doubt, like many of his naval colleagues, he objected to the blame being summarily pinned on his fellow officers in a series of what many in the Navy would have regarded as distasteful if not perfidious Admiralty press releases.

It was the second Naval Court of Inquiry (the other investigated the *Goeben* incident) in the course of less than two months of war, which in itself is a telling indictment of how the war was being conducted by the Admiralty. 'I am glad September is over. It has been a bad month for the Navy. You would hardly believe it, but we have already lost 120 officers and 2,000 men,' wrote Beatty two days later.[7]

Some must have suspected that, like the *Goeben* inquiry, the court might condemn the action of the officers at sea and even recommend another court martial, like that recently ordered for the widely respected Admiral Troubridge. The two surviving commanding officers, Captain Drummond of *Aboukir* and Captain Nicholson of *Hogue*, must have been fearing the worst. After all, Churchill and the Press Bureau had been working hard to establish their culpability in the press over the previous week.

However, the evidence suggests that Churchill also had another scapegoat in mind by the time the Court of Inquiry had assembled. A memo written by him, dated 29 September 1914, clearly shows that he was gunning for Admiral Campbell, the flag officer of the 7th Cruiser Squadron. Campbell was alongside in Chatham Dockyard on 22 September while his flagship *Bacchante* underwent repairs.

In the memo, Churchill seemed agitated and questioned, 'under whose orders did Admiral Campbell's squadron proceed to patrol on the day of the disaster?' He demands to know where Campbell was at the time the 'disaster occurred' and why his flag had not been transferred to another ship. Churchill seems unaware that it was Christian and not Campbell who was nominally in charge. It appears to be a desperate attempt to incriminate Campbell, just one day after the Court of Inquiry was ordered. 'Let me see the orders. Were they issued before my memo of the 18 September about the "*Bacchantes*" (attached)?'[8]

Fortunately for Churchill, he was holding the ace of spades in this particular round of the blame game that was about to be played out at the Court of Inquiry. The memo of 18 September to which he referred was the critical document that exonerated Churchill from any direct blame for the 22 September disaster. It is reproduced in full in his account of the incident in *The World Crisis*.

It was a neatly typed two-page minute on Admiralty-headed notepaper and addressed to the First Sea Lord, Prince Louis Battenberg, which among other naval matters, included his view on the current deployment of Cruiser Force C on the Broad Fourteens patrol. 'The *Bacchantes* ought not to continue on this beat,' wrote Churchill.[9]

The timing was extremely fortuitous too, written just four days before the incident. If it was any earlier, the court might ask why his opinion had not been followed up, or at least the patrol reviewed. If it was much later, it would have been too late for it to make any difference to the outcome. Those nine words on a flimsy memo rescued Churchill's reputation, at least for the time being. Despite many naval officers at sea having little confidence in the abilities of the Admiralty to run the war at sea, the First Lord could not be held personally responsible for the three cruisers being deployed in such a dangerous location.

According to Churchill, the memo had been written the day after his formal strategy meeting with Jellicoe and senior staff officers at Loch Ewe on 17 September, when he overheard a remark made by one unnamed officer about the so-called Live Bait Squadron. According to Churchill's account, this prompted a discussion with Tyrwhitt and Keyes and an immediate review of the ships deployed.[10]

Both Keyes and Tyrwhitt shared an official car with Churchill for several hours and talked in general while making their way north to attend the meeting but neither made any specific reference subsequently to any discussion of the three cruisers and their deployment in the Broad Fourteens. The issue had been raised by Keyes in a letter to the Admiralty War Staff on 21 August and on several personal visits to Whitehall, so it would be unusual not to make reference to it if it happened. It is possible that it was discussed during the formal talks with Jellicoe but, if it was, no one else mentioned it.

In his memoir published in 1918, Jellicoe recalls the conference of 17 September at Loch Ewe attended by Churchill, the Chief of Staff

(Sturdee), the Director of Naval Intelligence (Rear Admiral Henry Oliver), Commodore S (Keyes) and Commodore T (Tyrwhitt). He recalls that operations in the Baltic were discussed as well as the potential capture of Germany's naval base at Heligoland, which was unanimously opposed by Jellicoe and his senior flag officers.[11]

Later in the same chapter of his book, Jellicoe recalls the signal from *Cressy:*

> At 0745am on the 22nd [September] wireless telegraphy signals from the *Cressy* were intercepted indicating that the *Aboukir* and *Hogue* had been sunk by submarines in Lat 52° 18'N Long 8° 41 E. These vessels were patrolling the Broad Fourteens off the Dutch coast under Admiralty orders.

Given that the conference with Churchill was only five days earlier and merited a description, it is strange Jellicoe was not surprised that the cruisers were still on patrol if their withdrawal had been discussed on 17 September. It would not have reflected badly on Jellicoe because Cruiser Force C was under direct orders from the Admiralty – not the Commander-in-Chief.

Given the critical importance of the memo written after the Loch Ewe conference, it is curious at least that both the document which contains the reference to the 18 September memo (written on 29 September) and the memo itself appear to have been doctored.

In the Admiralty memo dated 29 September containing Churchill's questions about Admiral Campbell, which makes reference to the critical memo of 18 September, the date has clearly been left blank and then subsequently filled in by hand in pencil and overwritten in black and red ink. Churchill was known to use red ink to write, sign and amend his personal memos. 'I had for a long time been accustomed to write my minutes in red ink,' he wrote.[12]

Later, when joined at the Admiralty by Admiral Fisher, who customarily used a green pencil to sign and make notes on documents, their annotations were jointly known as 'port and starboard lights' (i.e. red and green).

Of course, there is quite possibly an innocent explanation for the apparently altered date. Perhaps Churchill could not remember the precise date of the memo he had apparently written only eleven days earlier but never thought to mention before. It may have been an Admiralty secretarial convention of some sort.

After the word 'attached' is a question mark suggesting Churchill is not sure that the critical 18 September memo has been attached or can be attached. And there are more curious anomalies with the crucial memo dated 18 September 1914.

The original first draft of the handwritten memo is contained in the classified Admiralty file, relating to the Court of Inquiry. This scruffy hand-scribbled single sheet contains semi-coherent ramblings with large sections crossed out. The heading indicates it was dictated by Churchill (FL – the official abbreviation for the First Lord) and presumably recorded by his secretary. It differs significantly from the neat type-written version on Admiralty-headed notepaper presented as evidence to the Court of Inquiry, though it does contain the same key sentence about removing the *Bacchantes* from their beat.

The date at the top of this memo has also clearly been changed or overwritten to 18 September 1914, in black ink (not red ink) in what appears to be the same hand as the handwritten insertion, in the memo of 29 September. There are no other documents in the file with dates similarly amended.

While this does not provide conclusive evidence of anything untoward, given how important the document was, it does arouse justifiable suspicion about the validity of the memo that possibly saved Churchill's political career.

The World Crisis is Churchill's own account of the First World War, published in six volumes between 1923 and 1931. In this account, Churchill dedicated no fewer than four pages (pp.196–200) to the 22 September incident, and references to the loss of the three warships return like Banquo's ghost in subsequent chapters.

The neat final version of the memo of 18 September presented as evidence to the Court of Inquiry was reproduced in full in his book:

> The force available for operations in the narrow seas should be capable of minor action without the need of bringing down the Grand Fleet. To this end it should have effective support either by two or three battle-cruisers or battleships of the Second Fleet working from Sheerness. This is the most efficiently air and destroyer patrolled anchorage we possess. They can lie behind the boom and can always be at sea when we intend a raid. Battle-cruisers are much to be preferred.

> The *Bacchantes* ought not to continue on this beat. The risk to such ships is not justified by any service they can render. The narrow seas, being the nearest point to the enemy, should be kept by a small number of good modern ships.
>
> The *Bacchantes* should go to the western entrance of the Channel and set Bethell's battleships – and later Wemyss' cruisers – free for convoy and other duties.
>
> The first four *Arethusas* should join the flotillas of the narrow seas. I see no sufficient reason to exchange these flotillas now that they know their work, with the northern ones.
>
> As the 'M' boats are delivered they should be formed into a separate half-flotilla and go north to work with the Grand Fleet. The *King Alfred* should pay off and be thoroughly repaired.[13]

Churchill knew how important this document was when he had been so widely accused of ignoring expert naval advice to withdraw the patrol and micromanaging naval operations at sea. It was his 'Get Out of Jail' card, though it differed from the original draft minute. It also revealed the prescriptive and highly authoritative role of the First Lord in the technical details of the deployment of naval assets in wartime. Churchill the politician was effectively issuing orders to the Royal Navy's senior officer. He also wrote that Prince Louis 'immediately agreed and gave directions to the Chief of Staff', though he might have used the word 'obeyed'.

Thomas Gibson Bowles, a former MP, was the editor of the *Candid Quarterly Review*, a brochure widely read in London's influential circles, which claimed that:

> Despite the warnings of Admirals, Commodores and Captains, Mr Churchill refused until it was too late to recall the cruisers from a patrol, so carried on as to make them certain to fall victims to the torpedoes of an active enemy.[14]

The criticism stung Churchill, who referred to it years later:

> The writer of a small but venomous brochure which was industriously circulated in influential circles in London, did not hesitate to make this

> charge [interference in naval operational issues and ignoring professional advice] in a most direct form.[15]

Perhaps the dates on these two minutes were left blank or altered for entirely legitimate secretarial reasons but, given the timing and the circumstances, it creates an unavoidable sense of unease.

Either way, the Court of Inquiry never saw the less coherent and rambling hand-scrawled draft memo with the dates changed but instead was only presented with the neatly typed official minute on Admiralty notepaper produced for the attention of the First Sea Lord. Churchill said he assumed Battenberg would take the necessary action as outlined in the memo, but he did not. Churchill did not follow up or check over the subsequent four days while he was otherwise engaged, overseeing amphibious operations in France and the air defence of Britain.

The President of the Court of Inquiry was Commodore Ernest Frederick Augustus Gaunt. He was assisted by Captain E.C. Villiers, Captain of HMS *Actaeon*, and Captain P.H. Colomb, Flag Captain, The Nore, the naval anchorage near Sheerness Dockyard in Kent.

Gaunt was a no-nonsense, old-school sea officer with little time for airs and graces or, it seemed, the unorthodox methods and random innovations of the First Lord of the Admiralty. Gaunt was promoted to captain in 1903 and had already successfully commanded three battleships by 1911, when Churchill was appointed as First Lord. He was fiercely loyal to Jellicoe, whom he worshipped, but he had little time for the flashy playboy image of Beatty, of whom he supposedly said: 'Friend of Churchill. Rich wife. Helped Churchill with his polo ponies. [Should] never have been allowed to cross the threshold of a quarterdeck. [Self]-Advertiser. No place inside the Senior Service.'

Edward Cecil Villiers was captain of HMS *Actaeon*, an old hulk that formed part of the torpedo school. He was promoted to the rank of Captain on 30 June 1906 and was renowned as an accomplished marine watercolour artist.

The inquiry was certainly no whitewash or establishment cover-up. It was exhaustive and comprehensive. Testimonies were submitted, witnesses of all ranks interviewed from all three ships and signals studied, during the course of the seven days the inquiry was convened. At its conclusion, a submission classified 'secret' with all the supporting documents was sent to Churchill at the Admiralty for review on 5 October 1914.

More than a century later, the inquiry documentation still makes shocking reading. So do the comments made about it by Churchill and the Sea Lords before, during and after the inquiry report was submitted and contained in the classified Admiralty file.

The succinct two-page summary report submitted by the court did not adhere to Churchill's preferred script about old ships and incompetent commanding officers acting with humanity instead of battle awareness. Much to Churchill's dismay, the inquiry focused more on the question that many naval officers and several newspaper correspondents were asking: what in God's name were those ships doing in such a highly vulnerable location without escort in the first place?

In paragraph three of the opening page of the report, the court states that:

> It is not possible for the court to measure the degree of blame, if any, attached to those who directed the movements of the three Cruisers concerned, since they are not acquainted with the war plans and policy of the Admiralty; but the responsibility for the presence of the cruisers undoubtedly rests with the Admiralty telegram of 19 September 1914: 'The Dogger bank patrol need not be continued. Weather too bad for destroyers to go to sea. Arrange with cruisers to watch Broad Fourteens.'

Paragraph five made even more uncomfortable reading for Churchill:

> In the opinion of the Court, a cruiser patrol established in a limited area at so short a distance from an enemy's submarine base was certain to be attacked by submarines and the withdrawal of the destroyers increased the chance of a successful attack, while diminishing those of saving life.[16]

The report added as a caveat that it could not comment on the 'expediency of making the cruisers take the risk they ran'.[17]

The court's finding was unequivocal. An attack by submarine on the three cruisers was inevitable in the Broad Fourteens and it was the Admiralty that ordered them there and without any supporting destroyers.

The Court of Inquiry could not comment on whether the risk was worthwhile from a strategic point of view because they were not aware of the objective of their presence. An officer with Gaunt's experience would have known full well there was almost certainly no strategic justification for the cruisers being placed in such obvious danger. It was simply abject incompetence, but he was in no position to make this accusation about his direct superiors and employers. The three cruisers were left 'paddling up and down', as First Sea Lord Prince Louis later put it, isolated and highly vulnerable to submarine attack, for no good reason whatsoever.

Without the apparently doctored memo of 18 September 1914, Churchill, already under mounting pressure and with a growing reputation for micro-management and interference in front-line naval operations, would have been held directly responsible for the loss. His career would have sunk almost as quickly as *U-9* had dispatched the three cruisers, and he acknowledged as much: 'My own position was already to some extent impaired. The loss of the three cruisers had been freely attributed to my personal interference. I was accused of having overridden the advice of the Sea Lords and of having wantonly sent the squadron to its doom,' he wrote.[18]

And behind the summary findings that were so damning for Churchill and the Admiralty, the Court of Inquiry gathered astonishing testimony from senior officers that exposed the Admiralty's command and control arrangements as shambolic. Rear Admiral Henry Hervey Campbell CVC provided shocking testimony, given that he was the flag officer in command of all the *Cressy*-class cruisers of the 7th Cruiser Squadron and was alongside in Chatham Dockyard while his flagship, *Bacchante*, was under repair. When asked by counsel if he could 'give the court any opinion as to the purpose for which this patrol was established on the Broad Fourteens,' Campbell simply replied, 'No.' He added, 'But I am speaking without knowledge of our war plan or information of which the Admiralty is in possession.'

This senior naval officer of flag rank being formally examined in time of war about the loss of the ships of his squadron, stated that he had no idea what his squadron was supposed to be doing or why. At times during his testimony, Campbell sounded more like a recalcitrant and sulky teenager than an experienced Admiral in wartime. As Marder observed, 'Rear Admiral Campbell's evidence is extraordinary (questions 949–968) in that he states that he does not know the object why the patrol was formed, received no instruction and apparently issued none.'[19]

Campbell's testimony was clear evidence that the Admiralty under the high-energy and forceful political leadership of Churchill was micro-managing the war with the new toy of wireless telegraphy, violating long-established chains of command and bypassing senior commanders at sea. The Admirals and Captains at sea in wartime had lost confidence in, and respect for, the Admiralty and its direction of the war effort.

This feeling of operational dysfunctionality is supported by Admiral Christian's testimony that, although he was in charge of all Southern Forces, his assets were often deployed on missions by the Admiralty without him being consulted or, on some occasions, even being informed. Specifically, Admiral Christian testified that, despite him being the senior flag officer for all operations in the southern North Sea, his cruisers were deployed to Ostend without his knowledge under direct orders of the Admiralty. He also testified that on 18 September 1914 his destroyers of the Southern Force were dispatched to the Dogger Bank without any reference to him. It's hard to imagine a more ridiculous situation in wartime than an Admiral not knowing where his ships were.

Christian also testified that he was not provided with any submarine threat reports, despite these being issued daily, because the Admiralty refused to send them by wireless telegraph – so the ships at sea most at risk from submarine attack were only able to receive vital intelligence in harbour, while coaling ship or when delivered by another ship with the mail.

The comments later added to the findings of the Court of Inquiry by the Third Sea Lord, Rear Admiral Sir Frederick Tudor, are also revealing given that he is one of the official Lords of the Admiralty, apparently being blamed squarely by the Court of Inquiry for the needless loss of three ships and 1,459 men. He wrote:

> With regard to the whole incident, I think we have to remember that whilst cables and more especially WT have put into the hands of the Admiralty very great power and very great advantages in directing movements and operations of fleets and units, this power involves certain disadvantages … weakens the sense of responsibility of the Officers in command.[20]

In doing so, Tudor made the important point that if authority is taken away, so is initiative. This also corresponded with the Nelsonian traditional disdain for obeying signalled orders with which he disagreed.

The evidence and findings of the Court of Inquiry painted a vivid picture of a dysfunctional Admiralty organisation. Contradictory and misleading orders were issued by wireless telegraph signal and the Admiralty indulged in the micromanagement of naval operations from Whitehall, without properly consulting commanders at sea.

Of course, those senior officers at sea were not entirely free of blame for the events of 22 September 1914. The Sea Lords disagreed about how critical it was that no flag officer was present during the submarine attack and Drummond did receive criticism but not at the expense of his honour or reputation.

There were six secondary court findings on page two of the report: Drummond should have ordered zigzagging, he was mistaken in ordering the other two cruisers to close on him, Captains Johnson and Nicholson made an 'error of judgement' in stopping their ships to rescue the survivors from *Aboukir*, watertight doors should have been shut while on patrol and there should have been more lookouts placed before the attack.[21]

The final finding (number six) was an official tribute to the courage and discipline shown at all times by the ship's companies of the three cruisers: 'The Court wishes to place on record its appreciation of the magnificent courage, discipline, and devotion to duty shown by officers and men,' concluded the report and made special mention of Engineer Lieutenant Commander Huxham of HMS *Aboukir* and Engineer Lieutenant Commander Fendick of HMS *Hogue*, who were both last seen entering the engine rooms of their respective ships to assess damage while their vessels were 'practically sinking'.[22]

The paragraph was not only a tribute to the ship's companies. It was also intended as a rebuke for the Admiralty and for Churchill in particular for placing them in needless danger and then blaming them for the loss.

Churchill was furious with the content of the report. This was a complete contradiction of the narrative he had carefully fashioned and issued to newspaper editors via the Press Bureau over the previous two weeks. He did not feel in any way responsible and possibly did not appreciate the gross offence he had caused to the Navy by hanging naval officers out to dry in the press. Churchill was in desperate need of some good news.

However, the loss of the three cruisers refused to fade from public consciousness as other events in October and November 1914 conspired against Churchill and further increased the pressure on him.

13

NOT HIS FINEST HOUR

Apart from the campaign of spin, Churchill did not initiate much in the way of radical practical actions within the Admiralty following the loss of the three cruisers. Perversely, the evidence suggests he became even more distracted from naval issues and further involved in matters of questionable relevance to the Admiralty – while the blame game continued in the background.

Around this time, Lloyd George told his secretary and mistress, Frances Stephenson, who kept a diary: 'Churchill is too busy trying to get a flashy success to attend to the real business of the Admiralty.'[1]

Two days before the Court of Inquiry convened (26 September), Churchill departed for France and began touring a 15-mile section of British front on the north bank of the River Aisne. By 29 September he was back in London pondering and issuing lengthy minutes on the merits of Dutch neutrality.

On 30 September, he dispatched Admiral Oliver to destroy merchant shipping in the Scheldt Estuary but he was not at his desk for long. On 2 October, Churchill was instructing the Director of Naval Ordnance to come up with new projectiles suitable to destroy German Zeppelin airships.[2] This was only ten days after three cruisers had been destroyed by a submarine.

On the same day he departed for France again, this time to view the naval airfields in Dunkirk and to refine his plans to defend these mobile air bases with a new fleet of armoured cars. It also gave him an opportunity to visit his so called 'private army', the Naval Brigade, also in Dunkirk.

Churchill's train was turned around at 2300 on the night of 2 October, not by an impatient Asquith, incredulous as to how the First Lord's expeditions to continental Europe aided the war at sea, but by Kitchener and Lord Grey, the Foreign Secretary, alarmed by the news from Belgium.

The day before the Court of Inquiry convened, on 28 September, a German bombardment of the fortifications of the Belgian port city of Antwerp commenced. Churchill, en route to the Western Front, was urgently recalled from his intended visit to a Royal Navy airfield in Dunkirk to discuss the military situation in Belgium. To the horror of the assembled ministers, the Belgian Government had announced it was considering the abandonment of Antwerp. In what became known as the 'Antwerp Expedition', or later, the 'Antwerp Escapade', Churchill dispatched himself to the front line to tour defence fortifications in a Rolls-Royce in an attempt to stiffen the resolve of the Belgian defenders.

Antwerp was considered to be of crucial strategic significance and the defence of Belgium was the cause for Britain entering the war. No one could question the First Lord's courage or determination, and certainly not his self-belief, in his personal intervention to defend the small country. However, Churchill was also desperate for positive action, for glory and, of course, for some much-needed positive press coverage. His responsibility for the land defence of Antwerp, as First Lord of the Admiralty, was tenuous in the extreme. Yet, in defiance of a barrage of professional advice, he also dispatched two hugely inexperienced and poorly trained naval brigades of volunteers and reservist sailors, often in blue rather than khaki uniforms and issued with antique rifles. They arrived in Antwerp in requisitioned London double-decker buses.

These men were civilian volunteers and seamen reservists for whom there were no berths available aboard warships. On 16 August 1914, two brigades of these surplus civilian sailors were added to an existing brigade of some 2,000 Royal Marines to create a composite Royal Naval Division. It was Churchill's pet project but was regarded with disdain by his staff, who referred to it as the First Lord's private army.

About 8,000 sailors were formed (often to their chagrin) into quasi-military units and billeted in tents pitched on the Walmer Downs near

Deal in Kent and at the nearby mining village of Betteshanger. The Royal Navy sailor possessed many traditional virtues and attributes but marching about with a rifle, living in tents and fighting conventional land battles had never been among them – unless short amphibious attacks and so-called 'cutting out operations' are included. Despite their obvious lack of readiness, training or suitable equipment, Antwerp presented Churchill with the opportunity to deploy his own land forces, and the 'maritime Marlborough' could not resist.[3]

'The First Lord is sending his army there. I don't mind his tu'penny untrained rabble going but I do strongly object to 2000 invaluable Royal Marines being sent to be locked-up in a fortress and becoming prisoners of war if the place is taken,' wrote Captain Richmond, Assistant Director of Operations at the Admiralty.[4]

Despite the arrival of the Royal Naval Division beginning on 3 October 1914, German forces penetrated the outer ring of Antwerp's forts and on 9 October the garrison surrendered. Some 57 British combatants lost their lives in Churchill's Antwerp operation, 1,480 escaped to the neutral Netherlands to be interned for the rest of the war and 900 were captured by the enemy. It was a shambles bordering on farce and represented another public humiliation for Churchill, who was again rounded on in the press.

In one editorial, *The Morning Post* felt it necessary to remind Churchill that 'he is not, as a matter of fact, a Napoleon,' and its editor, H.A. Gwynne (a fierce critic of Churchill), wrote to Cabinet members insisting that Churchill was 'unfitted for the office he now holds'.[5]

Churchill offered to resign from the Cabinet and take personal charge of land forces in Belgium if he was given the 'necessary military rank and authority'. His offer was received in Cabinet by what Asquith later described as a 'Homeric laugh' and Churchill was told to get himself back to London immediately. Some naval officers feared that Churchill had lost the plot.

'Churchill had made an awful hash of the Antwerp show. His business is at the Admiralty not dabbling about on land expeditions,' wrote Midshipman Scrimgeour in his diary later that month,[6] and Captain Richmond was even less impressed: 'It is a tragedy that the Navy should be in such lunatic hands,' he wrote in his diary entry for 4 October.[7]

The criticism hurt Churchill, who felt it was unjustified, and he insisted he was fully authorised to deal with what was generally viewed as a military emergency. He maintained that it had been a worthwhile exercise, writing in a secret Cabinet report submitted the following year:[8]

> I believe that it will be proved that the three or four days which were gained by the prolongation of the defence delayed the main German advance for at least an equal period, thus enabling the battle in which the main army was about to engage to be fought on its seaward flank three or four marches further north than would otherwise have been the case.

His colleagues were unconvinced and his foes were outraged. Conservative Party leader Bonar Law branded the mission 'an utterly stupid business'.[9]

By October, an anticyclone was developing over the North Sea, and low cloud and fog were reported from Dover to the coast of Norfolk. It might have represented Churchill's gloomy mood.

On 7 October 1914, at the height of the furious public response to the Antwerp escapade, Churchill's third child, Sarah Millicent Hermione, was born. It might have been a good omen and the First Lord desperately needed more good news – but it was not forthcoming.

Five days after receiving the classified findings of the Court of Inquiry, there was no statement in the press about its conclusion, which pointed the finger at the Admiralty, but it must have been common knowledge within senior naval circles. Instead, Churchill ignored the official version of events and allowed the commanding officers of the three cruisers to be further hung out to dry in the press.

The Illustrated London News report of Saturday, 10 October 1914, was a good example, complete with a photo of a submarine firing a torpedo:

> Captain (Weddigen) is an enterprising and experienced officer, well known in this country and he deserves all the praise that his comrades and the German Emperor can give him for his brilliant achievement. From the British point of view, however it must be enforced that his opportunity was made easy for him and that had it not been for the error of judgement of those in command it is exceedingly unlikely that he could have attained so complete a success.[10]

The 'error of judgement' might have been copied and pasted from the supplementary findings of the Court of Inquiry, but the court's primary conclusion about the flawed deployment of the cruisers by the Admiralty and the inevitability of attack did not form part of the same newspaper report. It was covered up.

As though to avenge the reputation of his former opponent, five days after that report, on 15 October 1914, Weddigen and *U-9* struck again. This time the victim was the *Edgar*-class cruiser HMS *Hawke* patrolling in the North Sea as part of the 10th Cruiser Squadron. The cruiser was on patrol off the coast of Aberdeen when it performed the risky move of stopping to pick up mail from HMS *Endymion*, demonstrating that the lessons learned on 22 September in the Broad Fourteens were still being ignored by the Admiralty. Without zigzagging, *Hawke* moved on at 13 knots to regain her station within the squadron and was hit by a single torpedo. The 8,000-ton warship quickly capsized, and the rest of the squadron failed to notice its absence for several hours. When the destroyer HMS *Swift* eventually began a search mission, it found a life raft carrying one officer and twenty-one men, while forty-nine other survivors were rescued by a Norwegian steamer. Overall, 524 men died, including Hugh P.E.T. Williams, the ship's captain.

In his diary, Scrimgeour, serving in HMS *Crescent*, the flagship of the same cruiser squadron, added a confidential note to the loss of *Hawke*, which if discovered he feared would 'lead to my dismissal from the service'. According to the Midshipman's diary entry, *Hawke*'s commanding officer, Captain Williams, came aboard *Crescent* prior to sailing to ask the Admiral (de Chair) for an extra two hours in harbour to make vital engine repairs. This was refused on the grounds that *Hawke* could still make 10 knots. On departing the Moray Firth, all ships were required to proceed at full speed to reduce the risk of submarine attack, but this would still have been very slow for *Hawke* in her impaired mechanical state. Scrimgeour claims that Williams was overheard saying to the Flag Lieutenant that 'it is pure murder sending the ship with over 500 officers and men to sea in this state'.[11]

'The story of *Hawke* being stopped for boarding ship when hit by the submarine was invented by the Admiralty to prevent unpleasant questions and a public outcry,' wrote Scrimgeour.[12]

On 31 October, there was news of another ship lost to a U-boat attack. Assigned to the Nore Command, HMS *Hermes* was used to ferry aircraft and stores to France. On 30 October, *Hermes* arrived at Dunkirk with a cargo of seaplanes. The cruiser set off on its return journey the next morning, before being recalled by reports of a German submarine in the area. Despite zigzagging at a speed of 13 knots, she was torpedoed by *U-27* and sank in the Strait of Dover, losing twenty-one men. On 4 November, the Admiralty issued a casualty list and emphasised that 'at once, it would take steps to pay all pensions and gratuities payable under the regulations'.

Evidence indicates that by late October Churchill was feeling the strain as the litany of defeats and blunders continued and the blame game for the three cruisers disaster was still at full throttle as it reached Cabinet level. 'I do not remember any period when the weight of the war seemed to press more heavily on me than these months of October and November, 1914,' he wrote.[13]

In his minute, dated 24 October 1914, contained within the secret Cabinet papers on the Court of Inquiry, the First Sea Lord, Prince Louis of Battenberg, responded at length to Churchill's aggressive questions about the actions of Admiral Christian, Admiral Campbell and Captain Drummond. Living up to his moniker in the Admiralty, the First Sea Lord concurred with most of the Court of Inquiry's comments and recommendations. He rejected the notion of a court martial for Captain Drummond and could find little specific cause for blame except in the case of Drummond's interpretation of weather conditions. Drummond was put on half-pay and was not recommended for major commands after that.

The First Sea Lord did not see any need for contrition on his part or the part of the Admiralty, and he resented the overt criticism contained in the Court of Inquiry report: 'Such criticism of Admiralty orders is, however, very improper (besides being quite uncalled for in this case) and it is for consideration whether the officers concerned should be so informed.'[14]

More importantly, Prince Louis had failed to dish up a suitable scapegoat for Churchill and he had no idea at that stage that it was he who was to be made the scapegoat for the disappointing naval failings to date.

Churchill's state of mind is referred to on the same day (24 October) as Battenberg wrote the minute about the Court of Inquiry. Captain Herbert Richmond, who had been so scathing of the First Lord's use of the Naval Division in the futile defence of Antwerp, hosted Churchill for dinner that evening. Richmond noted that Churchill was 'oppressed with the impossibility of doing anything'.[15]

According to research undertaken by Nicholas Duncan Black for his thesis, 'The Admiralty War Staff and its influence on the conduct of the naval war between 1914 and 1918': 'With no great battle, and no sudden decisive economic impact, and with examples of major errors, such as the loss of three cruisers on 22 September, the pressure was on Churchill to show that the Navy could do something.'[16]

His Admirals were pleading for improved anti-submarine measures but Churchill still seemed more interested in a grand plan that would deliver glory. On 17 October 1914, Beatty wrote an impassioned private letter to Churchill urging him to take immediate action on submarine defences to avoid what he called a 'catastrophe of a very large character':

> No *seaman* [his italics] can dispute that these three bases [Scapa, Rosyth and Cromarty] could have been made absolutely safe from submarine attack during the two and a half months that the war has been in progress.[17]

Instead, Churchill was coming up with increasingly eccentric and elaborate schemes. He had long believed that a forward base, for example, on Germany's western-most Friesen Island of Borkum, would either prompt the German High Seas Fleet out of harbour or at least allow the British to take the war to the German coast. The War Staff viewed the prospect with alarm. 'Stopping Churchill became almost a habit at the Admiralty in the autumn and winter of 1914,' writes Black.[18]

At a crucial time, when the Admiralty should have been fully focused on stopping the German High Seas Fleet and addressing the urgent and covert threat of mines and submarines, they were instead engaged in trying to stop an increasingly desperate and irrational First Lord of the Admiralty.

There was some good news during this bleak period. The vital anti-submarine defences demanded by Jellicoe and Beatty eventually left the naval dockyards for Scapa Flow on 24 October 1914, some eighty days after war had commenced.

However, worse was to come. Elements of the Grand Fleet, including Beatty's battlecruiser squadron, had redeployed from Scapa Flow to Lough Swilly in Ireland, following the 22 September incident. Here they were thought to be beyond the reach of German minelayers and U-boat patrols. On 26 October, the eight *Orion*- and *King George V*-class dreadnoughts of the 5th Battle Squadron, commanded by Vice Admiral Sir George Warrender, left Lough Swilly to carry out gunnery exercises.

At 0850, HMS *Audacious* struck a mine and was badly damaged about a mile from where a merchant ship, the *Manchester Commerce*, had been sunk earlier. The signal informing the Royal Navy of the possible presence of mines was misplaced and failed to reach Jellicoe. Thinking the damage had been caused by a U-boat torpedo, other large ships were reluctant to come to her aid and, as a result, *Audacious* eventually capsized and sank, once her crew had been removed safely.

In an unprecedented case of censorship and news manipulation in time of war, the mining and subsequent loss of HMS *Audacious* on 26 October 1914 was completely covered up. It was concealed from the British public, a policy that was described by one official history as 'so contrary to all British tradition and sentiment, that the Admiralty would not decide without reference to the Cabinet'.[19]

In the light of recent events and the loss of the three cruisers, the news of *Audacious* was considered so negative that it would be disastrous for public morale and a huge fillip to the ambitions of the German High Seas Fleet. It would also be disastrous for Churchill's image as political head of the Royal Navy, though in this case it seems the cover-up was requested by Jellicoe and encouraged by Fisher. It was opposed by Brownrigg, the Naval Censor, who thought it best to publish bad news quickly. The episode demonstrated that Churchill had no compunction about manipulating the news to suit the war effort or himself when he believed it to be necessary. To further add salt to the wounds, von Müller and SMS *Emden* were fast becoming what one historian called a 'cause célèbre' and even provoked reluctant admiration in wartime Britain.

The *Emden*'s reputation achieved legendary status on 28 October in what one Hong Kong newspaper headlined 'The *Emden*'s escapade at Penang'.[20] Von Müller had slipped into the strategic British Malayan port with a dummy fourth funnel erected so that she resembled the British cruiser HMS *Yarmouth*. The German warship, flying British colours, sailed unopposed into the heart of the anchorage, just beneath the red-brick walls of Fort Cornwallis in Georgetown, and sank the Russian cruiser *Zhemchug* at anchor. At the time of the attack, the Russian captain was ashore, apparently engaged in frenetic sexual activity with a local female friend. It was widely rumoured at the time that Captain Cherkassov watched, half-naked, at the window of his bedroom at the Eastern and Oriental Hotel, as his ship sank. He was later court-martialled.

On exiting the harbour, *Emden* also sank the French destroyer *Mousquet* as it returned from patrol, before disappearing into the Strait of Malacca.

The prosecution of the war at sea was so abject for Britain by late October 1914 that even the normally ebullient Churchill described the situation in a private letter to Jellicoe as 'grim'. Things were difficult for the First Lord and there was a drastic need for a change of course. The pressure had not relented since the Broad Fourteens incident on 22 September. It was this pressure that forced Churchill to turn to Fisher.

The opportunity to return the fiery Fisher to the Admiralty as First Sea Lord followed the resignation of his predecessor. Prince Louis of Battenberg had been forced to quit in late October after a series of venomous, press-inspired insinuations about his German heritage, which raised unfounded questions regarding his loyalty to the British cause. These were inflamed by the still-vocal Admiral Lord Beresford in Parliament. Churchill and Fisher's nemesis had inadvertently done them a huge favour by dishing up the scapegoat that Churchill so desperately needed. The forced resignation of Prince Louis was an act of craven political manipulation, but he departed obediently and with enormous dignity.

Given Fisher's age (he had turned 73 the previous January) and his divisive reputation, it was a high-risk move. However, only Fisher had the strength of character to confront Churchill, curb some of his more outlandish impulses and keep him on track. Only Fisher had the profile sufficient to steady the ship and reassure the public and Parliament. And only Fisher was capable of restoring Churchill's much-tarnished reputation.

'The advent of Jackie Fisher to the Admiralty in place of Prince Louis of Battenberg will probably put a stopper on Winnie's gambols,' wrote Scrimgeour in his diary entry for 3 November, reflecting the general sentiment in the Navy.[21] These two autocrats and powerful personalities were mutually attracted but they were too similar to ever survive as a long-term team. However, it might be enough to stop the rot.

Lord Beaverbrook wrote that a cold wind was blowing on Churchill in October 1914 and that 'he co-opted Fisher to relieve the pressure against himself'.[22] The appointment of Fisher on 30 October did not mark an immediate reversal in fortunes for the Navy. The lowest point of the naval war for Britain had yet to be reached.

That was to come on 1 November with the ignominious defeat of Admiral Sir Christopher 'Kit' Cradock by the German Asiatic Squadron commanded by Admiral Maximilian von Spee at the Battle of Coronel off the coast of Chile. Two ships were lost, HMS *Monmouth* and Cradock's flagship, HMS *Good Hope*, with all hands, as Cradock was overwhelmed in a classic gunnery action. Needless to say, the defeat was partly attributed to more Admiralty bungling, which implicated Churchill. The First Lord was accused of failing to communicate effectively with Cradock about the withdrawal of the *Minotaur*-class armoured cruiser HMS *Defence*.

'Two of the greatest wartime disasters of his wartime period in office for which he was held to blame by the Conservatives, were the sinking of the *Aboukir*, *Hogue* and *Cressy* and the Coronel defeat,' wrote one historian.[23]

By November, the continuing loss of confidence in Churchill that had started with the *Goeben* incident continued via the loss of the three cruisers and increased during the Antwerp escapade now left the First Sea Lord floundering in a stormy political sea after the Coronel defeat. He was accused of personally presiding over an ignominious naval humiliation for which he bore direct responsibility and his critics connected a line between these events, which they claimed demonstrated the First Lord's incompetence. He also blamed Cradock for the loss, which further infuriated and alienated the Navy.

After the Cabinet meeting of 4 November, Asquith wrote to King George V: 'The Cabinet are of opinion that this incident [the Coronel defeat] like the escape of the *Goeben*, the loss of the *Cressy* and her two sister cruisers … is not creditable to the officers of the Navy.'[24]

The Royal Navy now held their political boss in contempt. He was trashing the glowing reputation of the service constructed over centuries and was seeking to discredit respected senior officers and blame them for the Admiralty's incompetence. Beresford was seething that Cradock had been blamed for the Coronel defeat without the late Admiral having the opportunity to defend his reputation. Beresford launched a broadside attack on Churchill and a vehement defence of Cradock in Parliament in late November:

> Some small attempt has been made to throw blame upon this Admiral [Cradock], but again I say that the Service bitterly resents any remarks

> of that sort, He fought a superior force and he had ineffective ships and reserve crews, but he maintained the old tradition of our Navy.[25]

In the same speech Beresford drew a direct connection between the Coronel defeat and what he called 'the *Cressys*', which was still a raw wound two months after the event.

Even Beatty, who was Churchill's former Naval Secretary and who admired his former boss, was exasperated: 'If only we had a Kitchener at the Admiralty we could have done so much and the present state of chaos in naval affairs would never have existed,' he wrote to his wife.[26]

Churchill was accused by some of being personally responsible for telling Cradock to engage superior forces at Coronel, charges he vehemently denied: 'I cannot accept for the Admiralty any share of responsibility [for the Coronel defeat],' he wrote,[27] and again he sought to blame the front-line commander, in this case Cradock, who had been confused by contradictory orders from Whitehall. This was a more extreme example of the *Goeben* debacle in August, with commanders at sea undermined and confused by cascades of wireless telegraph signals from Whitehall.

'It was no part of my duty to deal with the routine movements of the Fleet and its squadrons, but only to exercise a general supervision,' he wrote,[28] but no one believed this statement reflected the reality at the Admiralty.

While it was not part of his duty, Churchill sought to micromanage the parts of naval operations that took his fancy. He also forced through his own favourite innovations – even those his staff officers fiercely resisted – while ignoring the most urgent operational priorities. These distractions included the naval air force in Dunkirk, the Antwerp escapade, anti-Zeppelin munitions, armoured car operations and a forward naval base in Borkum.

Churchill's insistence on interfering in the details of front-line operations was renowned and resented throughout the service. Churchill and the War Group's newfound ability to issue instantaneous instruction, via wireless telegraphy, only compounded the problem.

This new communications technology quickly became a tool for counter-productive micromanagement of ships at sea and miscommunication that regularly created confusion. It was a significant contributory factor, not only in the loss of the three cruisers on 22 September but also in the escape of the *Goeben* in the Mediterranean in August and the defeat at Coronel on 1 November.

'Developments in signals technology made possible for the first time the operation of a centrally controlled war by the Board,' writes Black,[29] and Churchill could not resist the urge to take instant prescriptive action. Wireless telegraphy became a dangerous weapon in the hands of someone as impetuous and impatient for success as him. 'It happened in a large number of cases that seeing what ought to be done and confident of the agreement of the First Sea Lord, I myself drafted the telegrams and decisions in accordance with our policy and the Chief of Staff took them personally to the First Sea Lord for his concurrence before dispatch,' wrote Churchill, and by all accounts, before his replacement by Fisher, Prince Louis always concurred.[30]

The next year, after repeated failures to silence gun batteries in the Dardanelles in 1915, an officer at sea on the front line wrote privately in response to one of the numerous Admiralty signals received from London:

> It is one of those peculiarly objectionable messages in which the man on the spot is not only urged to attack but told how to do it. In its easy and superficial reference to very difficult or impracticable tasks, it bears the unmistakable impress of the First Lord's hand.[31]

During November more humiliating disasters piled up, even with Fisher now at the helm and claiming to be astonished by the 'apathy' at the Admiralty as he tried to beat some urgency into the languid and atavistic organisation.

On 3 November 1914, German warships commanded by Admiral von Hipper bombarded Great Yarmouth on the Norfolk coast and slipped away unscathed. Only a few shells were fired and there was minimal damage but it was yet another high-profile blow to public confidence in Churchill and the Navy. On 26 November, HMS *Bulwark* was destroyed by a huge accidental explosion while she was at anchor in Sheerness, which claimed 741 lives. The Navy appeared to be destroying its own ships and saving the enemy the trouble.

On 9 November, the German thorn in Churchill's side, the seemingly indefatigable *Emden*, was finally destroyed. Von Müller's intrepid cruiser had been disabled by HMAS *Sydney* and grounded off the Cocos Islands in the Indian Ocean. The Admiralty could hardly claim significant credit for an Australian success but it was good news for the war effort, if not for Churchill personally.

The appointment of Fisher had also opened old wounds. The Chief of Staff, Sturdee, was a protégé of Beresford and Fisher hated him, branding him a 'pedantic ass'.[32] The solution was to make Sturdee the Commander of the Battlecruiser task force led by *Invincible* and *Inflexible* dispatched to the South Atlantic by Fisher to avenge Coronel and sink von Spee's squadron. As Sturdee made his 8,000-nautical-mile passage south to the Falkland Islands in search of von Spee, the schism had been diplomatically managed but the heat was still on Churchill. More questions were asked in Parliament about the management of the war at sea and the three lost cruisers were still very much on the agenda for Churchill's foes.

On 16 November, the Conservative MP William Joynson-Hicks continued his bitter criticism of Churchill for sending teenage cadets to their deaths in *Aboukir*, *Hogue* and *Cressy*. Many of these criticisms were often led by Churchill and Fisher's bête noire, Beresford. During a parliamentary debate on 27 November, Beresford focused on the loss of the three cruisers and the failure to allow the opportunity for formal courts martial to establish the cause of these disasters that had so undermined public confidence:

> What I particularly want to speak about is this: It has come to my knowledge, and I think many honourable Members will concur in what I say – that there is a doubt in the public mind, and a want of confidence in the Navy to carry out its duties ... There was first the three '*Cressy*'s'.[33]

Beresford also attacked Churchill's interfering micromanagement style, which by now seemed to be common knowledge, and he brought it up in the same parliamentary debate on 27 November, when he objected to the scapegoating of Cradock for the Coronel loss:

> I would ask the right hon. Gentleman [Churchill] to remember this. The Duke of Wellington laid down a very fine maxim in fighting: 'Tell your admirals or your generals what your object is, but do not give orders to them how they are to carry out that object, as a circumstance may occur in which the general or the Admiral by obeying your orders will defeat the object.'[34]

Beresford had struck the proverbial nail on the head and Churchill had no way to defend himself. The First Lord responded tamely:

> If I take the incidents to which he has referred – the action in the Pacific [Coronel], the loss of the cruisers off the Dutch coast, or the expedition to Antwerp – as good examples of his principle I would say that before it is possible to form a judgment it is necessary that the orders should be disclosed, that the telegrams which have passed should be disclosed, and that the dispositions which prevail, not only at the particular point, but generally throughout the theatre of war, should also in their broad outline and even in considerable detail be made known. That is clearly impossible at the present time.[35]

Churchill was on the ropes and his career was in jeopardy. However, within a few days he was rescued by Fisher and the old Admiral's stubborn insistence on sending two prime battlecruisers to the South Atlantic to avenge Cradock and the Battle of Coronel.

While coaling in the Falkland Island's capital of Port Stanley on 8 December, Sturdee's squadron, with the two battlecruisers that had been urgently dispatched by Fisher, sighted von Spee's force heading for the harbour. It was a fluke encounter but they had bumped straight into the foe they were seeking. Despite some awful gunnery and questionable tactics, the superior British firepower was enough to sink von Spee's squadron with all hands and temporarily rescue Churchill's political career.

The Battle of the Falklands turned the fortunes of war around in Britain's favour, redressed the strategic balance and restored confidence. It was a long time coming.

Churchill was saved thanks to Fisher and by Christmas 1914 he was politically more secure than he had been since the outbreak of war. The critics were silenced at least for now. The First Lord appeared to be vindicated but the controversy caused by the sinking of *Aboukir*, *Hogue* and *Cressy* was still not quite behind him. The ghosts of the Broad Fourteens refused to rest in peace.

14

LEGACY

Let us now sing the praises of famous men,
our ancestors in their generations.
Some of them have left behind a name,
so that others declare their praise.
But of others there is no memory,
they have perished as though they never existed,
they have become as though they had never been born,
they and their children after them.
But these also were godly men,
whose righteous deeds have not been forgotten

Ecclesiasticus 44

Another naval setback early in 1915 threatened to obliterate any new-found optimism.

In the early hours of 1 January 1915, off Portland in the English Channel, the pre-dreadnought battleship HMS *Formidable* was sailing in formation with the light cruisers HMS *Topaze* and HMS *Diamond* at approximately 10 knots when she was targeted by two torpedoes launched by *U-24*. It was a clear night, and the ships had no destroyer escorts and were not zig-zagging. The first torpedo caused *Formidable* to begin listing badly, while a second torpedo hit the ship some forty-five minutes later. Less than two hours later, at 0445, the 14,500-ton ship capsized and sank with the loss of 35 officers and 512 men.

Confidence was partially restored three weeks later at the Battle of the Dogger Bank on 23 January, when a German battlecruiser squadron heading for the east coast of England was intercepted and destroyed by the Navy. Press reports included a photograph of the sinking SMS *Blücher*. Sweet public relations for the Admiralty and no accusations this time of the First Lord's micromanagement – that was never a possibility with the forceful Fisher back on the scene.

Churchill and Fisher's honeymoon proved to be short-lived. With a hiatus in political assaults against him and with Fisher furiously marching about the corridors of the Admiralty demanding action, Churchill was free to indulge his more esoteric enthusiasms and engage his mind with grand strategic thoughts. These included the seizing of the Baltic island of Borkum and then, from January 1915, an increasing intellectual occupation with a combined land–sea offensive on Turkey's Gallipoli peninsula to relieve pressure on Britain's Russian allies under attack by Ottoman forces in the Black Sea region. It was the latter campaign that was eventually sold to Cabinet by Churchill as a naval-only operation – something Fisher never fully supported.

The campaign to support Russia commenced on 19 February 1915 when a strong Anglo-French naval task force, including the British dreadnought HMS *Queen Elizabeth*, began a long-range bombardment of Ottoman coastal artillery batteries. In February 1915, the Allied fleet's attempt to force the Dardanelles failed and was followed in April 1915 by a disastrous amphibious landing on the Gallipoli peninsula.

Four days before the attack started, Churchill felt confident enough to deliver a 23,000-word statement to Parliament on Britain's command of the seas, during which he called for complete discretion over when and if to call for courts of inquiry and courts martial.[1] This was a delayed response to the Broad Fourteens Court of Inquiry, which had been highly critical of the Admiralty and subsequently hushed up. The response was predictably hostile.

Admiral Lord Beresford MP, the nemesis of Fisher and former Commander-in-Chief of the Channel Fleet, would not let Churchill off the hook for the long series of naval losses that had commenced with the three cruisers in the Broad Fourteens. Part of Beresford's vitriol may have been fuelled by sour grapes that had been fermenting for decades but the points he made created a big impact:

> With regard to the losses by submarines, I maintain with regard to those six ships [*Aboukir*, *Hogue*, *Cressy*, *Pathfinder*, *Hawke* and *Formidable*] that the losses were unwarrantable, avoidable and preventable, and that there was no adequate compensation, or could not have been any adequate compensation, for the risks run. It is due to the relatives and dependants that there should have been an inquiry and a court-martial. A court-martial ought to have been held to find out who was to blame for what they considered, and I consider, preventable disasters. I got a great number of letters from the relatives and dependants of those men lost by the submarine incidents, and the majority of them put this question, 'We consider so and so was murdered as he had no chance in a fair fight and the accident was preventable'. What does the Admiralty say about this?[2]

Beresford must have known about the findings of the Court of Inquiry and that they had been hushed up, and he also challenged the alternative Churchill-inspired press narrative of obsolete ships manned by part-timers. 'I find fault with the Right Hon. Gentleman and the Admiralty that all we have ever heard was that those ships were of no military value. Why put them in and why put officers in them? It is very poor consolation and, I think, an unfeeling and unmerited remark,' stated Beresford.

'Murder' was an extremely strong term to use in a parliamentary exchange with a government Cabinet minister in wartime but Beresford persevered: 'There was no sentiment of respect paid to the memory of one of those officers or men who went to their death under those circumstances,' he added.

And it was not only Beresford who wielded an oratorical knife. Bertram Falle, Member of Parliament for the naval town of Portsmouth, could hardly conceal his personal antipathy for Churchill:

> Those ships [*Aboukir*, *Hogue* and *Cressy*] were sent regularly into the danger zone, and they were sent without the small craft that were built for the purpose of accompanying the bigger ships, and guarding them from danger – built to be the very eyes and ears of the Fleet. Yet these three cruisers were sent without their accompanying smaller vessels, and, of

> course, were sunk. But that was not enough for the First Lord. He sent the *Hawke* without smaller craft, and it shared the fate, and her men shared the fate, of the *Cressy*, *Hogue* and *Aboukir*. What I should like to know is, what the ships were doing in those particular waters? Was it necessary for them to be there? That is to me the crucial question.[3]

It was the question that Churchill could not answer. He implied this was because of security concerns but the truth was there was no sound reason for the three armoured cruisers to be there, and everyone knew it.

In more litigious modern times, if all the information about the loss of *Aboukir*, *Hogue* and *Cressy* and the loss of 1,459 men had reached the public domain, it would no doubt have provoked outrage. There would be vociferous calls for a public inquiry and even emotionally charged accusations of corporate manslaughter from the victims' families. Of course, corporate manslaughter did not exist in 1914 and military combat operations are usually exempt in any case, but as far as many were concerned it might describe quite aptly the fate of the 1,459 killed in the three cruisers. 'Either it was criminal negligence or it was crass stupidity, or it was dictated by what I may describe as amateur strategy,' said Beresford.

It was a public mauling, but Churchill never acknowledged any fault on his part. 'Those who in years to come look back upon the first convulsions of this frightful epoch will find it easy with after knowledge and garnered experience to pass sagacious judgments on all that was done or left undone,' he wrote later.[4]

On 24 May 1915, Churchill's first tenure as First Lord of the Admiralty came to an ignominious close. He was sacked from the Admiralty by Asquith after Fisher's resignation following more embarrassing defeats in the Dardanelles. He was given the token Cabinet post of Chancellor of the Duchy of Lancaster. It was a humiliating setback to his career prospects in wartime and he was personally devastated. His wife, Clementine, thought he would 'die of grief'.[5]

Many believed Churchill was the sole architect of one of the most disastrous and ill-conceived military campaigns in British military history. After eight months of fighting and around 250,000 casualties, the land campaign at Gallipoli was abandoned and the invasion force withdrawn, but Churchill believed he had been made a scapegoat for joint decisions that had gone wrong.

As Jellicoe pointed out, Churchill's principal fault was an inability to realise his own limitations as a civilian, and that he 'thoroughly distrusted Mr Churchill because he consistently arrogated to himself technical knowledge which with all his brilliant qualities, I knew he did not possess'.[6]

Despite his determination to educate himself in all things naval, Churchill possessed little or no deep knowledge or understanding of naval strategy or administration. He had also shown himself to be guilty of micromanaging and interfering in every detail of naval operations and being quick to blame subordinates when it all went wrong. By 1915 this was common knowledge within the Royal Navy and by the time he was dismissed by Asquith in May, the First Lord of the Admiralty was almost universally held in contempt.

His departure from office was marked in the Royal Navy by a collective sigh of relief. Even Beatty, widely regarded as Churchill's man, wrote that 'the Navy breathes freer, now it is rid of the succubus Winston'.[7]

When Churchill eventually resigned from Cabinet in mid-November 1915, he made an extraordinary public statement, in which he sought to exonerate himself from any blame for past errors at the Admiralty and shifted responsibility to his former colleagues, including his former long-standing friend and confidant, Fisher.

According to the front page of *The Daily Mirror*, under the headline 'Churchill makes sensational revelations', the First Lord, pictured next to an image of Fisher, absolved himself of any responsibility not just for the loss of the three cruisers but also for the Antwerp escapade, the Coronel defeat and the initial Dardanelles fiasco. He blamed Fisher for tacitly agreeing to the Dardanelles campaign, he blamed Kitchener for initiating the Antwerp expedition and he blamed the entire Admiralty Board for Cradock's loss at Coronel.

According to Churchill's account of the 'three lost cruisers', briefed to *The Daily Mirror* and published on 16 November 1915 after his statement to Parliament: 'It was untrue that he overruled his naval advisers and kept the *Hogue*, *Cressy* and *Aboukir* at sea against their advice.'[8]

Churchill, who later described himself as the 'escaped scapegoat', rejoined the Army in November 1915 as a Major in the Queen's Own Oxfordshire Hussars and trained in the front lines for several weeks with the Guards Division. Churchill subsequently became a Lieutenant Colonel commanding the 6th (Service) Battalion, Royal Scots Fusiliers (RSF), part of the 9th (Scottish) Division, in January 1916.

As battalion commander he performed admirably, winning over dubious junior officers and enlisted men. He survived many close calls, and while on leave also engaged in politics. To use modern marketing parlance, he also rebuilt his brand. In May 1916 his unit, unable to replenish its losses, was amalgamated with another battalion and this offered Churchill an opportunity to leave the Army and return honourably to the political home front, where the Asquith government was under fire. Churchill returned to government as Minister of Munitions in 1917, in Lloyd George's new Cabinet.

From 1919 to 1921, he was Secretary of State for War and in 1924 returned to the Conservative Party, where two years later he played a leading role in the defeat of the General Strike of 1926. Out of office from 1929 to 1939, Churchill issued numerous, if mostly unheeded, warnings of the threat posed by Nazi and Japanese aggression. The rest, as they say, is history.

Churchill's efforts to minimise the events of 22 September 1914 and exonerate himself were more successful in later years than they were at the time. The narrative he wove of an inconsequential action involving obsolete ships and gallant but incompetent commanders and over-aged crews became etched into the official history and was rarely, if ever, challenged. This incomplete and inaccurate version of events meant the significance of the Broad Fourteens action never received the full attention it deserved from future generations. To some extent, as Beresford implied, the 1,459 men and boys who lost their lives that day were dishonoured and dismissed as being of negligible relevance.

While Churchill's own account in *The World Crisis* refers to the loss of cruisers at some length, it is only to exonerate himself from any responsibility using the curious phrase, 'an episode of peculiar character in human history', to describe it.[9] Further, he sought to imply that such an attack was somehow beyond the realms of reasonable analysis or planning. 'Up till the end of September, 1914 no one seriously contemplated hostile submarines in time of war entering the war harbours of either side and attacking the ships at anchor,' he wrote.[10]

This was untrue. Fisher and Scott had been highlighting the threat for years and the submarine menace to modern warships in harbour was proven at naval manoeuvres that Churchill had attended.

Naval warfare had changed forever. The days of long lines of immaculately maintained warships engaging in perfectly synchronised gunnery actions had ended abruptly. The new reality, to use Churchill's analogy, was that an entire regiment could be 'defeated with a single cavalry pistol'.[11]

The Broad Fourteens action was also the moment when a complacent peacetime cruising club dominated by the 'gin and bitters brigade' designed to fly the flag across the British Empire started to transform itself gradually into a modern wartime fighting force.

The loss of the three cruisers on 22 September 1914 and, more specifically, the 1,459 men who died in them, also helped thrust the issue of naval family welfare into the public domain. Newspapers led the calls for greater pensions provision, while the armed forces charity SSAFA extended its reach into naval territory in earnest for the first time. Prior to the loss of *Aboukir*, *Hogue* and *Cressy*, there was very little official recognition of a naval family and their loss helped change that forever. The SSAFA network of trained volunteer case workers remains a powerful and largely undervalued service within armed forces family welfare today. They visit the homes of armed forces families or veterans and their dependants on request, without pay or any other financial recompense other than their travel expenses.

Other more fundamental changes were adopted by the Navy triggered by the loss of the three cruisers. One of the key recommendations of the Court of Inquiry was the provision of lifejackets to warship crews and the issue of identity discs for rapid casualty identification so that, where possible, the next of kin could be informed promptly of their relative's status. By 18 November 1914, this measure was already in hand.

Despite the fact that history has obliged Churchill by relegating the Broad Fourteens action to relative obscurity, there are still some personal traces and memorials to the men who were lost that day.

While there is not sufficient space to do justice to the memories of all those men who died on 22 September 1914, there are a few examples where their lives – like many others who died in the wars of the last century – may still be traced on war memorials and the large number of online sites that now support them.

Names of the men who died that day in *Cressy* are etched in stone or picked out in steel on memorials in Ripon, Sheffield, Huddersfield, York, Flamborough, Lancaster, Salford, Hartlepool, Birmingham, Birkenhead, Ascot, Southampton, Hitchin and High Wycombe. Seven men from Liverpool died that day and are commemorated on the city's war memorial. Small villages in Norfolk including New Buckenham and Hardwick all lost men on *Cressy*. And there were men lost from the ports of Scotland, Wales and Ireland, too.[12]

Along the coast and ports of Kent, Essex, and Suffolk, where the men for Chatham division ships were traditionally recruited, there are more traces of the men of the *Cressy*.

In the small port of Whitstable on the north Kent coast there is no specific memorial to commemorate Seaman George J. Keam RNR, who died with five of his shipmates, all from the town and serving on *Cressy*, on 22 September 1914. It was his wife who collapsed with shock while picking hops in the nearby fields when she heard the news of the loss of the cruisers.

All the men are named on the town's war memorial outside the library in Oxford Street, while the special story of the brave oystermen of *Cressy* has been mostly forgotten.

Visitors to Whitstable can still drive to Keam's Yard car park, named after the Keam family. They can enjoy a pint or two of Whitstable Bay ale at the popular Royal Naval Reserve public house in the High Street or the Old Neptune, on the beach, which was once run by George Keam's father. Middle Wall, where his family home was located, is nearby.

In the pretty village of Westleton, Suffolk, the names of Leading Seaman Will Potter and Stoker First Class Spindler are both listed on the simple stone war memorial outside the Crown Inn. Their story is also recorded in the record of graves retained in the vestry of St Peter's church, just over the road. The book contains a black and white image of the *Cressy* and a brief biography of the two shipmates.

In Surrey, the distraught parents of Engineer Lieutenant Stacey Wise, who was lost in the machinery spaces of *Cressy*, and his elder brother, who died a month later on HMS *Severn*, erected a bronze and marble tablet in memory of their two sons at St Peter's Church in Woking. It is still there.

In Harwich, information panels outside the Essex town's maritime museum on the seafront are maintained by the Harwich Society. They describe the events of the First World War and the Harwich Force. The entire German submarine fleet surrendered in Harwich in 1918 but there is no specific mention of Captain Johnson, who was born in the town and lost his life on *Cressy*.

The Great Eastern Hotel, which still stands on the quayside, was used as a naval hospital during the First World War and wounded officers from the three cruisers were treated there. The Admiralty had requisitioned the entire quayside during wartime from where an irregular, and highly hazardous, passenger service was maintained between Harwich and the neutral Netherlands.

A short ferry ride away, on the other side of the River Stour, are the buildings of HMS *Ganges* or what was RNSE Shotley in 1914. Sadly, those structures, including the swimming pool where thousands of boys learned sea survival skills and the fleet medical centre where those rescued from *Aboukir*, *Hogue* and *Cressy* were treated, might be demolished. Planning consent was granted in 2017 to allow this unique piece of British maritime heritage to make way for a development of nearly 300 new upmarket homes. It is planned that its famous mast and the parade ground will be preserved and fortunately, there is no intention of closing the HMS *Ganges* Museum located nearby. It is run by enthusiastic volunteers, some of them former Shotley Boys, so its stories can be kept alive.

In Chatham Historic Dockyard, where a major centenary commemoration was hosted in 2014, artefacts from the three cruisers are displayed, including one of the few lifebuoys from *Cressy* recovered from the site of the attack by *U-9*. A model of the *Cressy* on loan from the Imperial War Museum is on display and a wonderful 1920 colour print. The print shows the silhouetted figures on the open bridge (possibly Captain Johnson and his navigator, Gabbett) and the desperate men struggling for survival in the sea. The caption below the print reads: 'Up until this point the Royal Navy had not taken the threat posed by submarines seriously. The loss of HMS *Hogue*, *Cressy* and *Aboukir* shook people's confidence in the Navy and was a portent of much worse to come.'

At the Royal Navy Submarine Museum in Gosport there are a number of artefacts from *U-9*. There is the brass engine room bell, a small ash tray and some commemorative medals minted in Germany to mark the famous victory by Weddigen and his crew.

U-9 survived the entire war, but Weddigen was not so fortunate. The ace submariner was killed while commanding *U-29* on 18 March 1915, when the submarine was rammed and cut in half by HMS *Dreadnought* in the Pentland Firth. *U-29* had broken the surface immediately ahead of the British battleship after firing a torpedo at HMS *Neptune*. There were no survivors from the submarine.

Some of those who survived the Broad Fourteens action also left curious postscripts to the story. Captain Drummond of *Aboukir*, who was criticised by Churchill and Battenberg and put on half-pay, was appointed in command of the battleship HMS *Illustrious* on 31 October 1914. There is probably no better training for a commanding officer than having been sunk in action. On 7 September 1915, he was appointed in command of the *Diadem*-class protected cruiser HMS *Europa* and took part in the disastrous Dardanelles campaign. Drummond retired as a Vice Admiral.

Commander Bertram Nicholson, Executive Officer of *Cressy*, who wrote to the mother of Able Seaman Midmer, was appointed to HMS *Iron Duke*, Jellicoe's flagship, as 'additional for command of Flotilla of Armed Trawlers'. These were the new anti-submarine patrol vessels urgently requested by Jellicoe, and who better to command them than the man who had witnessed three ships sunk by a single submarine? He married in 1915, was promoted to Captain and appointed in command of the requisitioned auxiliary vessel HMS *Zaria*. He later worked in naval intelligence before taking retirement in 1922. He moved to Kenya and became the first headmaster of the Prince of Wales school in Nairobi, now known as the Nairobi School.

After commanding the Harwich Force from 1915 to 1916, Captain Wilmot Nicholson, the commanding officer of *Hogue* and the bedraggled senior officer among the survivors in the Netherlands, enjoyed a successful naval career after he was repatriated to the UK. He was appointed to command the battleship HMS *Collingwood* in December 1916 and then commanded the battlecruiser HMS *Furious* from March 1917. After the war, Nicholson commanded the aircraft carrier HMS *Eagle* during her trials and went on to command the 2nd Cruiser Squadron in May 1921. With typical naval logic, he was made Chief of the Submarine Service in September 1923. He retired as a full Admiral in 1930.

In one curious aside, Nicholson's wife, Christabel Sybil Caroline Nicholson, was involved in a spy scandal. She was arrested for possession of a document obtained illegally from the United States Embassy in London in 1940 during the Second World War. She was an associate of Anna Wolkoff and the American diplomat and Nazi sympathiser Tyler Kent, who worked at the London Embassy.

Kent removed classified documents from the embassy and in 1940 Nicholson was arrested in possession of a copy of a secret paper, obtained illegally by Kent. She was an admirer of the Nazi regime and took part in activities of the so-called 'Right Club', which sought to prevent the USA joining the war against Nazi Germany. However, she was found not guilty of offences under the Official Secrets Act in May 1941. The Admiralty expressed its severe displeasure over the incident.

In another minor scandal, the loquacious Gunner Dougherty made a reappearance in the national press. Having served as a trusted witness at the Court of Inquiry and been widely reported in newspapers for his gallant attempts to defend *Cressy* from multiple submarine attacks with a single 12-pounder gun, his name reappeared in the media in a less heroic context.

The front page of the 16 February 1915 edition of the *Scottish Evening Telegraph* reported that Dougherty had pleaded guilty at Kent Assizes to two charges of bigamy. In mitigation the defence counsel noted the valuable service the Warrant Officer had provided to the country. The judge was unmoved, remarking that 'the country would have to do without that prisoner's service for some time' before sentencing Dougherty, the former hero, to twelve months' hard labour.

Cressy's ship's chaplain, Rev. George Collier, who had awoken Surgeon Martin with news of the U-boat attack and who had lost consciousness in the cold sea but was miraculously rescued from the freezing waters, wasted no time in getting married. On 2 October 1914, the *Western Times* reported his wedding to Gladys Norton at St Stephen's church in Launceston in Cornwall by special wartime licence.

In December 1928, *The Courier* reported the case in Croydon, Surrey, of ex-convict George Pugh, who fraudulently posed as a *Cressy* survivor in order to defraud a sick mother of £20. The man he impersonated, Stoker First Class Benjamin E. Batchelor, was killed on 22 September 1914. The Chairman of Magistrates said: 'It is the most despicable case since I have been on this bench. Our great regret is that we cannot give you more than the maximum penalty [of six months' hard labour].'

The wrecks of the three cruisers are still on the bottom of the Broad Fourteens in about 30m of water, making them accessible to sports divers using air. The hull and superstructures are present but senior British Sub-Aqua Club (BSAC) instructor Dave Lock, who led an expedition on them in 2015, reported they 'are all smashed to pieces' due to explosives being used during salvage operations. Underwater video footage taken by a Dutch TV production company, shot as part of an excellent documentary about the disaster, shows an old sea boot and a plethora of marine life at the shipwreck site.

In 1954, in an astonishing act of insensitivity, the British Government sold off the salvage rights to the wrecks of the three cruisers to a German scrap metal contractor. Ironically, the rights were granted by the government of Prime Minister Winston Churchill (1951–55). It is inconceivable that he would not have known about it.

In 2017, the three wrecks were finally added to the list of designated protected places under the 1986 Protection of Military Remains Act.

The original memorial service for those lost on *Aboukir*, *Hogue* and *Cressy* was held at Chatham in early October 1914 and reported in the local press. The address, by Rev. J. Edgar Williams, was transcribed word for word, including his tribute to the lost: 'Each one left behind an unperishing name and a vacancy which no one could fill.'

A century later, a centenary commemoration service was held at Chatham Historic Dockyard. It was initiated by Henk van der Linden, founder of the Live Bait Squadron Society, who has done tireless work to obtain proper recognition of the three cruisers and those who served on them. The ceremony was attended by the then First Sea Lord, Admiral Sir George Zambellas, and featured a full naval ceremonial guard and Royal Marines band. Bishop Dr Stephen Venner addressed a congregation of the men's relatives and descendants, each wearing a coloured enamel lapel broach to designate on which ship their family member served:

> We remember all those who were killed in action, or by disease, the bereaved, the lost, the families which were shattered, the wounded, maimed and injured, those who held in silence unspeakable memories of warfare.

Afterwards, the Duke of Kent unveiled a commemorative plaque and a reading was given by Julie Cook, the granddaughter of Able Seaman John Richard Back of *Cressy*. Back was one of the four Dover RFR men listed as missing from *Cressy* in the local newspaper, and his remains most likely lie with his shipmates in the depths of the Broad Fourteens.

High above Chatham Dockyard, the home port of the three cruisers, an impressive obelisk exposed on a grassy hill dominates the skyline. The open space is part of the Great Lines Heritage Park, which, according to the local council, is Medway's most prominent green space, connecting Gillingham,

Chatham and Brompton. Together, its fortifications, massive ditches and field of fire were intended to defend Chatham Dockyard from landward attack, and now these 70 hectares of open space offer an unexpectedly wild and remote atmosphere in the middle of an urban area. It offers a splendid view west over the roof of the much-maligned Pentagon shopping centre to the River Medway and north west, over Fort Amhurst to the naval dockyard, which once employed tens of thousands of men and women.

The Chatham Naval Memorial commemorates the officers, ranks and ratings of the port of Chatham in the two world wars. It is marked by two huge black iron gates and guarded by two impressive stone statues of sailors on watch. The memorial honours those who lost their lives at sea in the two great wars and did not receive proper burials. The architect of the First World War memorial was Sir Robert Lorimer and the sculptor Henry Poole. The memorial was unveiled by the then Prince of Wales (later King Edward VIII) on 26 April 1924. An extension was designed later for those who lost their lives in the Second World War.

There are similar memorials in Plymouth and Portsmouth, and merchant seamen who lost their lives at sea during the two world wars are also commemorated in Liverpool and Tower Hill in London.

The names of 18,654 men and women are recorded on the Chatham memorial, maintained by the Commonwealth War Graves Commission. Of those men and women listed, 8,517 are from the First World War. The names are listed by year of death, and then by rank, in alphabetical order.

On a grey and blustering autumn afternoon, just as parents are gathering to collect their children from the nearby Brompton Westbrook primary school, it is a haunting spot to visit.

The victims from the early part of the First World War can be found on the west face of the obelisk, furthest from the entrance gates.

There are lots of familiar names from *Cressy* on the memorial: Lieutenant Commanders Grubb and Harvey; Lieutenant Stacey Wise (his brother Edward is listed too); 16-year-old Midshipman Froude; and Engineer Commander Grazebrook.

The names of the Penn brothers are there, as is Stoker First Class Spindler and Leading Seaman Potter. W.J. Potter was a man from a different social universe from his commanding officer but he was killed on the same day, on the same ship and commemorated with his name listed less than 2m away from that of his captain, on the same stone memorial.

The first name on the first scroll of names in the left corner as you face the monument is immediately recognisable. Listed under 1914, Royal Navy, Captain, is Johnson R.W. The commanding officer adored by his men, known as 'father' or 'the old man', was the man blamed unjustly for the Broad Fourteens disaster – stitched up for the purposes of political expediency and given no opportunity to defend his actions or his reputation.

Above all those familiar names is a large plaque bearing a simple commemorative statement:

> In honour of the Navy and to the abiding memory of these ranks and ratings of this port who laid down their lives in the defence of the empire and have no other grave than the sea.

NOTES

Chapter 1: North Sea Patrol

1 Traditional naval rhyme posted on the door of HMS *Ganges* Museum, Shotley, Essex, UK.
2 *Gloucester Journal*, Saturday, 13 January 1913.
3 Beynon, Mark and Hallam, Richard, *Scrimgeour's Small Scribbling Diary* (London: Conway, 2008).
4 Corbett, Julian S., *History of the Great War: Naval Operations* (London: Naval and Military Press, 1996).
5 Wells, John, Captain, *The Royal Navy: An Illustrated Social History 1870–1982* (Stroud: Sutton, 1999).
6 Beatty, David, Earl, *The Beatty Papers: Selected from the Private and Official Correspondence of Admiral of the Fleet Earl Beatty* (London: Scolar Press for the Navy Records Society, 1993).
7 Shane Leslie, a Beatty biographer, who knew both Beattys well, wrote that she was 'beautiful, opulent, ambitious and unhinged by her hereditary fortune and by an insane streak … she brought him many gifts; great beauty, a passionate and jealous love, sons, wealth, houses, and a personality he could not conquer, for against him was arrayed a distraught spirit which brought their home life to utter misery'.
8 *Naval Staff Monographs (Historical) Volume XI Home Waters Part 2. September and October 1914* (London: HMSO, 1924).
9 Court of Enquiry. Loss of ABOUKIR, CRESSY and HOGUE on 22 September 1914. TNA, ADM 1/8396/356.
10 *Sunderland Daily Echo*, 1 October 1914.
11 According to *Naval Staff Monographs (Historical) Volume XI Home Waters Part 2*, Chapter 6, Admiral Campbell was in charge of Cruiser Force C, which

comprised the four *Cressy*-class cruisers with *Euryalus* only attached as Admiral Christian's flagship.

12 Shewell, H.W.B., Surgeon Captain, HMS *Euryalus*, Private Remark Book, 13 July 1914 to 20 January 1915, held by Imperial War Museum.

13 Friedman, Norman, *British Cruisers of the Victorian Era* (Barnsley: Seaforth Publishing, 2012).

14 *Cressy HMS: Stations and Orders* (Portsmouth: Gale and Polden, 1906).

15 *Naval Staff Monographs (Historical) Volume XI Home Waters Part 2*, p.52.

16 J.A. Froude was the grandson of the historian James Froude of Salcombe and the great nephew of the engineer William Froude (1810–79). William Froude joined the practice of I.K. Brunel in 1837.

17 Lavery, Brian, *Able Seamen: The Lower Deck of the Royal Navy* (London: Conway, 2011).

18 Ibid.

Chapter 2: A Single U-Boat

1 The World War One Document Archive, wwi.lib.byu.edu/index.php/U-9_Submarine_Attack.

2 Ibid.

3 Spiess, Johannes, *Six Years of Submarine Cruising* (Miami: Trident Publishing, 2019).

4 Ibid.

5 Ibid.

6 Ibid.

7 Ibid.

8 Ibid.

9 Ibid.

10 Ibid.

11 Ibid.

12 Thanks to former submariner Commander Tony Dalton RN for this detail.

13 Spiess.

14 Ibid.

15 Ballantyne, Iain, *The Deadly Trade: The Complete History of Submarine Warfare from Archimedes to the Present* (London: Weidenfeld & Nicolson, 2018).

16 Scott, Admiral Sir Percy, *Fifty Years in the Royal Navy* (London: John Murray, 1919). Scott was one of the few senior naval figures who warned of the threat of submarines, to no avail.

17 *Naval Staff Monographs (Historical) Volume XI Home Waters Part 2.*

18 Gayer, Albert, Rear Admiral, *German Submarines and their Warfare 1914–1918* (Miami: Trident Publishing, 2020).

19 Beynon and Hallam.

20 Hough, Richard, *First Sea Lord: An Authorised Biography of Admiral Lord Fisher* (London: George Allen & Unwin, 1969).

21 Scott.

22 Ibid.

23 Jameson, William, *The Most Formidable Thing: The Story of the Submarine from its Earliest Days to the End of World War I* (London: Rupert Hart Davies, 1965).
24 Spiess.
25 Ibid.
26 The World War One Document Archive, wwi.lib.byu.edu/index.php/U-9_Submarine_Attack.
27 Ibid.
28 Ibid.

Chapter 3: Whitehall at War

1 Massie, Robert K., *Dreadnought: Britain, Germany and the Coming of the Great War* (London: Pimlico 2004), p.769.
2 Purnell, Sonia, *First Lady: The Life and Wars of Clementine Churchill* (London: Quarto Publishing Group, 2015).
3 Ibid.
4 Brownrigg, Douglas, *Indiscretions of the Naval Censor* (New York: George H. Doran, 1920).
5 Churchill, Winston S., *The World Crisis, Volume 1: 1911–1914* (London: Rosetta Books, 1923).
6 Ibid.
7 Marder, Arthur J., *From the Dreadnought to Scapa Flow, Volume II* (Barnsley: Seaforth Publishing, 2013).
8 Klein, Christopher, 'The Daring Escape that Forged Winston Churchill', www.history.com/news/the-daring-escape-that-forged-winston-churchill.
9 Kemp, P.K., *The Papers of Admiral Sir John Fisher, Volume One*, edited by the Navy Records Society.
10 Churchill, *The World Crisis, Volume 1.*
11 Ibid.
12 Ibid.
13 Hough, p.222.
14 Churchill, *The World Crisis, Volume 1.*
15 Ibid.
16 Eade, Charles (ed.), *Churchill by his Contemporaries* (London: Hutchison, 1953). Chapter 11, 'Churchill and the Navy' by Admiral Sir William James.
17 Hough, Richard, *Former Naval Person: Churchill and the Wars at Sea* (London: Weidenfield & Nicholson, 1985), p.49.
18 Churchill, *The World Crisis, Volume 1.*
19 Ibid.
20 Ibid.
21 Marder, *Volume II.*
22 Ibid.
23 Black, Nicholas Duncan, 'The Admiralty War Staff and its Influence on the Conduct of the Naval War between 1914 and 1918', PhD Thesis 2005 University College, London (Michigan: ProQuest, 2013).

24 Churchill, *The World Crisis, Volume 1.*
25 Black.
26 Ibid.
27 Jellicoe, John, *The Grand Fleet 1914–1916: Its Creation Development and Work* (London: George H. Doran Company, 1919 [2017 edition]).
28 Scott.
29 Marder, *Volume II.*
30 Churchill, *The World Crisis, Volume 1.*
31 Thompson, Julian, *The War at Sea 1914–1918* (London: Sidgwick and Jackson, 1996).
32 Scott.

Chapter 4: The Morning Watch

1 Spiess.
2 The World War One Document Archive, wwi.lib.byu.edu/index.php/U-9_Submarine_Attack.
3 *Dover Express and East Kent News*, 25 September and 2 October 1914.
4 Hook, Herewood, Commander. Private Papers held by Imperial War Museum, London.
5 Padfield, Peter, *Rule Britannia: The Victorian and Edwardian Navy* (London: Pimlico, 2002).
6 *The Whitstable Times*, 26 September 1914.
7 The World War One Document Archive, wwi.lib.byu.edu/index.php/U-9_Submarine_Attack.
8 Board Minutes on the loss of HM Ships Aboukir, Cressy and Hogue dated 4 December 1914. TNA, ADM 1/8396/356.
9 Ibid.
10 *Sheffield Daily Telegraph*, 26 September 1914.
11 Spiess.
12 *Naval Staff Monographs (Historical) Volume XI Home Waters Part 2.*
13 Board Minutes on the loss of HM Ships Aboukir, Cressy and Hogue dated 4 December 1914. TNA, ADM 1/8396/356.
14 Ibid.
15 *Naval Staff Monographs (Historical) Volume XI Home Waters Part 2.*
16 *Birmingham Gazette*, 29 September 1914.
17 Board Minutes on the loss of HM Ships Aboukir, Cressy and Hogue dated 4 December 1914. TNA, ADM 1/8396/356.
18 *Sunderland Daily Echo*, 1 October 1914.
19 *The Times*, 24, 25 September and 14 October 1914.
20 Board Minutes on the loss of HM Ships Aboukir, Cressy and Hogue dated 4 December 1914. TNA, ADM 1/8396/356.
21 The World War One Document Archive, wwi.lib.byu.edu/index.php/U-9_Submarine_Attack.
22 Board Minutes on the loss of HM Ships Aboukir, Cressy and Hogue dated 4 December 1914. TNA, ADM 1/8396/356.

23 The World War One Document Archive, wwi.lib.byu.edu/index.php/U-9_Submarine_Attack.
24 *The Derbyshire Courier*, 2 October 1914.

Chapter 5: Liverpool, Rats and Sinking Ships

1 *Hartlepool Northern Daily Mail*, 17 September 1914.
2 *Liverpool Echo*, 22 September 1914.
3 Ibid.
4 Churchill, *The World Crisis, Volume 1.*
5 Marder, *Volume II.*
6 Keyes, Roger, *Private Papers. Volume 1. 1914–18.* Navy Records Society.
7 Hansard, 'Mr Churchill and the Press', vol. 65, Friday, 7 August 1914, hansard.parliament.uk/commons/1914-08-07/debates/9df32867-adbb-4d3b-ac41-af9282ef15cc/MrChurchillAndThePress.
8 Hansard, 'GERMAN AUXILIARY CRUISER SUNK BY H.M.S. "HIGHFLYER."', HC Deb, 27 August 1914, vol. 66, cc.176-81, api.parliament.uk/historic-hansard/commons/1914/aug/27/german-auxiliary-cruiser-sunk-by-hms.
9 Ibid.
10 Heaver, Stuart, 'SMS *Emden*: Hong Kong's favourite foe', *South China Morning Post*, www.scmp.com/magazines/post-magazine/article/1411712/sms-emden-hong-kongs-favourite-foe.
11 Asquith, Margot, *Great War Diary 1914–1916: The View from Downing Street* (Oxford: OUP, 2014).
12 Churchill, *The World Crisis, Volume 1.*
13 Klein.
14 *Manchester Evening News*, 21 September 1914.
15 Hansard, 'Mr Churchill and the Press'.
16 Morgan, Ted, *Churchill 1874–1915* (London: Jonathan Cape, 1983), p.381.
17 Churchill, *The World Crisis, Volume 1.*
18 Churchill, Winston S., *Secret Minute on Defence of Antwerp.* TNA, CAB/37/134/33, dated 7 September 1914.
19 Churchill, *The World Crisis, Volume 1.*
20 Purnell.
21 Keyes.
22 Board Minutes on the loss of HM Ships Aboukir, Cressy and Hogue dated 4 December 1914. Court of Enquiry. TNA, ADM 1/8396/356.
23 Churchill, *The World Crisis, Volume 1.*
24 Ibid.
25 Jenkins, Roy, *Churchill* (London: Macmillan, 2001), p.248.

Chapter 6: The Final Touch

1 Jameson.
2 *Cressy HMS: Stations and Orders.*

3 *Sunderland Daily Echo*, 1 October 1914.
4 *The Whitstable Times*, 26 September 1914.
5 *Sunderland Daily Echo*, 1 October 1914.
6 *Sheffield Daily Telegraph*, 26 September 1914.
7 *The Derbyshire Courier*, 2 October 1914.
8 Spiess.
9 Ibid.
10 Ibid.
11 Ibid.
12 Board Minutes on the loss of HM Ships Aboukir, Cressy and Hogue dated 4 December 1914. Court of Enquiry. TNA, ADM 1/8396/356. Witness statement by ERA William Taylor.
13 Board Minutes on the loss of HM Ships Aboukir, Cressy and Hogue dated 4 December 1914. Court of Enquiry. TNA, ADM 1/8396/356. Witness statement by Chief Stoker James.
14 Hook.
15 *The Times*, 24, 25 September and 14 October 1914.
16 *Dover Express and East Kent News*, 25 September and 2 October 1914.
17 *The Times*, 24 ,25 September and 14 October 1914.
18 Board Minutes on the loss of HM Ships Aboukir, Cressy and Hogue dated 4 December 1914. Court of Enquiry. TNA, ADM 1/8396/356. Witness statement by Lt McCarthy.
19 *Birmingham Gazette*, 29 September 1914.
20 Ibid.
21 Board Minutes on the loss of HM Ships Aboukir, Cressy and Hogue dated 4 December 1914. Court of Enquiry. TNA, ADM 1/8396/356. Witness statement by PO Durrant.
22 *The Derbyshire Courier*, 2 October 1914.
23 Spiess.
24 Board Minutes on the loss of HM Ships Aboukir, Cressy and Hogue dated 4 December 1914. Court of Enquiry. TNA, ADM 1/8396/356. Witness statement by Lt Harrison.
25 Ibid.
26 Live Bait Squadron Society, www.livebaitsqn-soc.info.
27 Spiess.
28 *Sunderland Daily Echo*, 1 October 1914.
29 Board Minutes on the loss of HM Ships Aboukir, Cressy and Hogue dated 4 December 1914. Court of Enquiry. TNA, ADM 1/8396/356. Witness statement by Lt McCarthy.
30 *Sheffield Daily Telegraph*, 26 September 1914.
31 Wykeham-Musgrave, W.H. (Kit), Lt Commander. Private papers held by Imperial War Museum.
32 Beynon and Hallam.
33 Board Minutes on the loss of HM Ships Aboukir, Cressy and Hogue dated 4 December 1914. Court of Enquiry. TNA, ADM 1/8396/356. Witness statement by ERA William Taylor.

34 *Harwich and Dovercourt Standard*, 26 September 1914, courtesy of the Harwich Society.
35 Spiess.
36 Board Minutes on the loss of HM Ships Aboukir, Cressy and Hogue dated 4 December 1914. Court of Enquiry. TNA, ADM 1/8396/356. Witness statement by Lt McCarthy.
37 *The Manchester Guardian*, 25 September 1914.
38 Board Minutes on the loss of HM Ships Aboukir, Cressy and Hogue dated 4 December 1914. Court of Enquiry. TNA, ADM 1/8396/356.
39 *The Times*, 24, 25 September and 14 October 1914.
40 Spiess.
41 Gayer.
42 The World War One Document Archive, wwi.lib.byu.edu/index.php/U-9_Submarine_Attack.
43 Ibid.

Chapter 7: The Coal Black Sea

1 *The Derbyshire Courier*, 2 October 1914.
2 *Dover Express and East Kent News*, 25 September and 2 October 1914.
3 *Hull Daily Mail*, 30 September 1914.
4 *The Derbyshire Courier*, 2 October 1914.
5 Ibid.
6 *Sunderland Daily Echo*, 1 October 1914.
7 *Sheffield Daily Telegraph*, 26 September 1914.
8 *Sunderland Daily Echo*, 1 October 1914.
9 Ibid.
10 *Gravesend and Dartford Reporter*, 1914.
11 Board Minutes on the loss of HM Ships Aboukir, Cressy and Hogue dated 4 December 1914. Court of Enquiry. TNA, ADM 1/8396/356.
12 *Birmingham Gazette*, 29 September 1914.
13 Hook.
14 Board Minutes on the loss of HM Ships Aboukir, Cressy and Hogue dated 4 December 1914. Court of Enquiry. TNA, ADM 1/8396/356.
15 Ibid.
16 *The Western Times*, 2 October 1914.
17 *Dover Express and East Kent News*, 25 September and 2 October 1914.
18 Ibid.
19 Ibid.
20 *The Times*, 24, 25 September and 14 October 1914.
21 Ibid.
22 Curtis, Alan John, *Lowestoft Fishermen's War 1914–1918* (Lowestoft: Poppyland, 2018).
23 Board Minutes on the loss of HM Ships Aboukir, Cressy and Hogue dated 4 December 1914. Court of Enquiry. TNA, ADM 1/8396/356.
24 *The Derbyshire Courier*, 2 October 1914.

25 Board Minutes on the loss of HM Ships Aboukir, Cressy and Hogue dated 4 December 1914. Court of Enquiry. TNA, ADM 1/8396/356.
26 *Sheffield Daily Telegraph*, 26 September 1914.
27 *Framlingham Weekly News*, 26 September 1914.
28 Ibid.
29 Board Minutes on the loss of HM Ships Aboukir, Cressy and Hogue dated 4 December 1914. Court of Enquiry. TNA, ADM 1/8396/356.
30 *The Times*, 24, 25 September and 14 October 1914.
31 British Newspaper Archive.
32 *Hull Daily Mail*, 30 September 1914.
33 *West Sussex Courier*, 21 October 1914.
34 Board Minutes on the loss of HM Ships Aboukir, Cressy and Hogue dated 4 December 1914. Court of Enquiry. TNA, ADM 1/8396/356.
35 *Gravesend and Dartford Reporter.*
36 Buckland, Gary, *De Ruvigny's Roll of Honour 1914–18*, Volume 1 (London: Naval and Military Press, 2009).
37 Board Minutes on the loss of HM Ships Aboukir, Cressy and Hogue dated 4 December 1914. Court of Enquiry. TNA, ADM 1/8396/356.

Chapter 8: A Neutral Country

1 *Dover Express and East Kent News*, 2 October 1914.
2 *Framlingham Weekly News*, 26 September 1914.
3 *Birmingham Gazette*, 29 September 1914.
4 McKee, Christopher, *Sober Men and True: Sailor Lives in the Royal Navy, 1900–1945* (Cambridge MA: Harvard University Press, 2002).
5 *Sunderland Daily Echo*, 1 October 1914.
6 *The Times*, 24, 25 September and 14 October 1914.
7 Ibid.
8 *The Manchester Guardian*, 25 September 1914.
9 *Dover Express and East Kent News*, 25 September and 2 October 1914.
10 Board Minutes on the loss of HM Ships Aboukir, Cressy and Hogue dated 4 December 1914. Court of Enquiry. TNA, ADM 1/8396/356.
11 *The Times*, 15 October 1914.
12 Loss of Aboukir, Hogue, Cressy, 22 September 1914. (Described at item level). Part 1: Reports of losses and proceedings of Court of Enquiry, schedule of docketed papers (ff 9–436). Part 2: Rescue and treatment of survivors (ff 437–600). TNA, ADM 137/47.
13 Ibid.
14 *Naval Staff Monographs (Historical) Volume XI Home Waters Part 2.*
15 Identification and disposal of effects of bodies of seamen washed ashore in Holland. Late crew members of HM ships ABOUKIR, HOGUE and CRESSY. TNA, ADM 1/8400/395.
16 Ibid.
17 Ibid.

Chapter 9: The Shock Ashore

1 Manchester, William, *The Last Lion, Winston Spencer Churchill: Visions of Glory 1874–1932* (London: Michael Joseph, 1983), p.486.
2 Marder, *Volume II.*
3 *Justice: The Organ of Social Democracy*, 24 September 1914.
4 Churchill, Winston S., *The World Crisis 1916–18 Part 1* (London: Thornton Butterworth, 1927).
5 Morgan, p.388.
6 *Harwich and Dovercourt Standard*, 26 September 1914, courtesy of the Harwich Society.
7 Ibid.
8 Information kindly supplied by Roger Jones at HMS *Ganges* Museum, Shotley, www.hmsgangesmuseum.com.
9 Information kindly supplied by the Harwich Society, www.harwich-society.co.uk.
10 *Harwich and Dovercourt Standard*, 26 September 1914, courtesy of the Harwich Society.
11 *The Manchester Guardian*, 23 and 25 September 1914.
12 Ibid.
13 *The Daily Mirror*, 26 September 1914.
14 Live Bait Squadron Society, www.livebaitsqn-soc.info.
15 *The Whitstable Times*, 26 September 1914.
16 *Dover Express and East Kent News*, 25 September and 2 October 1914.
17 Ibid.
18 *The Times*, 24, 25 September and 14 October 1914.
19 *Harwich and Dovercourt Standard*, 26 September 1914, courtesy of the Harwich Society.
20 Keyes.
21 Beatty.
22 Beynon and Hallam.
23 *The Manchester Guardian*, 23 and 25 September 1914.
24 Marder, *Volume II.*
25 The World War One Document Archive, wwi.lib.byu.edu/index.php/U-9_Submarine_Attack.
26 *Westminster Gazette*, 28 September 1914.
27 Morgan.
28 *Naval Staff Monographs (Historical) Volume XI Home Waters Part 2.*
29 Churchill, *The World Crisis, Volume 1*, Chapter XIV, 'In the Narrow Seas'.
30 Scott.
31 Churchill, *The World Crisis, Volume 1.*
32 *Naval Staff Monographs (Historical) Volume XI Home Waters Part 2.*

Chapter 10: Wives and Sweethearts

1 *Gloucester Journal*, 26 September 1914.
2 *Walsall Advertiser*, 6 October 1914.
3 *Hull Daily Mail*, 30 September and 7 October 1914.
4 *Sussex Courier*, 16 October 1914.
5 *Faversham and North East Kent News*, October 1914.
6 *The Whitstable Times*, 26 September 1914.
7 *Shields Daily News*, October 1914.
8 Live Bait Squadron Society, www.livebaitsqn-soc.
9 *Whitstable Times*, 10 October 1914.
10 Live Bait Squadron Society, www.livebaitsqn-soc.info.
11 Information kindly supplied by family members.
12 Information kindly supplied by Anna West.
13 Ibid.
14 Lomas, Janis and Andrews Maggie (eds), *The Home Front in Britain: Images, Myths and Forgotten Experiences since 1914* (Basingstoke: Palgrave Macmillan, 2014).
15 Barnes, Alison, 'Our History', www.ssafa.org.uk/about-us/our-history.
16 Ibid.
17 Lomas, Janis, '"Delicate duties": Issues of Class and Respectability in Government Policy Towards the Wives and Widows of British Soldiers in the Era of the Great War', *Women's History Review*, 2000.
18 *Framlingham Times*, 26 September 1914.
19 *The Globe*, 7 October 1914.
20 Live Bait Squadron Society, www.livebaitsqn-soc.info.

Chapter 11: Spin

1 Churchill, *The World Crisis, Volume 1.*
2 Ibid.
3 Klein.
4 Brownrigg.
5 Hansard, 'Mr Churchill and the Press'.
6 Brownrigg.
7 Sanders, M.L. and Taylor, Philip, M., *British Propaganda During the First World War, 1914–18* (London: Macmillan,1982).
8 Brownrigg.
9 Ibid.
10 *The Manchester Guardian*, 23 and 25 September 1914.
11 *The Globe*, 7 October 1914.
12 Ibid.
13 *West Sussex Courier*, 1 and 21 October 1914.

14 Hansard, 'NAVAL CADETS', HC Deb, 16 November 1914, vol. 68, cc.182–4, api.parliament.uk/historic-hansard/commons/1914/nov/16/naval-cadets.
15 Churchill, *The World Crisis, Volume 1.*
16 Marder, *Volume II.*
17 *The People*, 27 September 1914.
18 *The Daily Mirror*, 26 September 1914.
19 Ibid.
20 Ibid.
21 Ibid.
22 Brownrigg.
23 Churchill, *The World Crisis, Volume 1.*
24 Beatty.
25 Beynon and Hallam.
26 Churchill, *The World Crisis, Volume 1.*
27 Marder, *Volume II.*
28 Corbett.
29 Hammerton, Sir John, 'The Great War I was there', edited extract from Part 4, *Suicide Squadron*, narrative of Commander Austin Tyrer RD RNY or HMS *Hogue* held by Imperial War Museum.

Chapter 12: The Blame Game

1 Keyes.
2 Ibid.
3 Beatty.
4 Jellicoe, John, Admiral, *The Jellicoe Papers: Vol. I*, ed. A. Temple Patterson (London: Routledge, 2019).
5 Ibid.
6 *Naval Staff Monographs (Historical) Volume XI Home Waters Part 2.*
7 Beatty.
8 Board Minutes on the loss of HM Ships Aboukir, Cressy and Hogue dated 4 December 1914. Court of Enquiry. TNA, ADM 1/8396/356.
9 Ibid.
10 Churchill, *The World Crisis, Volume 1.*
11 Jellicoe, *The Grand Fleet.*
12 Churchill, *The World Crisis, Volume 1.*
13 Ibid., p.197.
14 Morgan.
15 Churchill, *The World Crisis, Volume 1.*
16 Board Minutes on the loss of HM Ships Aboukir, Cressy and Hogue dated 4 December 1914. Court of Enquiry. TNA, ADM 1/8396/356.
17 Ibid.
18 Churchill, *The World Crisis, Volume 1.*
19 Marder, *Volume II.*
20 Board Minutes on the loss of HM Ships Aboukir, Cressy and Hogue dated 4 December 1914. Court of Enquiry. TNA, ADM 1/8396/356.

21 Ibid.
22 Ibid.

Chapter 13: Not His Finest Hour

1 Manchester, p.485.
2 Churchill, *The World Crisis, Volume 1.*
3 Hough, *Former Naval Person.*
4 Morgan, p.394.
5 Manchester, p.503.
6 Beynon and Hallam.
7 Morgan, p.394.
8 Cabinet papers on defence of Antwerp. 29 September 1915. TNA, ADM 1/6396/256, CAB/37/1341.
9 Manchester, p.504.
10 *The Illustrated London News*, 3 and 10 October 1914.
11 Beynon and Hallam.
12 Ibid.
13 Churchill, *The World Crisis, Volume 1.*
14 Admiralty papers on Report of Court of Enquiry. *Aboukir*, *Hogue*, *Cressy*, Loss of. TNA, ADM 1/6396/256, CAB/37/1341/34.
15 Hough, *Former Naval Person.*
16 Black.
17 Churchill, *The World Crisis, Volume 1.*
18 Black.
19 Corbett.
20 *China Mail*, 28 October 1914.
21 Beynon and Hallam.
22 Manchester.
23 Hough, *Former Naval Person.*
24 Jenkins, p.248.
25 Hansard, 'MESSAGE FROM THE LORDS', HC Deb, 27 November 1914, vol. 68, cc.1597–600, api.parliament.uk/historic-hansard/commons/1914/nov/27/message-from-the-lords.
26 Beatty.
27 Churchill, *The World Crisis, Volume 1.*
28 Ibid.
29 Black.
30 Churchill, *The World Crisis, Volume 1.*
31 Hough, *Former Naval Person.*
32 Hough, *First Sea Lord.*
33 Hansard, 'MESSAGE FROM THE LORDS'.
34 Ibid.
35 Ibid.

Chapter 14: Legacy

1 Hansard, 'MR CHURCHILL'S STATEMENT', HC Deb, 15 February 1915, vol. 69, cc.919–79, api.parliament.uk/historic-hansard/commons/1915/feb/15/mr-churchills-statement#S5CV0069P0_19150215_HOC_204.
2 Ibid.
3 Ibid.
4 Churchill, *The World Crisis, Volume 1*.
5 Purnell.
6 Hough, *Former Naval Person*, p.117.
7 Ibid.
8 *The Daily Mirror*, 26 September and 16 November 1914.
9 Churchill, *The World Crisis, Volume 1*.
10 Ibid.
11 Hansard, 'MR CHURCHILL'S STATEMENT'.
12 Live Bait Squadron Society, www.livebaitsqn-soc.info.

SELECTED BIBLIOGRAPHY

Admiralty Manual of Seamanship Volume 1 & 2 (London: HMSO, 1909).

Admiralty Manual of Seamanship Volume 1 (revised and reprinted 1915) (London: HMSO, 1905).

Admiralty Manual of Seamanship Volume 1 (revised and reprinted 1943) (London: HMSO, 1937).

Archibald, E.H.H., *The Fighting Ship of the Royal Navy* (New York: Sterling, 1984).

Arthur, Max, *Lost Voices of the Royal Navy* (London: Hodder, 1985).

Arthur, Max, *The True Glory: The Royal Navy 1914–1939* (London: Hodder & Stoughton, 1996).

Asquith, Margot, *Great War Diary 1914–1916: The View from Downing Street* (Oxford: OUP, 2014).

Ballantyne, Iain, *The Deadly Trade: The Complete History of Submarine Warfare from Archimedes to the Present* (London: Weidenfeld & Nicolson, 2018).

Beatty, David, Earl, *The Beatty Papers: Selected from the Private and Official Correspondence of Admiral of the Fleet Earl Beatty* (London: Scolar Press for the Navy Records Society, 1993).

Beynon, Mark and Hallam, Richard, *Scrimgeour's Small Scribbling Diary* (London: Conway, 2008).

Black, Nicholas Duncan, 'The Admiralty War Staff and its Influence on the Conduct of the Naval War between 1914 and 1918', PhD Thesis 2005 University College, London (Michigan: ProQuest, 2013).

Brownrigg, Douglas, *Indiscretions of the Naval Censor* (New York: George H. Doran, 1920).

Buckland, Gary, *De Ruvigny's Roll of Honour* 1914–18, Volume 1 (London: Naval and Military Press, 2009).

Churchill, Winston S., *The World Crisis, Volume 1 1911–1914* (London: Rosetta Books, 1923).

Churchill, Winston S., *The World Crisis 1916–18 Part 1* (London: Thornton Butterworth, 1927).
Coles, Alan, *Three Before Breakfast* (London: K. Mason, 1979).
Colville, Quintin, *The British Sailor of the First World War* (London: Shire Publications, 2015).
Corbett, Julian S., *History of the Great War: Naval Operations* (London: Naval and Military Press, 1996).
Cressy HMS, Stations and Orders (Portsmouth: Gale and Polden, 1906).
Curtis, Alan John, *Lowestoft Fishermen's War 1914–1918* (Lowestoft: Poppyland, 2018).
Dingle, Nicholas, *British Warships 1860–1906: A Photographic Record* (Barnsley: Pen & Sword Books, 2009).
Eade, Charles (ed.), *Churchill by his Contemporaries* (London: Hutchison, 1953).
Felton, Mark, *China Station: The British Military in the Middle Kingdom 1839–1997* (Barnsley: Pen & Sword Books, 2013).
Freeman, Richard, *Unsinkable: Churchill and the First World War* (Stroud: The History Press, 2013).
Friedman, Norman, *British Cruisers of the Victorian Era* (Barnsley: Seaforth Publishing, 2012).
Gayer, Albert, Rear Admiral, *German Submarines and their Warfare, 1914–1918* (Miami: Trident Publishing, 2020).
Goldrick, James, *The King's Ships Were at Sea: The War in the North Sea August 1914 to February 1915* (London: Naval Institute Press, 1984).
Grant, Heathcoat S., *My War at Sea 1914–16: A Captain's Life with the Royal Navy during the First World War*, ed. Mark Tanner (warletters.net, 2014).
Gray, Edwyn A., *The Killing Time: The German U-boats 1914–18* (New York: Charles Scribner's Sons, 1972).
Gunns, G.H., *The Log of HMS Sutlej 1904–1906* (London: Westminster Press, 1906).
Hoehling, A.A., *The Great War at Sea: The Dramatic Story of Naval Warfare 1914–1918* (London: Corgi, 1967).
Hough, Richard, *First Sea Lord: An Authorised Biography of Admiral Lord Fisher* (London: George Allen & Unwin, 1969).
Hough, Richard, *Former Naval Person: Churchill and the Wars at Sea* (London: Weidenfield & Nicholson, 1985).
Hough, Richard, *The Great War at Sea* (Oxford: Oxford University Press, 1983).
Jameson, William, *The Most Formidable Thing: The Story of the Submarine from its Earliest Days to the End of World War I* (London: Rupert Hart Davies, 1965).
Jellicoe, John, Admiral, *The Grand Fleet 1914–1916: Its Creation Development and Work* (London: George H. Doran Company, 1919 [2017 edition]).
Jellicoe John, Admiral, *The Jellicoe Papers: Vol. I*, ed. A. Temple Patterson (London: Routledge, 2019).
Jellicoe, John Rushworth, *The Crisis of the Naval War in WWI* (Oklahoma: Musaicum, 2018).
Jenkins, Roy, *Churchill* (London: Macmillan, 2001).
Keegan, John, *The Price of Admiralty: War at Sea from Man of War to Submarine* (London: Hutchinson, 1988).

Kemp, P.K., *The Papers of Admiral Sir John Fisher, Volume One*, ed. Navy Records Society.
Keyes, Roger, *Private Papers, Volume 1, 1914–18* (Navy Records Society).
Lavery, Brian, *Able Seamen: The Lower Deck of the Royal Navy* (London: Conway, 2011).
Lewis, Michael, *The History of the British Navy* (London: Pelican Books, 1957).
Lomas, Janis, '"Delicate Duties": Issues of Class and Respectability in Government Policy towards the Wives and Widows of British Soldiers in the Era of the Great War', *Women's History Review*, 2000.
Lomas, Janis, and Andrews, Maggie (eds), *The Home Front in Britain: Images, Myths and Forgotten Experiences since 1914* (Basingstoke: Palgrave Macmillan, 2014).
MacDonald, Lyn, *1914: The Days of Hope* (London: Penguin, 1987).
MacDougall, Philip, *The Chatham Dockyard Story* (Rainham: Meresborough Books, 1987).
McKee, Christopher, *Sober Men and True: Sailor Lives in the Royal Navy, 1900–1945* (Cambridge MA: Harvard University Press, 2002).
Manchester, William, *The Last Lion, Winston Spencer Churchill: Visions of Glory 1874–1932* (London: Michael Joseph, 1983).
Marder, Arthur J., *From the Dreadnought to Scapa Flow, Volume I, The Road to War* (Barnsley: Seaforth Publishing, 2013).
Marder, Arthur J., *From the Dreadnought to Scapa Flow, Volume II, The War Years: to the Eve of Jutland 1914–16* (Barnsley: Seaforth Publishing, 2013).
Massie, Robert K., *Dreadnought: Britain, Germany and the Coming of the Great War* (London: Pimlico, 2004).
Morgan, Ted, *Churchill 1874–1915* (London: Jonathan Cape, 1983).
Naval Staff Monographs (Historical), Volume III, Monographs 6, 7, 8 and 11 (London: HMSO, 1921).
Naval Staff Monographs (Historical), Volume XI, Home Waters, Part 2, September and October 1914 (London: HMSO, 1924).
Navy List September 1914 (London: HMSO, 1914).
Nicholson, Virginia, *Singled Out: How Two Million Women Survived Without Men after the First World War* (London: Penguin, 2008).
Padfield, Peter, *Rule Britannia: The Victorian and Edwardian Navy* (London: Pimlico, 2002).
Parkinson, Jonathan, *The Royal Navy China Station 1864–1941 as Seen Through the Lives of Commanders in Chief* (London: Troubador, 2018).
Purnell, Sonia, *First Lady: The Life and Wars of Clementine Churchill* (London: Quarto Publishing Group, 2015).
Roskill, Stephen, *Admiral of the Fleet Earl Beatty: The Last Naval Hero* (Barnsley: Seaforth Publishing, 2018).
Roskill, Stephen, *Churchill and the Admirals* (Barnsley: Seaforth Publishing, 2014).
Sanders, M.L. and Taylor, Philip M., *British Propaganda During the First World War, 1914–18* (London: Macmillan, 1982).
Scott, Sir Percy, Admiral, *Fifty Years in the Royal Navy* (London: John Murray, 1919).
Seligmann, Matthew S., 'A Service Ready for Total War? The State of the Royal Navy in July 1914', *The English Historical Review*, Vol. 133, Issue 560, February 2018, pp.98–122.

Spiess, Johannes, *Six Years of Submarine Cruising* (Miami: Trident Publishing, 2019).
Tanner, Mark, *War Letters 1914–1918, Volume 2, Philip Malet de Carteret 1898–1916* (warletters.net, 2014).
The King's Regulations and Admiralty Instructions for the Governance of His Majesty's Naval Service 1914 (London: HMSO,1914).
Thompson, Julian, *The War at Sea 1914–1918* (London: Sidgwick and Jackson, 1996).
Tyrell, James, *World War One at Sea: An Introduction* (CreateSpace Independent Publishing Platform, 2016).
Van der Linden, Henk, *The Live Bait Squadron* (Amsterdam: Aspekt B.V., 2012).
Wells, John, Captain, *The Royal Navy: An Illustrated Social History 1870–1982* (Stroud: Sutton, 1999).
Women of the Empire in War Time, Souvenir pamphlet published in 1916.

The National Archives

Admiralty papers on Report of Court of Enquiry. *Aboukir*, *Hogue*, *Cressy* Loss of. ADM 1/6396/256, CAB/37/1341/34.
Board Minutes on the loss of HM Ships Aboukir, Cressy and Hogue dated 4 December 1914. Court of Enquiry. ADM 1/8396/356.
Cabinet papers on defence of Antwerp. ADM 1/6396/256, CAB/37/1341.
Court of Enquiry. Loss of ABOUKIR, CRESSY and HOGUE on 22 September 1914. ADM 1/8396/356.
CRESSY. ADM 53/13182:
HMS Aboukir, Cressy and Hoque: board minute referring to Court of Enquiry. ADM 178/13.
Identification and disposal of effects of bodies of seamen washed ashore in Holland. Late crew members of HM ships ABOUKIR, HOGUE and CRESSY. ADM 1/8400/395.
Loss of Aboukir, Hogue, Cressy, 22 September 1914. (Described at item level). Part 1: Reports of losses and proceedings of Court of Enquiry, schedule of docketed papers, (ff 9–436). Part 2: Rescue and treatment of survivors, (ff 437–600). ADM 137/47:
Churchill, Winston S., *Secret Minute on Defence of Antwerp*. CAB/37/134/33, dated 7 September 1914.

Imperial War Museum

Hammerton, Sir John, 'The Great War I was there', edited extract from Part 4, *Suicide Squadron*, narrative of Commander Austin Tyrer RD RNY of HMS *Hogue*.
Hook, Herewood, Commander, Private Papers.
Shewell, H.W.B., Surgeon Captain, HMS *Euryalus* Private Remark Book 13 July 1914 to 20 January 1915.
Wykeham-Musgrave, W.H. (Kit), Lt Commander, Private papers.
Wallace, Thomas, Signalman, HMS *Lysander* oral history, Cat. Number 731.

Newspapers

Birmingham Gazette
China Mail
Daily Sketch
Dover Express and East Kent News
Framlingham Weekly News
Gloucester Journal
Gravesend and Dartford Reporter
Hartlepool Northern Daily Mail
Harwich and Dovercourt Standard
Hong Kong Telegraph
Hull Daily Mail
Justice, the Organ of Social Democracy
Liverpool Echo
Manchester Evening News
Sheffield Daily Telegraph
Shields Daily News
Sunderland Daily Echo
The Courier
The Daily Mirror
The Derbyshire Courier
The Globe
The Illustrated London News
The Manchester Guardian
The People
The Times
The Whitstable Times
Walsall Advertiser
Westminster Gazette
West Sussex Courier

Hansard

'GERMAN AUXILIARY CRUISER SUNK BY H.M.S. "HIGHFLYER."', HC Deb, 27 August 1914, vol. 66, cc.176–81, api.parliament.uk/historic-hansard/commons/1914/aug/27/german-auxiliary-cruiser-sunk-by-hms.

'MESSAGE FROM THE LORDS', HC Deb, 27 November 1914, vol. 68, cc.1597–600, api.parliament.uk/historic-hansard/commons/1914/nov/27/message-from-the-lords.

'Mr Churchill and the Press', vol. 65, Friday, 7 August 1914, hansard.parliament.uk/commons/1914-08-07/debates/9df32867-adbb-4d3b-ac41-af9282ef15cc/MrChurchillAndThePress.

'MR CHURCHILL'S STATEMENT', HC Deb, 15 February 1915, vol. 69, cc.919–79, api.parliament.uk/historic-hansard/commons/1915/feb/15/mr-churchills-statement#S5CV0069P0_19150215_HOC_204.

'NAVAL CADETS', HC Deb, 16 November 1914, vol. 68, cc.182–4, api.parliament.uk/historic-hansard/commons/1914/nov/16/naval-cadets.

'Naval Operations HMS Formidable', HC Deb, 4 February 1915, vol. 69, c.164W.

Websites and online resources

Live Bait Squadron Society, www.livebaitsqn-soc.info.

The World War One Document Archive, wwi.lib.byu.edu/index.php/U-9_Submarine_Attack

Barnes, Alison, 'Our History', www.ssafa.org.uk/about-us/our-history.

BBC, *The First World War 7/10 Blockade*, www.youtube.com/watch?v=GXwOZylYHzw.

Dunley, Richard, 'The Live Bait Squadron', blog.nationalarchives.gov.uk/blog/live-bait-squadron.

Heaver, Stuart, 'SMS *Emden*: Hong Kong's favourite foe', *South China Morning Post*, www.scmp.com/magazines/post-magazine/article/1411712/sms-emden-hong-kongs-favourite-foe.

Klein, Christopher, 'The Daring Escape that Forged Winston Churchill', www.history.com/news/the-daring-escape-that-forged-winston-churchill.

Watson, Graham, 'From Imperial Policeman to North Sea Battle Fleet: The Evolution of British Naval Deployment 1900–1914', www.naval-history.net.

INDEX

INDEX